AF510191

# ALGOINTELLIGENCE

A Critical Study of Artificial Intelligence

# ALGOINTELLIGENCE

## A Critical Study of Artificial Intelligence

**Domenico Talia**
University of Calabria, Italy

**World Scientific**

NEW JERSEY • LONDON • SINGAPORE • BEIJING • SHANGHAI • HONG KONG • TAIPEI • CHENNAI • TOKYO

*Published by*

World Scientific Publishing Europe Ltd.
57 Shelton Street, Covent Garden, London WC2H 9HE
*Head office:* 5 Toh Tuck Link, Singapore 596224
*USA office:* 27 Warren Street, Suite 401-402, Hackensack, NJ 07601

Library of Congress Control Number: 2026026789

**British Library Cataloguing-in-Publication Data**
A catalogue record for this book is available from the British Library.

**ALGOINTELLIGENCE**
**A Critical Study of Artificial Intelligence**

Copyright © 2027 by World Scientific Publishing Europe Ltd.

*All rights reserved. This book, or parts thereof, may not be reproduced in any form or by any means, electronic or mechanical, including photocopying, recording or any information storage and retrieval system now known or to be invented, without written permission from the publisher.*

For photocopying of material in this volume, please pay a copying fee through the Copyright Clearance Center, Inc., 222 Rosewood Drive, Danvers, MA 01923, USA. In this case permission to photocopy is not required from the publisher.

ISBN 978-1-80729-063-4 (hardcover)
ISBN 978-1-80729-081-8 (paperback)
ISBN 978-1-80729-064-1 (ebook for institutions)
ISBN 978-1-80729-065-8 (ebook for individuals)

For any available supplementary material, please visit
https://www.worldscientific.com/worldscibooks/10.1142/Q0604#t=suppl

Desk Editors: Murali Appadurai/Cian Sacker Ooi

Typeset by Stallion Press
Email: enquiries@stallionpress.com

*A special thanks to all my relatives, past, present, and future.*

# Preface

Since his appearance on Earth, humankind has undergone continuous transformations, some of which have been radical, while others have been less so. These transformations have contributed to the evolution of the species and the societies that humans have created over time. Evaluating and judging past and distant transformations is relatively straightforward; however, assessing nearby transformations can be more challenging. Most notably, accurately assessing transformations is difficult when one is immersed in them. The everyday routine often obscures our awareness of humans as subjects or objects of transformations that possess non-contingent and occasionally historical significance.

Without giving in to the temptation of exaggeration, it is noteworthy that the social, cultural, and economic transformations we have observed since the late 20th and early 21st centuries are largely due to remarkable advancements in science and technology. In particular, a significant proportion of the changes observed in our era are the result of major innovations in the fields of telecommunications and information technology.

Thanks to the widespread use of these innovations, over the past few decades, we have been living in a world in which the physicality of things is gradually being lost. Objects and relationships are increasingly immaterial, digital, and mediated by "smart" and soft machines. Distances have been reduced – or even disappeared altogether – through instantaneous communications, even when those communications occur between people living thousands of miles apart. News and information no longer wait for the newspaper in the morning or the appointment with the TV news to spread.

Almost everything is being transformed into digital data and information. Time and space are different now from what we knew even in the last decades of the past century; they have shrunk, and we can no longer manage them quietly. In factories, in large distribution centers, and in warehouses, armies of robotic machines work tirelessly and increasingly replace human labor. The reality we are confronted with every day and which is in front of our eyes is the one we see in the screens of our smartphones, tablets, and computers.

We live in a reality extended by machines taking on novel roles, such as robot priests, avatar girlfriends, and lawyer chatbots, that have appeared recently. Digital machines are opening up new digital spaces in which they push us to live, enhancing, limiting, or sometimes disrupting our experiences and our usual physical relationships.

The most recent developments in the artificial intelligence (AI) field reinforce this picture even more and increase the scope of digital influence and action on humans, their daily lives, and their future. Thanks to machine learning algorithms and AI tools, computers are now widely believed to be able to give advice to people and to make decisions on complex issues in very important areas such as justice, healthcare, finance, and education.

In these and other contexts, computers, smartphones, and other digital devices have become aids (appendages) that we can no longer do without – that we no longer want to do without. Based on these scenarios, there are quite a few experts who believe that the changes taking place in this area constitute an irreversible transformation, with the risk that machines and their automated procedures will take over from humans and become more capable, faster, and more powerful decision-makers than people.

It is not easy to say how many concrete possibilities there are for this scenario to come true in the next few years. However, the latest extraordinary developments in generative AI systems, as well as the fact that this future possibility is being discussed and that there are different opinions even among AI specialists, is a clear demonstration of the very important role that information technology systems and applications have acquired in the lives of human beings and in the transformative changes of historical significance we are facing. Some, among the most concerned, invoke the risk of the end of the world and the danger of the extinction of the human species because of its hubris that pushes it to conceive and implement ever-new machines, which will one day threaten its very existence.

It is not useful to be catastrophic; however, it must be recognized that, as other times announced in the past, we are not facing the end of the world this time. However, we are certainly at the end of a historical phase in which human-invented machines served to ease his labors and make life more comfortable and at the beginning of a new phase in which machines are being used for the first time to replace human thinking, language, and decision-making. Large language models (LLMs) such as ChatGPT, Gemini, DeepSeek, and Claude are becoming the new "mouth of truth" for many people who listen to these systems and interact with them, viewing them almost as if they were oracles to be totally trusted, when in fact, though very capable of processing text and dialogues, they are equally capable of generating erroneous, inaccurate, and deficient information and spreading misinformation that can do harm to the individuals who use them and to society.

Therefore, we are not at the end of the world, but we are certainly at the end of a world. We are at the final sunset of the world that began with the end of the 20th century and continued into the first two decades of the 21st century. We are at the terminal stage of the classical tradition that has always seen the centrality of the human being in imagining and building civilizations, in governing nature, in thinking about and knowing the living universe, its potentials, and its limits. A tradition also founded on millennia-old religious beliefs for which man was created in the image and likeness of God. Over the past several decades, man has been developing machines in his own image and likeness and preparing to entrust so much of his exclusive prerogatives to them. Now, we can say that we are at the end of a world in which machines were only operational means, devices that were also highly sophisticated but never able to compete with human knowledge, never able to aspire to make decisions that have always been the human prerogative. Instead, for some time now, the new digital machines have been designed and built to be decision-making agents, conceptual entities, personal assistants, and choice makers that humans are also willing to follow.

This "technocentric" approach aims to put digital machines and their algorithms at the center of human processes in the organization of society, the world of work, and even social relations. Thus, people's lives and the functioning of society tend to be reorganized around automatic processes and algorithmic procedures. In many cases, AI systems can help people solve so many real problems and manage so many aspects of their daily activities. But the many benefits should not be traded off for the risks and dangers that can result from the misuse of these systems. On the ability to limit or nullify the risks while at the same time harnessing the great capabilities of intelligent artificial systems, the future is at stake.

The ever-faster development of information technologies is causing continuous and profound changes. Failure to discern these major transformations that digital is introducing on Earth can be a serious problem for citizens and governments. If we do not perceive this "functional" leap by machines, we will not be ready to deal with the current deep revolution, and above all, we will not be capable of handling with awareness the end of a world in which many of us were born and which today is in fact largely outdated and dissolved. Failure to take note of this transformative phase and the need to deal with it proactively weakens the role of humans in the world and reinforces the automatic processes that tend to overshadow them. In other words, it does not allow us to understand how to deal with the advent of a new world in which we are obliged to live anyway. A new world in which we must be able to act fully as protagonists, governing technological developments without losing our human nature.

This book explores these developments and discusses how digital technologies and advancements in AI are transforming our lives and our world. It aims to introduce and critically examine the fundamental concepts and principles of advanced computing, learning algorithms, and AI. To do that, the chapters investigate main issues and topics concerning the human–machine relationship in the age of AI.

The book examines the profound influence of technologies such as data analysis, machine learning, and generative AI on individuals and organizations across various sectors, including industry, justice, politics, culture, human relationships, and the workforce. Key topics explored throughout the chapters include data privacy, the AI Act, deep learning, LLMs, AI ethics and explainability, automatic decision systems, digital government, and digital administration, demonstrating how these technologies are reshaping our world.

Domenico Talia

# About the Author

**Domenico Talia** is a full professor of computer engineering at the University of Calabria, Italy, and an honorary professor at Noida University, India. He is a co-founder of the start-up DtoK Lab. His research interests include big data analysis, high-performance computing, parallel and distributed machine learning, cloud computing, generative artificial intelligence, sustainable AI, and parallel programming models and languages. Domenico Talia has published 10 books and about 500 papers in archival journals. These include publications of the Association for Computing Machinery (ACM), such as *Communications of the ACM* and *ACM Computing Surveys*; several journals published by the Institute of Electrical and Electronics Engineers (IEEE), including *Computer, IEEE Micro, IEEE Internet Computing, IEEE Transactions on Parallel and Distributed Systems (TPDS), IEEE Transactions on Knowledge and Data Engineering (TKDE), IEEE Transactions on Software Engineering (TSE)*, and *IEEE Transactions on Systems, Man, and Cybernetics: Systems*; as well as *Future Generation Computer Systems (FGCS), Parallel Computing*, and leading conference proceedings. He is a member of the editorial boards of *Computer*, *ACM Computing Surveys*, *FGCS*, and several other archival journals. He has served as program chair or a member of the program committee for several international conferences. Talia is a senior member of the ACM and the IEEE Computer Society and is a recipient of the Euro-Par Achievement Award.

# Contents

# Chapter 1

# Introduction

*How will man avoid being dehumanized by the machine, dominate it, make it a moral weapon of progress?*

—Giuseppe Ungaretti

The exponential growth of digital technologies, with hardware devices and software programs, has opened up enormous possibilities and, at the same time, is posing equally great challenges. The world of production is now entirely based on computers, their algorithms, and their data. The same occurs in transport, communications, and public administrations. On a daily basis, the creative abilities of programmers must be increasingly closely connected to the imaginative and strategic abilities of managers of companies and public and private organizations. The creative act of the head of an organizational structure or an entrepreneur must increasingly find technological support from software engineers, data scientists, and developers of that code and the procedures supporting organizations and production. In the processes of digital transformation, the human factor continuously enters into a relationship with machines (hardware) and with their procedural expressions (software).

This relationship is therefore becoming increasingly important in the creation, design, and implementation of digital applications that make intensive use of the internet, the Internet of Things (IoT), Big Data, machine learning, generative artificial intelligence (AI), or robots. The use of digital systems and applications offers extraordinary opportunities to human beings. They change people's lives while giving rise to new risks that people are not entirely ready to face. These opportunities and risks require the human factor to deal with more and more often, and with increasing complexity, algorithms and the large quantities of data that they are capable of processing and the effects that their "intelligence" is capable of producing on the reality of work and collective life.

Along with this necessary interaction and osmotic cooperation, which occurs during the design and development stages of digital solutions, among all the parties that contribute to the definition and creation of procedures entrusted to machines, there is also an obligatory cooperation between humans and machines during the activities they perform for us.

In their daily operations, in a public office, in professional work, and in personal and family activities, ongoing relationships occur between people and algorithms. These relationships are often collaborative, supportive, and helpful for humans, but sometimes they lead to friction, rigidity, disagreements, or conflicts. Automated procedures, through rigid coding and little attention to the human element, sometimes exceed their scope, generating strain and conflict with the people who use them. When computing machines and their applications are not designed (by humans) with the necessary care and flexibility and when they are inspired by mechanistic ideas, they may become straitjackets within which it becomes difficult to move and operate. They become instruments of power exercised by those who create them over those who use them.

In these cases, machines act in opposition to human nature; they demean it, and they construct rigid relationships that are distant from or in opposition to the principles of humanism that should inspire technological achievements at the service of society. For these reasons, necessary care must be taken in designing and implementing digital transformation processes, focusing on building hybrid collective intelligence environments that foster complementarity and synergies rather than rigidity and contradictions.

The great flexibility of digital machines is sometimes limited by the decisions of those who design them and define their algorithms. It is therefore necessary to conceive, design, and implement thoughtful forms of human–machine interaction that preserve and prioritize the human element and, in doing so, make the automatic processes governed by machines more natural.

In his book *The Coevolution*, Lee [1], questioning the trajectories of technological development, asks whether "*are humans defining technology or is technology defining humans?*" The question is entirely legitimate, given the enormous developments being generated by extraordinary technologies such as AI or CRISPR/Cas9 gene editing. Lee argues that it might be more realistic to think of the technological advances of the coming decades as the realization of a Darwinian coevolution between humans and machines, in which humans – aware that digital machines are better at performing various tasks (computing, communicating, and processing huge amounts of data) – learn to improve their rational, empathetic, creative, dialectical, cultural, and pragmatic abilities and increase their capacity to govern technological processes not only by using their technical and scientific knowledge but also by employing their culture, ideals, and know-how. These skills can never be fully expressed through coded sequences and are essential to the humanization of processes managed by digital machines.

## 1.1 Humans Facing Accelerationism

Today, we are witnessing a seemingly unstoppable trend, according to which digital objects (hardware and software) depend on the humans who code them, but humans also depend on the digital objects they produce. This phenomenon seems to respond to accelerationist theories that, after originating in the imagination of the science fiction writer Roger Zelazny in his novel *Lord of the Light* [2], have spread among the followers of a movement that sought to elevate society to a higher level of technological awareness, rapidly transforming its attitude toward digital technology.

This movement was most notably represented by Nick Land, a philosopher at the University of Warwick who, in the 1990s, theorized the need for an increasingly accelerated capitalist system, finally freed from political constraints, capable of maximizing the potential offered by new technologies. Accelerationist ideas have aimed to intensify automation of work, pushing for robots to perform the majority of jobs with the utopian goal of allowing humans to gradually achieve the ideal of a post-work society. This scenario should achieve full and complete automation, including through the introduction of a universal income guaranteed to all, regardless of class or citizenship.

The ideas of various accelerationist theorists seem to entrust intelligent machines with the role of agents of societal transformation, in which technologies become a central element of political, economic, and social processes. These theories seem to engender a certain naiveté (when it's not self-serving ideology) that embraces the choices of "technological solutionism," which claims to be able to solve every human problem through a new technical solution or a new technological product. The naiveté of accelerationists and solutionists lies in their underestimation of the complexity of human nature, its strengths, and even its weaknesses. On the contrary, what is needed in the digital transformation taking place across different spaces and contexts of our society is precisely to begin with the human factor, from its characteristics – the product of a slow evolution that cannot make leaps.

Technological accelerations always need to consider the human being. This is true in the world of work, where greater training, higher levels of competence, and skills that combine culture and specialized knowledge are required, but it is also true in other areas, such as schools and training centers, where new content and new teaching methods are needed that recognize the human element as central to work processes and their purposes.

Technological accelerationism appears to fail to adequately consider the impact of the ever-increasing speed of innovation processes on organizations and individuals. Accelerationists seem to ignore the ethical inevitability of the human element becoming the object of automatic procedures that ultimately manipulate it and of increasingly frequent deskilling processes that push skilled labor out of an industrial or economic sector due to the introduction of technologies used by workers with lower skills and qualifications [3].

This process is often motivated by savings in production costs due to reduced investment in human capital, which weakens the bargaining power of individual workers. In this case, the machine becomes the competent party, and the worker's role is limited to a simple facilitator of the processes encoded in the device. Humans become part of these processes because they lack significant skills and are the weaker element. These types of conditions can be avoided through reskilling processes that enable employees to acquire new skills, allowing workers to take on a new role within the organization they work for, enhancing their know-how that extends beyond the operational nature of machine actions.

Finally, as previously mentioned, increasing the operational capabilities of machines must be matched by an upskilling process for those who interact with them and those who use them, but also those who program them or integrate them into an organizational context in which the human factor remains significant. Through training and the acquisition of higher levels of knowledge, upskilling workers can expand their know-how and build new skills that enhance the human element and improve its relationship with digital transformation processes in which machines are no longer negotiable.

## 1.2 Cultural Factors and Digital Technologies Toward the Future

One of the challenges posed by the digital revolution is ensuring that digital machines do not become a factor in the exercise of human supremacy over other humans, risking, over time, becoming subjects of supremacy over the entire human race. Along with the need to develop new generations of professionals with advanced skills and a multidisciplinary background, it is necessary to consider digital transformation processes that enhance the role of the human component, without which no transition to digital can be considered effective and secure [4]. We must not make the mistake of believing that injecting large doses of technology is sufficient to streamline processes without understanding that digital transformation is essentially a cultural process in which technologies act as facilitators, not as exclusive or primary agents.

The success of digital transformation will not be achieved solely because of its technological nature, but above all if its cultural complexity and the social role of the technologies upon which it is based are managed. Sophisticated digital technologies such as IoT devices, robotic systems, cloud computing, machine learning applications, generative AI bots, and autonomic computing systems are certainly playing an enabling role, but their use in relation to their impact on people will determine the real benefits. Indeed, the effects of digital transformation must be positive and meet the interest and acceptance of significant segments of the population. Digital solutions must be sustainable and prevent a potential attitude of trust in new technologies, as potential solvers of personal and social problems, from turning into skepticism and rejection. This can especially occur in social classes that have experienced impoverishment in the last decade and now feel threatened or marginalized by automation processes. For these reasons, they also become victims of populism [5].

The software solutions being developed every day, fueled by the ever-increasing availability of Big Data [6], offer almost unceasingly original and innovative solutions for managing individual and social life. Digital machines, through their algorithms, are building an increasingly procedural future, and they build it as they foresee it. Automatically predicting our future is one of the primary goals of data science. Data analysis and machine learning algorithms are used extensively and massively to generate forecasts. New professions and skills, such as those of data scientists and data detectives, have emerged from a new data science that builds methods for obtaining correlations between information, connections between events, classifications of facts, and people capable of proposing what will happen to us tomorrow.

This new science and associated technology rapidly and analytically perform processing and predictions, even if in many cases (for example, with deep learning techniques) it cannot explain the underlying reasons behind a relationship or predicted phenomenon. Are the machines, through their software, learning from data just as we learn from experience, even though we often lack a clear explanation of the events unfolding around us? In recent years, these systems have often been referred to as "artificial intelligence," yet it would be more appropriate and useful to emphasize that they are essentially rational, automatic systems capable of learning and constantly adapting the operational choices of their algorithms to the information they acquire, unlike traditional imperative software systems that always execute the same sequences coded by their programmers. These new adaptive capabilities are changing the use of digital machines and their interactions with humans, and therefore they require new skills and unprecedented relational abilities from people to govern these increasingly complex digital systems.

The future has always been one of the greatest enigmas for human beings. Today, we face the future primarily using computers, software, and data. This new practice is transforming our approach to reality and pushing us to address the challenges and unknowns of tomorrow using analytical and computational tools. The results are sometimes surprising, but it would be a mistake to consider science and technology (even those underlying the digital universe) as subjects alien to our consciousness, distant from the values that make us human [7], or detached from the social body that generated them.

As digital civilization pushes for the affirmation of computational thinking to the detriment of emotional thinking and consciousness, the role of science, technology, and their proponents is becoming increasingly influential and prescriptive. In this role of ever-increasing importance, technoscience, along with other sectors of society, must take on the "shape" of our future and must necessarily assume ethical and social roles, contributing to the development of a new well-being that thrives not only on rationality but also on creativity and human consciousness. As technologies expand their role, they must therefore be not only important operational tools but also agents capable of pushing forward, along with their productive capabilities, the frontiers of human evolution, operating with ever greater responsibility and a higher social vision.

## 1.3 The Intelligence of Machines

The term "artificial intelligence" was first coined by John McCarthy and his co-authors Marvin Minsky, Nathaniel Rochester, and Claude Shannon in 1955, when they wrote the proposal for the Dartmouth Summer Research Project on Artificial Intelligence (held in summer 1956 at Dartmouth College). In 2023, "artificial intelligence" was named the word of the year by the authoritative Collins Dictionary. The reasons for this decision are multiple, but they all boil down to the fact that AI was one of the defining themes of the 2020s. Systems such as ChatGPT, Gemini, DeepSeek, DALL-E, and Midjourney quickly became known to billions of people around the world. Indeed, it's worth noting that ChatGPT, launched at the end of November 2022, had already reached one hundred million users by January 2023. No product or system had ever achieved such record numbers in just over a month.

As we were taught in school, the term "intelligence" has its origins in the two Latin words *intus*, meaning "inside," and *legere*, meaning "to read." Reading inside, in this case, indicates the ability to investigate deeply and to understand what is happening around us, the ability to distinguish, and the capacity for reasoning and thought to investigate reality. Intelligence is also the ability to use knowledge to achieve our goals and solve the problems we face every day. In saying this, we must also recognize that human intelligence is such a complex matter that no one can claim to know how it develops or what exactly the natural faculties are that underlie it.

Since life appeared on Earth, different forms of intelligence have emerged: that of animals, that of plants, and only later, human intelligence. No one can reasonably deny that various animal species have developed forms of intelligence, be they bees, dolphins, crows, foxes, or other species. The same can be said of the intelligence of plants, which is certainly different from that of animals, but allows them to adapt to their environment and climate, to reproduce by spreading seeds through the air or soil, and to communicate through their roots and the subsoil. Among these natural intelligences, human intelligence has developed the most, becoming predominant over the others. For this reason, it is the intelligence that has governed life on the planet for many thousands of years.

In recent years, a new form of intelligence has been added to these natural intelligences: machine intelligence, which was dubbed "artificial intelligence" in 1955. This new type of intelligence, certainly different from others, is rapidly gaining an increasingly important role on planet Earth and has been used for several years to generate knowledge, solve numerous problems, and make complex decisions of varying complexity. While, as mentioned, the various characteristics of intelligence in a general sense include the ability to solve problems and adapt, these capabilities are undoubtedly also expressed by AI systems.

It may be helpful to clarify that AI systems are not intended to reproduce human intelligence processes but are content to execute data processing procedures whose results are similar to, or even better than, those produced by an intelligent human when solving the same problem. Therefore, AI as it exists today is not created in the image and likeness of human intelligence. It is a different way of understanding that is proving effective in many cases. For example, it can drive a car in traffic, recognize one person's face among many, learn people's behaviors, discover new medical treatments, and translate texts into hundreds of languages.

Recently, many have focused their attention on generative AI systems, which, among AI systems, are demonstrating the most ingenious capabilities. These are systems that can communicate with us in our own language, answer our questions, write texts, and produce extremely realistic images and videos. Generative AI systems, such as ChatGPT and Gemini, possess immense memories and a remarkable ability to listen, write, speak, and explain many things to us humans by conversing in natural language. Despite these extraordinary capabilities, we shouldn't believe that these systems possess the faculties and talent of Einstein or Galileo. They don't possess the brilliance of Picasso or Mozart, and they are not capable of making great discoveries, even if in many cases they can reach levels of intelligence equal to or even greater than those of normal people.

Unlike other forms of intelligence, this new form of intelligence we call "artificial" was created by human intelligence; therefore, it has a natural origin and is generating new senses, different feelings that complement those known to date. These are sensitivities and perceptions that machines are creating and with which we must necessarily engage. Indeed, in addition to expanding the ways in which we humans relate to one another, digital machines, brimming with intelligent software, have altered our feelings, the forms of our expression, and our perception of everyday reality, often mediated by computers. In doing so, machines are creating new senses and generating elements such as artificial empathy (between humans and machines and between machines themselves), digital friendship (between humans through machines, between humans and machines, and, finally, between machines), and so forth.

We are faced with a new form of intelligence which many fail to recognize as such and which is based on enormous quantities of data and highly complex, fast mathematical operations. This is an intelligence born of human artifice, but, as mentioned, it is more capable than many of us at solving several problems. It does so even better than many who don't recognize it as such, perhaps out of a fear of feeling inferior to a machine. Or because they cannot comprehend this novel type of intelligence due to cultural limitations. Or simply because they cannot grasp the sophisticated technology behind and within it.

While it's understandable that some don't accept that machine intelligence is true intelligence and that, in many cases, it's even better than us in solving problems, we should at least agree that this new form of intelligence is contributing to the advancement of the world's collective intelligence. A thousand years ago, the Spanish philosopher Averroes hypothesized the existence of a single intellect for all humans, upon which individuals draw to think and deliberate. At the time, this thesis was not well received by the Catholic Church and sparked much discussion. Without wishing to provoke the reactions of philosophers and theologians, today we could envision a new collective intellect that could also include AI systems, which, combined with human and natural intelligence, contribute to a more powerful and insightful overall intelligence of the world we live in. To achieve this goal, it will be necessary to find appropriate hybrid forms of interaction and collaboration between living beings and machines that benefit humanity rather than harm it, improve its quality of life, and create new freedoms rather than new inequalities and discrimination.

## 1.4 Toward a Hybrid Future

Despite the positive aspects, it's important to consider that current AI systems lack some elements that are an important part of human intelligence. For example, doubt is absent from AI systems, making them overly assertive and sometimes fallible because they always try to provide an answer even when they are incapable of doing so. AI systems don't express problematic opinions; they don't know how to expose problems because they are designed to provide solutions, even when they are imprecise or incorrect, and AI systems present themselves as correct, misleading a human interlocutor who lacks the skills to interpret them.

We have grown up comparing ourselves with the intelligence of other human beings and even with the intelligence of other life forms. Now, in a very short time, we are being called upon to confront a new form of intelligence that we didn't know before and that, in part, seems more like magic than science. We must think of it as an advanced form of the human ability to create machines – in this case, made of billions of chips and bits – and to instruct them to do things and solve problems that we humans need to solve. Problems that, in some cases, take too long or that we don't know how to solve because their resolution would require inhuman effort.

The relationship between human and machine intelligence is one of the key elements that will characterize the years to come. The outcome of this collaboration or antagonism, which seems to characterize the digital century we live in, will determine the future of the human race more than any other factor. For our part, we should act to avoid what Günther Anders predicted half a century ago: that human beings would become obsolete, unable to manage their relationship with AI systems, and become subordinate to the technologies they themselves have created [8].

We must ensure that individuals have a critical and informed view of them, preventing them from being sidelined by the new and extraordinary abilities of digital intelligent machines. Preparing future citizens and nurturing talent in the new digital century is essential for the proper use of innovations and for living as humans aware of the impact of AI and its applications. The more we work in this direction, the more effective our ability to live and work in the new world will be. It is a new world where this innovative form of intelligence will certainly find its place and will have to coexist with others.

## 1.5 The Plan of the Book

The primary goal of this book is to offer the reader an exploration of how intelligent machines work and how the worldwide use of AI systems is changing our lives. The book aims to illustrate and carefully analyze the concepts and impacts of machine learning algorithms, generative AI, and pervasive computing systems. With this objective in mind, the chapters examine key issues and themes regarding the human–machine relationship in the age of AI.

The book discusses the main aspects of the deep influence of new computing technologies, such as data analytics, machine learning, LLMs, and generative AI, on individuals and organizations. Key topics such as data and AI ethics, AI safety, algorithmic responsibility and accountability, digital governmentality, and artificial general intelligence (AGI) are examined. The author's desire is to help the reader inspect the main facets of intelligent technologies and discover hidden features that must be evidenced to help humans to find the best way to interact with intelligent machines that are populating our world.

Chapter 2 introduces algorithms and illustrates the role they play in our society. The chapter also discusses the massive utilization of algorithms in personal digital devices we utilize wherever we are on a daily basis. We all spend most of our lives inside a global computing machinery connected by the internet. Chapter 3 discusses how the network works to connect billions of computers that make up a large digital machine. Chapter 4 introduces basic concepts and models of AI and discusses how AI algorithms are programmed and trained today. Data-driven programming, natural language programming, and other new approaches are discussed in the chapter. Chapter 5 examines how the profiling algorithms of social media influence people's privacy and decisions. The role of AI chatbots is also discussed. Digital non-things made of combinations of bits and lines of code incessantly take shape in our digital devices and on their screens. Chapter 6 discusses this new class of immaterial objects we daily handle.

The properties of Big Data are introduced in Chapter 7, and their different types and formats are discussed with special attention on personal data, of which neural data are a critical class that must be considered and protected. The advent of digital systems has generated a rapid transition to artificial narratives that include reticular, relational, and generative AI, which are introduced and analyzed. Chapter 8 discusses relationships between artificial narratives and generative AI.

LLMs are highly capable of combining words and sentences; however, they do not think. Chapter 9 illustrates this new way of generating concepts provided by conversational AI. Chapter 10 discusses the role of the human factor in a world full of computing devices that interact with each other and take decisions for human beings. Then, Chapter 11 illustrates the concepts of data ethics and ethics of AI, discussing how both must be considered to protect users of information technology systems.

In Chapter 12, we discuss two key concepts of AI, accountability and explainability, that must be embodied in AI development for achieving safe systems. Chapter 13 introduces the principles of safe AI systems and discusses the implementation of safety features in machine learning and generative AI.

Chapters 14 and 15 discuss the relationships between digital systems and society. In particular, Chapter 14 considers how theories of Herbert Marcuse about modern one-dimensional man can be reconsidered due to the advent of AI systems in people's lives. Chapter 15 describes how politics became digital in a few years due to Big Data and machine learning.

The cultural influence of algorithms and digital devices is discussed in Chapter 16, and social regulations created by software applications are also presented. Chapter 17 analyzes the relationships between digital technologies and governmentality (as the relationship between the government and the forms of rationality) and the practical scenarios that these relationships are shaping.

AI is used today by lawyers and judges to make decisions in the court. Chapter 18 describes some recent cases and analyzes the opportunities and risks of artificial justice. Chapter 19 is the final chapter of the book. It outlines new scenarios that may originate from future advancements in AI, with a special emphasis on AGI expected to be developed within the next decades.

## References

1. Lee, E. A. (2020). *The Coevolution: The Entwined Futures of Humans and Machines*. USA: The MIT Press.
2. Zelazny, R. (2010). *Lord of the Light*. UK: Gollancz.
3. Eubanks, V. (2018). *Automating Inequality*. USA: St. Martin Press.
4. Nida-Rumelin, J. and Widenfeld, N. (2019). *Umanesimo digitale*. Italy: Franco Angeli (in Italian).
5. Frey, C. B. (2019). *The Technology Trap*. USA: Princeton University Press.
6. Talia, D. (2019). *Big Data and the Computable Society: Algorithms and People in the Digital World*. UK: World Scientific Publishing.
7. Rossi, F. and Mattei, N. (2019). Building ethically bounded AI. *Proceedings of 33rd AAAI Conference on Artificial Intelligence*. AAAI, pp. 9785–9789.
8. Anders, G. (2025). *The Obsolescence of the Human*. USA: University of Minnesota Press.

# Chapter 2

# In a World of Algorithms

*The art of programming is the art of organizing complexity.*

—Edsger W. Dijkstra

Every day, web portals, social media platforms, and billions of computers and smartphones we use at work or at home run numerous complex algorithms to personalize each user's browsing experience, manage billions of commercial and financial transactions, and exchange massive amounts of information. At the core of all computing systems are algorithmic procedures that control computers and support the interactions of billions of people every day. These algorithms exploit a huge amount of data (social media, for example, uses relentlessly collected personal data: posts, likes, searches, other contents we share and the pages we follow, and the times and places where we use them) and show us contents that are most likely to capture our attention and engagement.

We are therefore faced with a gigantic global algorithmic device that decides how to make people interact, how to assist them, and how to influence their choices, relationships, and opportunities. If this were not the case, it would be inexplicable, for example, why Elon Musk spent $44 billion to buy Twitter (now X). A platform that has become his digital Golem to influence customers, voters, governments, and wars. It would be inexplicable to understand Zuckerberg's political strategies or the US government's fight against TikTok.

For all these reasons, it is necessary to ask what the principles and logic of the algorithms that guide computers and digital platforms are and how these principles and logic, thanks to the flexibility of the software, can be adapted over time to meet different and changing objectives. Without examining the algorithms, we cannot understand what really happens in digital systems.

For example, it is certain that many social media users bear responsibility for their often spiteful, selfish, and offensive online behavior and for the many inappropriate things they post. However, the greatest responsibility lies with the algorithms created by the owners of those platforms, which determine the quality of content and interactions, their manipulation, the spread of fake news, and the various purposes to which the massive production of posts generated by billions of individuals can be directed, for good or evil.

## 2.1 What Are We Talking About When We Talk About Algorithms?

Algorithms are sequences of operations executed by automatic machines, such as computers. They are used nowadays to automate decisions. Every time we use a PC, a tablet, or a smartphone, we run algorithms that process data to compute results, provide solutions, make decisions, or generate new data.

Donald Knuth provided a definition of an algorithm as a "finite set of rules that gives a sequence of operations for solving a specific type of problem" [1]. Given the ubiquity and applicability of algorithms, it is useful to know their principles. Awareness of these very long chains of instructions, which programmers design and computers execute to produce answers or solve problems, is fundamental today.

Although algorithms are elements of modernity, their origins are very old. In some clay tablets from ancient Mesopotamia were reproduced the first known algorithms that solved practical problems, such as calculating the area of a terrain or solving an equation. Traces preserved in various museums demonstrate that as early as 4,000 years ago, the Babylonians defined and used algorithms to solve problems of calculating physical quantities or to create resolution procedures that used numerical values. From clay tablets to papyrus, parchments, and then books, the different supports and forms of writing and calculation have shaped the lives of peoples and nations.

For a long time, the term "algorithm" has indicated a procedure defined and used to solve a problem or calculate a result through a sequence of elementary operational steps. According to this general definition, each of us executes algorithms every day. We do it by preparing a cup of tea at home, boiling water in a kettle, cooking pasta in a pot, driving a motorcar, or going shopping in a mall. We may say that algorithms are operational processes that human beings have conceived and carried out in order to live. However, the word "algorithm" originates from the name of the Arab mathematician al-Khwārizmī, who lived around 800 CE and, in 825, wrote a book later translated into Latin with the title *Algoritmi de Numero Indorum* [2]. That book is considered the most important ancient treatise on the Indian numeral system and allowed the spread of the Hindu-Arabic numeral system in Europe. This volume, of which only the Latin translation is known, contains many calculation procedures expressed as sequences of mathematical operations, algorithms, in fact.

In the late Middle Ages, the Latin pronunciation, *algorismus*, used in Europe after the name of al-Khwārizmī, served to indicate the decimal numerical system. An important role in all this was played by the Tuscan mathematician Leonardo Pisano, better known by the name Fibonacci. In 1202, Fibonacci, also using material contained in al-Khwārizmī's book, wrote in Latin his *Liber Abaci* [3], which is one of the most influential and detailed mathematical treatises written in Europe after those of the ancient Greeks, though it did not achieve the same widespread diffusion as Fibonacci's work. *Liber Abaci* is a great book of calculation that contains various algorithms still frequently used today. Many of these have been implemented in the software programs that run on our computers today.

Algorithms have been used for centuries by a small number of mathematicians, engineers, and scientists as problem-solving procedures through the execution of a sequence of operational steps. Subsequently, the invention of the electronic computer around 1940 and its subsequent widespread diffusion since the last decades of the past century led to the design, implementation, production, and use of a vast collection of algorithms. Nowadays, algorithms are not only used as methods for solving mathematical calculations but also govern all computers and digital devices in the world and contribute to the automation of a large part of human activities.

## 2.2 Principles of Algorithms

An algorithm can be defined as a well-defined and unambiguous computational procedure composed of a finite set of operations that transform input data into output data (or results). To be valid solution methods, algorithms must hold the following main properties:

- **Algorithms must be *finite*:** Every time they are executed, algorithms must end after a finite, although high, number of steps. An algorithm that never ends while solving a problem through its execution will not lead to the generation of a complete result.
- **Algorithms must be *definite*:** Each phase of an algorithm must be defined exactly and unambiguously for every possible case in which the algorithm can be used. This means that all actions performed by an algorithm must be precisely expressed, thus avoiding the possibility that an executor (e.g., a human or a computer) does not understand exactly what the author of the algorithm intended to achieve. This property requires that each operation (step) of an algorithm must have a precise meaning (unambiguous semantics) that can be interpreted in a single way, without possible ambiguities that would lead computers or people who execute it to generate unwanted results.
- **Algorithms must be *effective*:** Each step of an algorithm must be not only defined but also feasible. This means that each instruction that belongs to the sequence of operations comprising an algorithm must be simple enough to be completed (by the machine or the human who executes it) in a limited period of time.
- **Algorithms must be *correct*:** They must reach the solution of the task for which they were defined without making mistakes in any operation; otherwise, the obtained results will not be the desired ones.

These four properties apply to all algorithmic procedures composed of logical-mathematical sequences that are used to solve a problem or compute a result. They are even more valid when an algorithm is coded in a programming language that expresses it as a software program executable by a digital computer.

## 2.3 Two Simple Algorithms

To illustrate how simple yet significant algorithms can be defined, we show here the operations that comprise an algorithm capable of finding the smallest number (the minimum value) in a sequence of positive numbers.

```
Algorithm "Find the Smallest Positive Number":
BEGIN
        READ the number N that is the length of a sequence of numbers
        ASSIGN the value 0 to MIN
        FOR I = 1 UP TO N REPEAT
            READ a positive number X
            IF X < MIN
                  ASSIGN the value of number X to MIN
                  INCREASE I by 1
        END REPEAT
        WRITE MIN
END
```

This simple sequence of operations defines an algorithm that receives as input a value *N* (for example, 100) and a sequence of *N* positive integers (for example, 100 positive values) and iteratively, i.e., scrolling the index **I** from the value 1 to the value *N*, computes and shows the minimum value among all the received numbers. The computed value is stored in the data variable, which, in the algorithm, is indicated by the name **MIN**. If this algorithm is executed by a computer, **MIN** is the name that can be given to a memory cell where the minimum value is stored.

This algorithm can be used in many applications to find the smallest number and can be executed by a person or a computer on short sequences of numeric values or on sequences of even billions of positive numbers. Whereas a person may require minutes or days to compute the minimum value of a sequence of numbers, a computer is capable of calculating the minimum value among all the numbers in a few milliseconds or a few seconds if the sequence is composed of millions of elements. A machine will still perform its computations much faster than a person can do them, no matter how good they are at mathematics. The algorithm will calculate the minimum value each time it is asked by executing the same sequence of instructions. Solutions similar to this one can be created for countless different cases and then executed on a huge set of problems that need to be addressed and solved.

Following the algorithm that computes the minimum value, we show a search algorithm for locating an item within a list of ordered values. This algorithm is used in many software applications that need to search for a target value within long sequences of ordered values. The algorithm we discuss here is called *Binary Search*, and it is efficient in finding a value if the list of values is ordered, as it works by cutting a sorted list in half until it finds the item or discovers that the item is not in the list. Each step eliminates half of the possibilities. For example, in a list of 1,000 items, you need at most 10 steps instead of the 1,000 steps that could be required if a linear search strategy is used.

---

```
Algorithm BinarySearch(LIST, TARGET):
BEGIN
        ASSIGN the value 1 to LOW
        ASSIGN the length of the LIST to HIGH
        WHILE LOW ≤ HIGH DO
            ASSIGN the value (LOW+HIGH)/2 to MID
            IF LIST[MID] == TARGET THEN
                WRITE LIST[MID]                         /target is found
            ELSE IF LIST[MID] < TARGET THEN
                ASSIGN LOW the value of MID+1   /search in the right half
                ELSE
                ASSIGN HIGH the value of MID-1 /search in the left half
        END WHILE
        WRITE "NOT FOUND"                           /target is not in the list
END
```

---

The binary search algorithm receives the list of items and the target element as input. Then, it starts a **WHILE** loop by looking at the middle item in the list (stored in the variable **MID**). If it is the one we are looking for, we are done, and the target value is written. If the middle item is smaller than what we are looking for, the algorithm ignores the left half and searches only in the right half. If the middle item is larger than what we are looking for, the algorithm ignores the right half and searches only in the left half. The **WHILE** loop is repeated, always cutting the list in half, until the item is found or the list becomes empty; that is, the target item is not in the list.

Each algorithm represents a small or large machine that is always ready to execute its operations. This highlights the power of algorithms, which, once codified in the form of software programs, will run their instructions without showing a hint of tiredness. They will do so to perform short numerical calculations, solve very long sequences of logical choices, or analyze enormous quantities of text, images, or videos. The programming languages used to implement algorithms today are able to represent every element of our reality, not only a single number, vector, or table but also sentences, entire documents, voice recordings, images, or videos, as a long sequence of bits upon which all the processing operations that we are capable of conceiving can be executed. Let's consider that a bit is the minimum unit of information represented by a binary digit, which can represent two values: 0 or 1. In computers, bits are grouped into sequences made up of 8 bits, called bytes, or of 16 or 32 bits, called words. All information can be coded in a set of bits, bytes, and words that represent the basic quanta for representing any kind of information we can conceive.

## 2.4 Algorithms Became Software

In the mid-20th century, the essential contributions of Alan Turing, John von Neumann, John Vincent Atanasoff, Konrad Zuse, and other mathematicians and scientists created computer science as a new science, capable of transforming algorithms from tools used exclusively by mathematicians, physicists, and engineers into automatic procedures available to everyone to execute with surprising speed using machines composed of billions of electronic circuits. Procedures designed as software code to process small or large quantities of data in various formats, representing the variety and quantity of information present in our world [4]. When, after the creation of the first programmable computers in the 1940s, algorithms were represented through sequences of software codes (data declarations and instructions) that electronic machines read and execute, they became a very powerful and pervasive machinery. These sequences of instructions are expressed through a set of programming languages that define a large set of instructions, which can be combined to express any algorithm we wish to implement and run on a computer.

Through computers, algorithms have emerged from the shell of mathematics and science to become the fastest and most efficient operational tools available to all individuals who can use them relentlessly to solve simple or complex problems, communicate with their peers, work, travel, and have fun – in short, to relate to the world.

Despite the numerous and complex means for representing experience that human beings have invented since their appearance on Earth, today the main intermediation between people and the outside world is carried out by algorithms. Endless sequences of operations that codify complex processes and calculate solutions to a very large number of problems. They and their operational form, which is embodied in the software programs that machines execute, are the new logos. They are words and thoughts entrusted to machines to make the humans of the new millennium powerful and efficient. They are executed at enormous speeds by computers, smartphones, and all digital devices that populate our world.

Software systems place us continuously in relation with reality, constantly circumscribing and modifying our daily lives. They guide men and women who, in many situations, experience difficulty managing and interacting, with full knowledge and awareness, with the ever-new digital tools in widespread use. Very sophisticated tools that feed bulimically on algorithms and execute them when requested, as well as in many cases where we do not want them or are unaware of them.

## 2.5 Algorithms and AI

Until about 20 years ago, algorithms and software systems were designed to explicitly perform a given task and transform input data into results through a series of imperative statements. Nowadays, algorithms based on machine learning strategies and used in artificial intelligence systems use input data to create new algorithms capable of acting autonomously on new data without the need for human intervention. This new scenario represents an epochal transition. Generative AI programs, such as ChatGPT and Gemini, have taken over our language and our forms of expression, and they are able to converse with us, create new information, instruct us, and operate autonomously in our daily lives. The challenges they put in place also open up the problem of human capabilities in comparison with machines and in studying, developing, and using new AI systems that require specialized skills.

Machine learning algorithms persistently offer new solutions in the management of individual and social relationships. They are building a procedural future, and they build it while they predict it. The automatic prediction of our future is one of the main objectives of the so-called data analysis. New professions and new skills, such as those of data scientists, prompt engineers, and data detectives, have emerged from data science and inductive algorithms that build methods for identifying links between information, relationships among events, classifications of facts and people, and synthetic systems capable of proposing what will happen to us tomorrow.

New sciences and technologies quickly allow for processing and predictions, even if, in many cases, they cannot explain the deep reasons for a relationship or predicted phenomenon. In fact, AI algorithms learn from data as we learn from experience; however, sometimes we do not understand how to give a clear explanation of the events we observe. Similarly, AI systems, in several cases, do not know how to explain a phenomenon to users, although they anticipate it, predict it, and suggest it to humans who very often follow their recommendations [5].

Digital society is increasingly configured as a very long "concatenation of procedures" that is subjected to a sort of "universal coding procedure," represented by information technologies that, driven by algorithms, promote the so-called "calculative thinking." They aim for total automatism and push for the success of computational action to the detriment of emotional action and consciousness. Obviously, the large impact of digital systems has significant social implications.

With the widespread use of AI, there is a risk of moving toward an "algorithmic life" in which the governance of individuals and community dynamics will increasingly be defined by automatic learning algorithms and data analysis software. The roles of science and technology are increasingly influential and prescriptive. In this continuous acquisition of relevance, the so-called techno-science should take charge, not alone, in "shaping" our future, and this role cannot be limited to the development of extraordinary and useful "algorithmic prostheses." It must assume ethical and social roles by contributing to the development of a new thought that is based not only on rationality but also on creativity and human consciousness.

The rapid expansion of technological domains, both as an operational tool and as a thinking tool, pushes forward the frontiers of human evolution. At the same time, this scenario of advancement requires greater responsibility, as well as increased public investment in research and development and a broader social vision. Technological innovation must be used to help us face the elusiveness of the present, together with the immense complexity of the future, and not to complicate the picture.

The relationship between human knowledge and machine knowledge, based on algorithms and data, will shape the future in which we will live. We will have to catch up with the procedural accumulation that machines are realizing through algorithms. This should also be made possible through the appropriate and responsible use of AI systems. We must work to improve ourselves and act toward the distribution of the benefits that machine intelligence is producing today and will produce in the future. We could emerge with new and wider inequalities or with better conditions of coexistence and justice. This certainly also depends on the use we will be able to make of the many solutions algorithms, computers, and AI are making available to society.

## References

1. Knuth, D. E. (1997). *The Art of Computer Programming, Fundamental Algorithms, Vol. 1*. USA: Addison-Wesley Professional.
2. Boyer, C. B. (1991). *The Arabic Hegemony. A History of Mathematics*. USA: John Wiley & Sons.
3. Sigler, L. E. (2002). *Fibonacci's Liber Abaci: A Translation into Modern English of Leonardo Pisano's Book of Calculation*. Germany: Springer-Verlag.
4. Talia, D. (2020). *Big Data and the Computable Society: Algorithms and People in the Digital World*. UK: World Scientific Publishing.
5. Talia, D. (2023). *From Algorithms to Thinking Machines: The New Digital Power*. USA: ACM Books.

# Chapter 3

# In a Planetary Computer

*The internet is a reflection of our society, and that mirror is going to be reflecting what we see.*
*If we do not like what we see in that mirror the problem is not to fix the mirror, we have to fix society.*

—Vinton Cerf

Every story, even the most important, begins with tiny events, and sometimes, when these tiny events occur, we don't realize they are merely the first microscopic grains of what will become a gigantic mountain. This is how many things in human history have begun, and very often, even the greatest scientific and technological discoveries begin with small events. The processes of discovery and innovation are never linear, and even when serendipity, which combines hard work, chance, and luck, is absent, inventions are never entirely predictable *a priori*.

## 3.1 The Night the Internet Was Born

What happened on October 29, 1969, in an area of California that a few years later would be called Silicon Valley, has changed the world. However, the protagonists back then had no idea what would happen next.

Something similar had happened to many other innovators before them (e.g., Guglielmo Marconi and Wilbur and Orville Wright), who had made discoveries that would have universal effects.

The student revolts of the 1960s in the United States originated and grew in Californian universities and from there spread throughout the West, leaving profound scars and epochal changes. In the same places and at the same time as the student activist movement and the Flower Children emerged, another revolution was born: a technological revolution based on silicon and telecommunications. Among the many fathers of this revolution, strangely enough, was the U.S. Department of Defense, which had decided to fund a small project to connect computers installed in different locations across the country to run complex calculation programs, rather than funding the purchase of new, more powerful, but much more expensive computers.

Thus, several research groups began working on an unprecedented project that, if it achieved its intended goals, would have connected only a very few North American computers. After several meetings, discussions, and phone calls, it was decided to try connecting the first two computers: one at the University of California at Los Angeles (UCLA) and the other at the Stanford Research Institute (SRI) in Menlo Park. Once the first prototype communications software was implemented, the first experimental test was needed to verify whether the data were reaching their destination. Due to several technical problems and tedious details to resolve, the test did not arrive until after sunset, when the California sky had lost its usual blue hue.

It was late that evening at the UCLA laboratories in Los Angeles. It was well after 9 p.m. when Charley Kline, a young programmer, typed the letter "L" on his computer keyboard and, a few seconds later, received a telephone confirmation from Menlo Park: "Yes. Let's see the L." Then, Kline typed the character "O" and transmitted it to the Menlo Park computer. At the computer at SRI, Bill Duvall, another long-haired programmer, sat waiting to receive the characters Charley had typed. The two of them, along with all of their colleagues from the two research groups, on that evening of Wednesday, October 29, 1969, conducted the first communication experiment on the ARPANET, the precursor to the Internet. Those two characters were the first tiny step in the worldwide network that today, after more than 50 years, connects people and things across the Earth and beyond.

## 3.2 The Network of Computers Grows

The Internet has now entered our lives in a pervasive and all-encompassing way, yet among the billions of people who use the network every day, few know the story of the first communication sent on what would become the Internet and its first two characters.[1] After approximately 50 years, annual data traffic transmitted on the Internet has reached 1,500 exabytes, while the number of Internet users is estimated to exceed 5.2 billion (over 60% of the Earth's population). The Web, the Internet's most popular application, now boasts about two billion sites (the first was created on a NEXT computer on August 6, 1991, at CERN by the inventor of the World Wide Web, English physicist Tim Berners-Lee), and for many users, especially younger ones, it is as if the Internet has always existed.

Yet, the history of the great network, like Marconi's radio and the Wright brothers' airplane, began with the communication of just two characters that were sent late in the evening of October 29, 1969, more than 50 years ago. They were sent from the Honeywell DDP 516 computer at the University of California at Los Angeles to the SDS 90 computer, where a software program was running and waiting for them at the Stanford Research Institute in Menlo Park.

That initial network, which also included two other computers, one at the University of Utah and the fourth at the Mathematics Center of the University of California, was not yet called the Internet. However, it was the first nucleus of the predecessor network that took the name ARPANET because it was funded by the Advanced Research Projects Agency (ARPA), later renamed DARPA, and which carried out research projects on behalf of the U.S. Department of Defense.

In front of the UCLA computer were members of Professor Leonard Kleinrock's group attempting to connect to the Stanford Research Institute computer. The reason for that choice as the first ARPANET node, intended to lead the first experiment, was also linked to the fact that Kleinrock had been the first and leading scholar to develop the theory of *packet switching* and conduct pioneering studies on the analysis, design, and measurement of message exchange between computers.

---

[1] The characters "L" and "O" were used because they are the first two letters of the word "LOGIN."

Kleinrock had published the first scientific paper on the theory of data packet switching, the basis of that experiment, in 1961 [1] and his first book on the subject in 1964 [2]. Indeed, in the years preceding that experiment, Leonard Kleinrock had successfully argued for the theoretical feasibility of computer communications based on packet switching rather than the creation of *ad hoc* circuits (*circuit switching*), and this represented a significant contribution to the creation of computer communication networks.

Packet switching is a technique of transferring data in a network in the form of packets. The data belonging to a message to be sent are broken into small pieces, called packets, and sent through one or more connections toward the destination. At the destination, all these small packets have to be reassembled to rebuild the message. With packet switching, the network capacity is used only when data are actually being sent, and thus many users/computers can share the same network infrastructure at the same time. On the contrary, in circuit switching, used in traditional telephone networks, a dedicated communication path is reserved between the sender and receiver for the entire duration of a session. Even if no data were being transmitted, the reserved capacity cannot be used by other users, leading to inefficiency and contention during setup.

In October 1972, Robert Kahn, then head of the ARPANET project for DARPA, organized the first public demonstration of the ARPANET network at the International Computer Communication Conference (ICCC) held in Washington, D.C. At that time, 40 computers were connected to the network, a number that was a surprising achievement. In 1972, one of the most widely used applications on the Internet was created: electronic mail, or email. In March 1972, Tomlinson created the first software for sending and receiving messages over the ARPANET, with the primary purpose of facilitating the exchange of information and collaboration among ARPANET project members. He was the first to use the now-famous @ symbol to distinguish the recipient's name from their address. That first version was expanded by Lawrence G. Roberts, who extended the email sending system by adding the necessary functions to read messages, display a list of incoming and outgoing emails, and automatically reply to a received message. Since then, email has become the most widely used tool for exchanging information among people.

## 3.3 The Importance of Protocols

Network protocols are standardized rules implemented by communication software to manage how computers communicate and exchange data. They are essential because they ensure interoperability, reliability, and efficiency across connected computers. Protocols are necessary in computer communications because they provide a common language and a set of rules that allow different machines, often developed by different vendors and running different software systems, to exchange data correctly.

In the early 1970s, the ARPANET network continued to expand and connect an ever-increasing number of computers, research centers, and universities. Researchers working on its design and implementation gradually realized the need to improve its functionality and, above all, increase the generality of its transmission protocol, the so-called Network Control Protocol (NCP), to accommodate a wide variety of contexts and integrate all interconnection technologies. Thus, in 1973, the development of the TCP/IP protocol began under the leadership of Robert Kahn and Vinton Cerf. This development led to the transition from the ARPANET to the Internet, followed by the invention of the World Wide Web (WWW) by Tim Berners-Lee and Robert Cailliau in 1991 at CERN, along with the spread of smartphones and mobile communications software, which completed the development and diffusion of the network as we know it today.

Kahn and Cerf's idea was that there was a need for a network, named the Internet, based on the ARPANET packet switching model, capable of connecting multiple independent networks based on different technologies, such as satellite networks, cable-based telephone networks, and radio frequency communications networks. In short, an open architecture was needed for computer internetworking. This open network model was proposed by Kahn in 1972 while working on a DARPA project. Kahn developed a communications protocol that defined the basic rules for exchanging data packets among different computers connected to an open network architecture. The project Kahn worked on was called "Internetting," and the protocol he designed, after a series of design and development phases, was named Transmission Control Protocol/Internet Protocol (TCP/IP).

In the spring of 1973, Robert Kahn asked Vinton Cerf, who was then working at Stanford, to join him in defining the details of the TCP/IP protocol. Kahn and Cerf completed the definition of the protocol, which included the rules and services for sending and transporting data packets, and in 1974, they published the first paper on the TCP protocol [3]. This first version of the protocol, which underpins the functioning of the Internet and all its applications, underwent modifications that became necessary to handle data communication errors and ensure the order of delivery of sent data packets. This work led to the reorganization of the original protocol, which was divided into two protocols: the IP protocol for addressing and sending individual data blocks between computers and TCP, which in the new version was designed to handle packet flow control between the sending and receiving computers and the recovery of any packets lost during communication.

After the TCP/IP protocol was developed, DARPA funded three research contracts for Vinton Cerf, Ray Tomlinson, and Peter Kirstein, with the goal of developing three independent implementations of the protocol. In less than one year, the three implementations were completed and were used to demonstrate TCP/IP's ability to exchange data using heterogeneous communications networks. From then on, TCP/IP began to spread, and with it, the Internet grew exponentially in number, services, applications, and complexity. The old NCP protocol used on computers connected to the ARPANET was completely replaced with the new TCP/IP protocol on January 1, 1983. On that day, the communications software on most ARPANET computers was replaced, allowing those computers to be open to connections outside the ARPANET and join the vast Internet.

From the US, computer networks spread throughout the world. The first connections were established between North America and Europe and within the Old Continent. England, Norway, and Germany were the first three European nations to connect to ARPANET, while Italy was the fourth.

## 3.4 From the Web to the Blockchain

The WWW emerged in the early 1990s as a distributed system of hypertext documents connected via hyperlinks and accessible through the Internet. Tim Berners-Lee and colleagues introduced the first version at CERN, with the first website going online in August 1991. In its first two years, the Web consisted of a small set of interconnected sites accessed through the first browser and server developed by Berners-Lee. Then, it rapidly expanded once the Mosaic browser was released in 1993, making available distributed websites accessible to a wider public.

In 1995, the Web was only a four-year-old infant, but its grid of links already connected tens of thousands of sites. The most widely used operating system was Windows 95. Google did not exist yet; it would appear in 1998, while Jeff Bezos was starting to launch his Amazon.com portal to sell books, and no one had yet realized that it would quickly revolutionize the commerce of goods and products.

By 1998, the Web had grown to approximately 2.5 million sites (today, the number is estimated at around 2 billion sites), and the arrival of Google that year came as a surprise to those who, upon using it, quickly realized how much more effective it was than Altavista and Yahoo! at finding pages and content on a Web that was becoming too large to navigate without an efficient guide, such as the one invented by two Stanford University doctoral students. PayPal was born that same year to become the fastest and most dynamic tool for electronic payments and to support purchases on e-commerce sites such as eBay.

In those same years, another innovation arrived from the US that would change the lives and ways of working for many people: Wi-Fi networks. It was no longer necessary to connect our laptops with a cable to modems or the local network. All we needed was a wireless connection card, and we could go online without using wires. Of course, in the early years, these were "magical" gadgets for a select few. The rest of us were happy with a PC that could connect even over a telephone line that transmitted a few dozen kilobytes per second, just to be able to use the sea of information that the Web "gave us". It was a dense and increasingly enveloping web, at that time free of advertising and other annoying digital hindrances.

The dawn of the new millennium brought other great innovations and opportunities, along with risks. The year 2004 marked the debut of Facebook, the brainchild of Mark Zuckerberg, then a 19-year-old Harvard University student, who initially called it Facemash and used it on campus to vote for the most attractive faces. To many users, Facebook seemed like a fun tool for catching up with old, long-lost friends. Only later did it reveal itself to be a colossal advertising machine and a gigantic source of fake news. YouTube arrived the following year and played its part in forever changing the way we watch videos and films, forcing all television channels worldwide to follow its "on-demand" model and leaving static television schedules to the few nostalgic viewers.

Meanwhile, smartphones had crept into our pockets and ladies' handbags. First, to be able to make phone calls from anywhere, and later, to stay constantly connected to the web, social media, email, and many other apps. The next step came in 2007 with the release of the iPhone, featuring a touchscreen that enabled us to do everything online with a simple tap of our finger. That convenient and elegant object, the brainchild of Steve Jobs, quickly outpaced other models, imposing a typing ease we can no longer live without.

Digital transformations did not end there, and other innovations continued to arrive: the cloud, intelligent voice assistants such as Alexa and Siri, cryptocurrencies, and the metaverse. In 2009, Satoshi Nakamoto (a pseudonym perhaps concealing multiple individuals) invented Bitcoin, the progenitor of cryptocurrencies that are poised to play an increasingly important role in the world of finance and which contributed to the birth of digital versions of state currencies that will replace paper currencies in the coming years. The story of the first Bitcoin purchase at a Papa John's pizzeria in Florida in 2010 is entirely true. Two pizzas cost 10,000 Bitcoins, which were worth about $40 at the time. The owner, unfortunately for him, resold those Bitcoins shortly thereafter for about $400. Had he held onto them until today, when one Bitcoin is worth about $100,000, he would have been worth a staggering $1 billion.

Bitcoin relies on a secure distributed architecture to record and verify all transactions associated with money transfers. This system is blockchain, a distributed ledger in which data are grouped into "blocks" and linked in chronological order, forming a chain. Each block contains a set of Bitcoin transactions and a cryptographic reference to the previous block, making the entire history tamper-resistant. Transactions are validated by a network of participants called miners, who use computational power to solve puzzles and add new blocks. Once a block is added, it becomes part of the shared record that every participant can access, ensuring transparency and consensus. In this way, the blockchain guarantees the integrity of Bitcoin and other cryptocurrencies without the need for central oversight. In summary, Bitcoin is a digital currency, while blockchain is the underlying technology that makes it possible. Since its invention, this technology has been recognized as useful well beyond monetary matters, with applications in supply chains, voting systems, and digital identity.

The widespread use of smartphones worldwide has generated a market for apps that we now use to do virtually everything. We have dozens or hundreds of them on our devices, and they occupy a large portion of our daily time, both at work and during leisure. As we use them, they collect enormous amounts of data that large tech companies use to profile us and serve us endless streams of advertising.

As if all this were not enough to fill four decades of continuous digital innovation, recent years have given us machine learning and generative artificial intelligence, which, in a short time, have become capable of driving self-driving cars, communicating with us in natural language, writing articles and books, composing songs, creating software, and producing entire artificial videos – in short, a technology capable of creating the oxymoron of synthetic reality, made up of tangible illusions and merely plausible truths.

## 3.5 The Network of Everything

Over its decades of existence, the Internet has changed a great deal, transforming our lives, the way we work, and the way we communicate. Yet, as we mentioned, the Internet was conceived in a very different era from today, when information technology was also very different from what we use today. The history of the Internet began with the goal of connecting a few large computers. Currently, there are billions of nodes (supercomputers, personal computers, personal digital assistants, smartphones, and sensors) connected to the network, along with thousands of different network applications and highly advanced services that would not be possible without the Internet. Today's network is primarily composed of mobile nodes, and the Internet is transforming from a network of computers into a network of smart objects, the Internet of Things (IoT), in which every object (e.g., a bracelet, a cup, a bicycle, or a t-shirt) can be connected to the network. The IoT is a network of physical objects, such as sensors, appliances, vehicles, and webcams, that are equipped with communication hardware, operating software, and data-processing capabilities, enabling them to collect, exchange, and act on information over the Internet without requiring direct human intervention.

It is clear that few decisions have had such a significant and pervasive impact on the lives of individuals and society as a whole as the one ARPA made at that time. Born from the need to share resources, the Internet is today the greatest sharing tool humanity has ever created. It happens cyclically that when something new, something unprecedented appears, we have difficulty defining it, and we tend to use already known names. In the case of the IoT, the word "thing" hides a universe of chips, circuits, and algorithms that transform and augment the functions of every traditional object such as a keychain, a watch, a mug, or a pair of glasses, transforming it into a postmodern artifact that only with time will we be able to call by an appropriate name.

The IoT, today, is made up of several billion new digital objects, devices that speak and communicate with us and, above all, with each other, often without human control. In short, they have enabled formerly passive things, like our car keys, wearable sensors, Wi-Fi refrigerators, home alarm devices, or radio frequency smart tags that, thanks to the chips and software they contain, become interactive. They are "neo-things" that communicate with us and the environment through the logic they enclose, which allows them to live and interact, removing the passivity that the "traditional things" of the world have always had, even as they continue to appear to us as mere objects. In other words, they are hidden computers – electronic micro-machines in disguise.

It is estimated that there are about 20 billion of these new "smart neo-things" on Earth, and within the next decade, there will be over 40 billion – many more than human beings. We program them, we help them connect, and they can cooperate even without us: wearable devices, cell phones, sensors, webcams, drones, household appliances, smartwatches, iBeacons, GPS devices, RFID tags, and smart cards of all kinds. There are countless of them, and they are capable of exchanging information, storing data, and processing information much faster than us and without our help. New technologies, such as compute continuum and edge, fog, and ambient computing, are all that bring to life the new things that inhabit our world, work with us, and constitute the Earth's new life system, which acts for us without depending on us, except for power.

They resemble vast colonies of digital ants, hives of billions of robotic bees, and countless "binary drops of water" that become an ocean, which organize and operate increasingly autonomously. They empower transportation, large cities, shopping malls, hospitals, cars, industries, homes, and all communication infrastructures that humans need. Unfortunately, they also go to war in new autonomous weapons, kamikaze drones, robot soldiers, thermal imaging goggles, and the latest-generation missiles. Moreover, in the military field, they are reshaping the landscape of battles and large-scale conflicts.

As we will discuss in the following chapters, Ludwig Wittgenstein, in his *Tractatus Logico-Philosophicus* [4], argues that our world is not a collection of objects but is rather made up of the relationships that exist between objects and, therefore, of the events that happen as a result of these relationships. The IoT is based on these principles and is defining the occurrences of our lives and of the world.

## References

1. Kleinrock, L. (1961). Information flow in large communication nets. RLE Quarterly Progress Report.
2. Kleinrock, L. (1964). *Communication Nets: Stochastic Message Flow and Delay*. USA: McGraw-Hill.
3. Cerf, V. G. and Kahn, R. E. (1974). A protocol for packet network interconnection. *IEEE Transactions on Communication Technology*, 22(5), pp. 627–641.
4. Wittgenstein, L. (2017). *Tractatus Logico-Philosophicus*. UK: Benediction Classics.

# Chapter 4

# Programming Artificial Intelligence

*By far, the greatest danger of Artificial Intelligence is that people conclude too early that they understand it.*

—Eliezer Yudkowsky

Alan Turing was one of the first scientists to reason how to build machines capable of thinking. Previously, several philosophers and, of course, some science fiction authors had done so. Around the end of the 1940s, Turing wrote a few essays on the possibility of a computer being programmed to respond appropriately to human questions (the so-called Turing test) [1–3]. In those essays, the English mathematician used the term "machine intelligence," which is a synonym of "automatic intelligence," wondering whether it was possible to create computers capable of thinking or, at least, capable of giving us the impression that they were thinking.

Despite his authority, the term Turing coined to indicate the ability of an electronic computer to, in certain situations, solve problems like a human was not very successful. The term that proved successful, however, and which is now used all too frequently by specialists and ordinary people, was created a few years later. It was in 1955, to be precise, that a group of American university professors and researchers led by John McCarthy, Marvin Minsky, Nathaniel Rochester, and Claude Shannon proposed a workshop to study how to build intelligent computers, which was to be held the following summer at Dartmouth College, New Hampshire [4]. The workshop was actually held at that university from mid-June to mid-August 1956 and was the first scientific conference on the so-called “artificial intelligence”.

That was the birthplace of a scientific discipline that, through ups and downs, has grown extraordinarily and developed to become a hotly debated topic not only in the scientific community but also across all social contexts. A subject that, thanks to research developments and especially the systems developed in recent years, is poised to have a huge impact on people’s lives. Indeed, AI systems are changing the world of work, communications, healthcare, education, transportation, and even tourism and agriculture. There is much to be said about the impact of AI systems on the social and political organization of nations and on the future of both democracies and authoritarian regimes, which are competing with great commitment and significant financial investment to gain leadership in the development of AI technologies.

The choice of the organizers of the 1956 workshop to use the term “artificial intelligence” to refer to computer systems capable of actions and choices that can be deemed intelligent has sparked much discussion and controversy regarding what this new kind of intelligence actually is and its relationship to human intelligence. Let’s clarify right away that computer systems that fall within the field of AI are hardware/software systems that, based on their algorithms (i.e., sequences of instructions) and input data, are able to calculate difficult results (such as the probability of success of a therapy or the answers required to win a TV quiz) or make decisions that are not easy for a machine (for example, regarding facial recognition or the most desired products among teenagers over the next 12 months). These include all problems that, when humans have to face them, we say it is necessary to use intelligence to solve them.

## 4.1 Programming Models for AI

Researchers in the AI field proposed several theoretical computational models of intelligence. At the same time, they developed languages and tools for implementing AI systems. If we look at the history of programming paradigms designed and used for developing AI systems, we note that from the 1950s to the 1970s, symbolic programming models were used. AI began with symbolic reasoning, where knowledge was represented explicitly as rules and logic. Languages like LISP (LISt Processing) [5] and Prolog (Programming in Logic) [6] were designed and used for manipulating symbols rather than numbers. These systems powered theorem proving, early work in natural language processing (NLP), and logic-based problem-solving. LISP focuses on symbolic computation through the manipulation of lists, which serve as both data and code structures. The syntax of LISP is simple and based on parentheses and recursive functions. The dual nature of lists as both data and programs makes LISP unique and powerful, especially for AI research where symbolic reasoning is key.[1] Prolog programs, instead, are written as sets of facts and rules, and computation occurs through logical inference and pattern matching. This makes Prolog especially well-suited for tasks requiring reasoning, such as expert systems, natural language understanding, and solving problems with constraints.

From the 1970s to the 1980s, the focus shifted to developing expert systems based on rule processing, primarily coded in logic languages such as Prolog. Inference engines used either forward or backward chaining to deduce conclusions from a set of rules. They had some success in medicine and business but found it difficult to scale for solving many real-world problems.

In the 1990s. AI moved from rule-processing models toward approaches aimed at learning from data. Machine learning systems[2] using decision trees, *k*-NN, and probabilistic models were implemented. Instead of hand-coding rules, learning algorithms discover patterns (semi-) automatically and adapt their code to the data domain on which they had been instructed.

In the last years of the 20th century and in the first decade of the new one, connectionist and neural network models demonstrated to be effective if provided with very large training sets of data. Matrix-based computation and gradient descent became core programming patterns for

---

[1] This very simple LISP program: (setq code '(+ 10 20)); (print (eval code)); evaluates the list composed of two elements (10, 20) and compute their sum (30).

[2] Machine learning defines a set of techniques that enable programs to improve their performance on complex tasks by learning patterns from data, rather than being explicitly programmed. It works by training algorithms on examples, allowing them to make predictions or decisions when exposed to new, unseen information. The term was popularized by Arthur Samuel in 1959, who defined "machine learning" as "the field of study that gives computers the ability to learn without being explicitly programmed." Samuel originally demonstrated this approach with a checkers-playing program, which improved its performance the more it played.

developing deep neural networks. As in other machine learning models, adapting a neural network to a given learning task did not require programming effort. What is needed is to train the network with a large dataset of examples and a training phase to improve its adaptation to a specific domain, for example, in image recognition, NLP, or control tasks.

In the first two decades of the new century, AI exploited big data and high-performance computing (HPC) [7]. Therefore, tools such as Hadoop, Spark, and parallel machine learning frameworks enabled AI systems implementation and training on massive datasets. Distributed and federated machine learning frameworks decentralized AI systems while increasing accessibility and performance. With the advent of HPC systems and massive datasets, deep neural networks have proven far more effective than symbolic manipulation in solving some of the most challenging problems in AI, including natural language modeling.

This novel scenario significantly influenced the ways developers program machine/deep learning and generative AI applications. Whereas imperative parallel programming models, such as CUDA, OpenMP, and MPI, are used to implement efficient and scalable AI frameworks, these frameworks do not require traditional programming approaches to implement AI applications such as chatbots, machine learning apps, and agentic systems. In fact, AI applications are developed by providing input datasets and parameter values to an AI framework, and it generates a learning program that executes complex tasks such as event classification, pattern recognition, sentiment analysis, content translation, and content generation.

The main trend for future AI programming is given by natural language programming (NLPg). This new technology refers to an approach where people write programs (or interact with a system) using natural human language (such as English or Italian), instead of a formal programming language. NLPg aims to let users describe instructions in plain natural language, which are then parsed, interpreted, or translated into executable code. A significant first step is represented by AI-assisted coding tools (e.g., GitHub Copilot and ChatGPT Code Interpreter), which let you describe what you want in natural language and generate the code automatically. However, these systems are error-prone and need attention and intervention from human programmers to fix errors and avoid the negative effects of ambiguity of human language that is not correctly resolved by AI-based coding frameworks [8].

## 4.2 Programming or Training AI Algorithms?

Following Alan Turing's initial contributions to machine intelligence, the idea of the proposers of the AI workshop held at Dartmouth College was "*to proceed on the basis of the conjecture that every aspect of learning or any other feature of intelligence can in principle be so precisely described that a machine can be made to simulate it. An attempt will be made to find how to make machines use language, form abstractions and concepts, solve kinds of problems now reserved for humans, and improve themselves.*"

During the workshop at Dartmouth College in the summer of 1956, two main ideas emerged for the creation of intelligent systems:

- the **logic-based** approach, which used the inference of logical rules to process sequences of symbols; it is also called the "symbolic approach," as it considers intelligence as the manipulation of symbols according to formal rules to deduce new rules and compute results.
- the **connectionist** approach, which mimicked the biological processes of human neurons and their connections. Intelligence was modeled as collective behavior arising from networks of simple units (neurons) connected together. This approach defined the concept of artificial neurons capable of learning by strengthening the connections between them. It is the precursor of today's deep learning.

As discussed above, neural networks are a class of systems that belong to machine learning models. Like other learning models (e.g., decision trees or support vector machines), neural networks are trained on large sets of data describing facts, items or phenomena. During training, they adjust their internal parameters (weights) to capture patterns in the data. Once trained, they can apply what they learned to new, unseen data, which is the core goal of machine learning.

Although McCulloch and Pitts demonstrated that any computable function can be represented by a specific artificial neural network [9], the logical approach, initially proposed by Newell and Simon at the 1956 conference at Dartmouth College in New Hampshire, was considered the most valid for three of four decades, while the neural network approach did not seem to show good results except in small cases. After the final decades of the last century, logic-based and expert systems failed to deliver on their promises, and at the beginning of the new century, systems based on neural networks underwent significant developments.

Thanks to the use of increasingly powerful computers that have enabled large, very fast deep neural networks and the availability of large amounts of data (Big Data) to train neural models, this approach has seen significant developments and very encouraging results in many application areas, such as image recognition, speech recognition, automatic text translation, and even text generation from just a few sentences.

As mentioned, when we use neural networks, it is not necessary to explicitly program the operations to be performed or the rules to be used to achieve a result. It is sufficient to provide the network of artificial neurons with a series of input data to which it can associate output data. The network is capable of adjusting its connections to produce the correct output, and after doing so, it will be able to provide further correct output results based on new inputs. In short, we don't program how the network should behave, but rather we program the network structure and define its initial connections. Then we train the network by providing input data and checking if it produces correct output. If results are correct, the network strengthens its connections, and if results are wrong, connections are adjusted to improve the learning process. Its algorithm will then adapt it to the problem we need to solve, learning from the data we provide. The network learns from examples, adapting to provide correct answers, much like our brains do when faced with a new situation and use their prior knowledge to react appropriately. In a neural network, errors are measured by a loss function, and then an optimization algorithm (e.g., gradient descent) updates parameters to reduce the error.

A similar procedure occurs in other machine learning algorithms, such as decision trees, logistic regression, *k*-nearest neighbors, support vector machines, and naïve Bayes. In the training phase, the model adjusts its internal parameters by comparing its predictions with the correct answers. When the accuracy of classification is good on training data, the model is evaluated on new, unseen data to check how well it generalizes. Once accurate enough, the model is used in real tasks, sometimes continuing to learn as more data arrive [10].

## 4.3 The Limits of Rule-Based Programming

One of the reasons the rule-based approach to implementing AI systems has not worked well so far is that we are unable to provide logic programming and expert systems with the entire set of rules, symbols, and facts humans know. While the logic-based approach can be effectively used in solving specific problems in restricted application domains, until today it was not successful as a general tool for implementing solutions in all fields. We are unable to program logic-based systems by transferring all of our knowledge into code, particularly the implicit (not entirely conscious) knowledge we possess. This transfer and communication of knowledge is sometimes impactful and inefficient. Therefore, programming large-scale logic systems and transforming them into algorithms was not feasible until today.

This scenario illustrates the fact that although a computer is capable of calculating everything computable (but not everything we would like to calculate), to do so we must program it appropriately, providing it with all the necessary strategies and procedures. This raises the issue of how we "communicate" with computers and how we transfer our knowledge so that they can solve problems on our behalf. The programming differences between the two approaches to AI illustrate the different ways in which we can transfer our knowledge to computers by providing them with algorithms, data, examples, and patterns. Much of the brief history of computer science is based on the explicit programming of computers using imperative programming languages that tell machines the sequences of operations that compose algorithms and must be executed to calculate a result or perform a given task. This type of programming approach has produced extraordinary results and made computers the most flexible, sophisticated, and fastest machines ever created. However, the approaches used in machine learning have produced new methods and strategies for programming computers, making them capable of new forms of intelligence.

Programming according to the machine learning paradigm (which also includes deep learning achieved through artificial neural networks) does not involve defining imperative algorithms that explicitly represent problem-solving procedures. On the contrary, it requires programming an algorithm that is ready to learn from data how to behave and therefore how to provide the solution to a given problem. In this case, we do not program explicit algorithms that provide the final solution to the problem, but rather we program algorithms that read large amounts of data and learn from them to compose the solution. They adapt to the data (input and/or output) they receive, building *ad hoc* software code that is capable of reading new data and providing new results. It must be said that these algorithms – because they depend on the data – are not always able to provide complete or perfect solutions but exhibit a behavior that leads to results with probabilistic characteristics, that is, results with an accuracy value that can vary and often does not correspond to 100%.

The ways in which computers have been programmed so far have significantly influenced the problems we have been able to solve with them. This issue unites at least three fundamental aspects of computer science: computers, algorithms, and programming languages with which algorithms are expressed so that they can be understood and executed on the available hardware. While numerous programming languages have been designed and developed, there is certainly much still to be researched and implemented to develop other computer programming models and techniques that will enable new applications and solutions. NLPg is one solution, perhaps the most interesting for many, but that does not mean it is the most promising or innovative.

In fact, as mentioned in a previous chapter, by using generative AI tools, such as Gemini, ChatGPT, or Claude, we can specify an algorithm in natural language and ask such large language models to generate the corresponding code in a programming language such as Java, C++, or Python. This is a kind of NLPg; however, code generated by LLMs often is not totally correct and requires the intervention of programmers to check the correctness of automatically generated programs, find bugs, and make improvements for getting an efficient version of those programs.

## 4.4 Two Different Intelligences

Many are passionate about the debate over whether AI is the same as human intelligence or different, and which of the two is superior. This debate would take us far, and perhaps we wouldn't even be able to sustain it fully, given the underlying uncertainty and complexity. What we are interested in discussing here, however, is a seemingly secondary but, in some respects, highly interesting aspect of the issue.

Although the proponents of the 1956 workshop [4] started from the idea that it was possible to simulate any characteristic of human intelligence with a computer, today many AI programs and systems don't aim to simulate human intelligence processes but are happy to execute data processing procedures whose results are similar to, or even better than, those produced by an intelligent human when solving the same problem.

A similar situation occurs with airplanes, which fly very well but don't do so by flapping their wings like birds, and it is also the case with helicopters, which don't fly by imitating birds, let alone bees or bumblebees. Therefore, the goal of AI systems is to find procedures that produce results similar to those people achieve using human intelligence, but without necessarily operating in the same way as the processes of the human brain. Even those computer systems that use a computational and communication structure inspired by that of the human brain (e.g., deep learning systems) employ extremely simplified models of the human brain, and on this basis alone, they cannot be considered intelligent systems capable of exactly replicating human intelligence. They simply draw inspiration from it.

To summarize, AI, beyond the highly evocative adjective, does not have as its primary goal reasoning like human intelligence (which, moreover, we don't fully understand how it works because many characteristics of the human brain and mind are still unknown to us), but rather intends to perform tasks, solve problems, and provide results that require people to use their intelligence. Tasks, solutions, and results that we humans cannot achieve without intelligence.

Therefore, we can conclude these brief considerations by saying that computers, through AI, can do many things that we consider intelligent, such as winning a game of chess, translating text from a foreign language, following a road and recognizing the signs they encounter, reading a book and summarizing it, diagnosing a disease from a series of medical tests, writing a newspaper article, designing new proteins, and many other things, but they do so without being truly intelligent according to the reference model for human intelligence.

Yet, what is increasingly being demonstrated through research and technological development in the field of AI systems is that they are capable of performing complex actions, achieving difficult goals, and making intelligent decisions. They accomplish these without showing flashes of genius, but simply by analyzing large amounts of data and seeking out the most significant and most interesting elements and patterns within them.

They do so without considering *qualia*, the qualitative elements (sensations) that various philosophers and many scholars of the mind, from Democritus to John Searle [11] and David Chalmers [12], have invoked to describe the aspects linked to an individual's consciousness that have emotional and sensitive characteristics. Currently, computers and AI systems don't know what *qualia* are and don't have consciousness, yet they are capable of doing complex things that only conscious humans can do. This could mean that consciousness isn't necessary to act intelligently, and besides, we have evidence that many conscious humans struggle to behave intelligently.

These aspects open up very interesting scenarios regarding the nature of intelligence (both human and artificial). On the one hand, these could lead to a reconsideration of the various theories on how intelligence is formed and recognized, and on the other, they could explain the mechanisms underlying the decisions of humans we deem intelligent. These decisions are often based on simple calculations performed repeatedly and rapidly, probabilistic assessments made on facts, events, and the many possible choices that can be made at any given moment, and on random factors that computers simulate very well through random functions, which are proving highly effective in AI, even for emulating human creativity. Creativity that, for example, is also implemented through the use of randomness in AI algorithms, when executed by a computer, can contribute to composing original pieces of music, writing accurate and even very long lyrics, or painting original and surprising portraits.

At this moment in history, the greatest concern for many seems to be preventing AI systems from becoming more "intelligent" than us humans (something that currently occurs in limited cases but cannot be ruled out as becoming the norm in the future). However, recent advances in AI systems could help demystify human intelligence by demonstrating that it can be achieved even without the extraordinary abilities we believe we alone possess, but through a series of simple methods, innate and/or acquired over time, allowing us to address the many everyday problems and find solutions to them much as digital machines have now learned to do.

## References

1. Turing, A. M. (1995). Lecture to the London Mathematical Society on 20 February 1947. *MD Computing,* 12, pp. 390–397.
2. Turing, A. M. (1969). Intelligent machinery. Report for National Physical Laboratory. Machine Intelligence, Vol. 5. UK: Edinburgh University Press.
3. Turing, A. M. (1950). Computing machinery and intelligence. *Mind,* LIX(236), pp. 433–460.

4. McCarthy, J., Minsky, M. L., Rochester, N., and Shannon, C.E. (1955). A proposal for the Dartmouth summer research project on artificial intelligence. jmc.stanford.edu/articles/dartmouth/dartmouth.pdf.
5. McCarthy, J. (1960). Recursive functions of symbolic expressions and their computation by machine, Part I. *Communications of the ACM*, 3(4), pp. 184–195.
6. Colmerauer, A. and Roussel, P. (1993). The birth of prolog. *ACM SIGPLAN Notices*, 28(3), pp. 37–52.
7. Talia, D., Trunfio, P., Marozzo, F., Belcastro, L., Cantini, R., and Orsino, A. (2024). *Programming Big Data Applications: Scalable Tools and Frameworks for Your Needs*. UK: World Scientific.
8. Wong, M.-F., Guo, S., Hang, C.-N. Ho, S.-W., and Tan, C.-W. (2023). Natural language generation and understanding of big code for ai-assisted programming: A review. *Entropy*, 25(6), p. 888.
9. McCulloch, W. S. and Pitts, W. (1943). A logical calculus of the ideas immanent in nervous activity. *Bulletin of Mathematical Biophysics*, 5, pp. 115–133. https://doi.org/10.1007/BF02478259.
10. Huyen, C. (2022). *Designing Machine Learning Systems*. USA: O'Really Media.
11. Searl, J. (1997). *The Mystery of Consciousnes*. USA: The New York Review of Books.
12. Chalmers, D. J. (2021). *Philosophy of Mind: Classical and Contemporary Readings*. UK: Oxford University Press.

# Chapter 5

# Social Media, Privacy, Chatbots and Narcissism

*Social media gives legions of idiots the right to speak when they once only spoke at a bar after a glass of wine, without harming the community ... but now they have the same right to speak as a Nobel Prize winner.*

—Umberto Eco

We can define social media as digital platforms that, through mobile and web applications, enable every individual to create and share content and interact with one another in virtual communities or networks. Unlike traditional media, social media allows anyone to be a producer and a consumer of content, a new kind of *prosumer*,[1] whose participation contributes to the value and visibility of the platform. Although in social media users produce content, we must consider that algorithms, not users, define the way content is distributed and shared.

The short but intense history of social media began in the late 1990s, when the internet became publicly accessible, the Web began to give many people the opportunity to write and read content online, and those

[1] Alvin Toffler in his 1980 book *The Third Wave* [1] is the originator of the term "*prosumer*," predicting today's interactive, participatory digital economy decades in advance. Toffler combined the words "producer" and "consumer" to describe a new kind of economic and social actor, the prosumer, who both produces and consumes goods or services.

people were excited to experiment with online communication platforms.

One of the earliest forms of social platforms was SixDegrees.com, created in 1997, which allowed users to create profiles and connect with friends, a concept that anticipated future networks. In the early 2000s, blogs and forums encouraged online self-expression and community interaction. Friendster and MySpace introduced more personalized networking and music sharing, attracting millions of users. Two years later, in 2004, Mark Zuckerberg, with a few classmates, launched Facebook at Harvard University, deeply transforming how people shared personal information online. YouTube followed in 2005, marking the beginning of large-scale user-generated video content. In 2006 Twitter appeared, pioneering microblogging with short, real-time messages.

Around 2010, Instagram and Snapchat emphasized instant sharing of photos and stories, changing how people documented their everyday lives. At the same time, LinkedIn grew as the dominant professional networking platform. During those years, social media became a central part of marketing, politics, and news dissemination. Profiling algorithms began to shape users' experiences, showing personalized content and targeted advertising according to the market policies of social media owners.

The late 2010s saw the rise of TikTok, a China-based social platform, bringing short-form video and AI-driven recommendations to global audiences. People began to realize how platform algorithms influence and manipulate them; therefore, social media began to face criticism for misinformation, addiction, and privacy issues [2]. In response, platforms introduced fact-checking tools and some moderation policies; however, users continued to encounter hate speech, fake news, and privacy violations.

By the 2020s, social media evolved into a mix of entertainment, communication, and commerce ecosystems. Live streaming and influencer culture became dominant trends. Following this trend, social media became content distributors rather than socialization tools for people. Today, social media platforms such as Facebook, Instagram, TikTok, and X (formerly Twitter) connect billions of users daily. They continue to evolve, integrating artificial intelligence, virtual reality, and personalization services. They are one of the most transformative technologies of the 21st century, reshaping how humanity communicates, learns, and shares identity, although some uses are unsafe for young people, and governments and parliaments of several countries are worried about their negative impact on communities and have passed laws and regulations to limit their use.

## 5.1 Social for Profit

The daily lives of individuals, their experiences, and their human feelings have for some time become the primary object and commodity of a new economy based on the consumption of endless digital elements, brilliantly exploited by many companies to obtain profits far greater than those generated by more traditional businesses. Production operations based on these "virtual quanta" are often hidden within sophisticated machines and within lengthy sequences of operations that process them in the form of data to generate economic value extracted from people's lives. The collection, processing, classification, and sale of data, information, and forecasts are operations that have created a mutation of capitalism, which has become increasingly digital and characterized by the vast accumulation of wealth, knowledge, and power held by a few individuals who make up a technological super-élite.

This economic-technological phenomenon has strong social impacts and is unprecedented in human history in terms of its pervasiveness and influence, surpassing the effects of traditional media in the past. The shift from a web model based on a limited set of "writers" (generators of content to be distributed worldwide to millions of readers via web pages, information portals, and blogs) to that of social media platforms where anyone can write and read has been taking hold for some time. This transition began at the end of the previous century and has captivated billions of people who are thrilled to have their own micro-communication channels through which they can meddle with other people's business while also allowing others to meddle with their own.

Facebook claims to manage over 3 billion accounts (with the number of Facebook's daily active users (DAUs) currently standing at more than 2 billion people), while Instagram (owned by the same company) claims just over 2 billion users. TikTok, X, and others follow suit, involving a billion or several hundred million users. These personal content-sharing platforms generate a wealth of information unknown to humanity until just a few years ago, and much of this information concerns people, their lives, their personal interests, friendships, tastes, and even the intimate moments that are paraded in public. Private quanta exhibited in a square as large as the Earth, defining a universe of facts and gossip never before shared, with unexpected and completely unpredictable effects.

As expected, this unprecedented technology has brought significant benefits and new ways of socializing, some previously impossible. It has connected people far apart, allowing them to find each other, to form new relationships, and to access continuous and massive information – all things that were impossible to experience until a few years ago. But like all medals, this one too has two sides, and the dark side has revealed the fueling of online hatred, the manipulation of the less astute, the massive spread of fake news, and the invasion and distortion of people's privacy, sometimes to the point of nullifying or distorting it against their rights. Adding to this is the phenomenon of influencers, followed by hundreds of thousands or millions of people who wait for a post or a like from the new social media stars and allow themselves to be influenced by them in their opinions, daily choices, and, in particular, in their purchases.

## 5.2 The Main Actor

The main actor governing the various social media platforms used by millions or billions of people is the algorithm that decides what to show to users on the screen of their devices. It is a multifaceted sequence of thousands of operations, implemented and continuously updated by the programmers of Meta, X, and TikTok. It is a complex software system that operates 24 hours a day to manage every event that occurs on the platform and guide, like a cyclopean director, the publication of hundreds of thousands of posts and several million likes per minute.

It is the instructions and choices made by the many software procedures that manage Facebook that call the shots, deciding what we can publish and what we can read, in what order we can do so, and according to what preferences. This obviously is the case with X and TikTok as well. In the latter two, it is the algorithms appropriately modified by Elon Musk, compared to the original ones of Twitter, that have turned X into an extraordinary megaphone for Musk's political propaganda, and it is the algorithms of the Chinese company ByteDance that have turned TikTok into a gigantic channel for advertising and the manipulation of young people.

In short, in addition to paying attention to what huge masses of people post on Facebook, those who want to analyze what happens on social media must consider the algorithms that compose the content of the *Timeline* posts we see on those social media every day. This becomes necessary because we have reached such an advanced stage of digital technology and, in particular, of AI that people's poor behavior on social media has become a collateral symptom accompanying the fundamental symptom of a disease caused by the algorithms of Zuckerberg, Musk, and other "gigacapitalists," owners of social platforms who use their opaque software procedures to guide billions of people and generate power and profit, not to improve social relationships between people.

This worrying scenario requires that those who study these massive online content generation and distribution systems devote the necessary attention to the true directors of social media programming. That is, the algorithms that profile users, moderate and sort content, and create chatbots and fake profiles with which millions of people interact, thinking they're dealing with a human but instead are fooled by a software program capable of greater interactive cunning than a real human user.

All of this has been going on for at least 15 years now, ever since the masters of the digital stream understood that relationships between individuals on the internet could be managed to make money and gain greater power, rather than to improve social relations. Thus, the algorithms that manage our posts and tweets are no longer limited to displaying what we publish in the same chronological order in which it occurs but, as mentioned, follow other logics: maximizing users' time (so-called user engagement), targeting advertising, the ideological and political orientation of user groups, and the commodification of their privacy.

Since social media, starting with Facebook, uses sophisticated algorithms to personalize each user's browsing experience, anyone investigating these tools should be willing to acquire even a basic understanding that they are based on algorithmic procedures that steer the social media landscape, influencing the interactions of hundreds of millions of people every day. These algorithms exploit an immense amount of relentlessly collected personal data (for example, our interactions, likes, searches, the content we share and the pages we follow, and the times and places we use them) and show us content that is most likely to capture our attention and engagement.

We are therefore faced with a gigantic global device that decides how people interact and influences their choices, relationships, and opportunities. If this were not the case, it would be inexplicable, for example, why Elon Musk spent $44 billion in 2022 to buy Twitter – a platform that has become his digital Golem to influence customers, voters, governments, and wars. It would be inexplicable why Zuckerberg changed his strategy with the new White House administration or why the US government is fighting against TikTok, which risked being shut down in that country and was bought by US investors.

For all these reasons, scholars of digital platforms, regardless of whether they study anthropology, computer science, sociology, mass media, philosophy, or law, would do well to ask themselves what the principles and logic of the algorithms that drive these platforms are and how these logics, thanks to the flexibility of software, can be adapted from time to time to meet diverse and changing objectives. Without examining these algorithms and their strategies, we cannot understand what really happens on social media and who is truly responsible for the many atrocities committed there.

Ultimately, it's evident that many social media users bear some responsibility for their often spiteful, selfish, and offensive behavior and for the many inappropriate things they post online. However, the greatest responsibility lies with the algorithms developed by the owners of these platforms, which determine the quality of content and interactions, their manipulation, the spread of fake news, and the various objectives to which the massive output of posts generated by billions of individuals, which can be combined for good or evil, is directed. In particular, these algorithms are currently being used to increase the power of the likes of Musk, Zuckerberg, and their associates, who wield them like clubs against certain governments or other subjects. These are giant capitalists who refuse to filter fake news, because it would be part of what they consider freedom of information, and who foment protests against states that are passing appropriate laws to limit the harm their platforms cause to minors.

Two recently published books illustrate interesting and troubling themes. The first is *The Tech Coup* by Marietje Schaake [3], which describes how large tech companies have amassed enormous political and economic power, often under the guise of creating innovation, and how this power could undermine democracy if not properly regulated. The other is *The Chaos Machine* by Max Fisher [4], which explores in depth the impact of social media platforms, including Facebook, Twitter, and YouTube, on human behavior, society, and global political dynamics.

More studies and books are forthcoming on the topic of social media and its impact on people, especially now that AI is fueling them to generate more complex and sophisticated apps, bots, and fake content. On Facebook, it is estimated that there are, on average. several hundred million fake accounts or accounts managed by chatbot programs. These accounts do not correspond to real people, but many people interact with them unknowingly. The impact of these social avatars is massive and, in many cases, very damaging. In conclusion, there is enough to address these platforms, not only to blame users for their erroneous behavior, which does exist, but also to competently investigate their algorithms, which have become highly skilled manipulators of large numbers of people.

## 5.3 From Networking to Content Consumption

As some social media scholars have noted, some platforms are losing their original function of enabling people to interact and communicate and are transforming into continuous sources of content distribution, especially short videos, reels, and advertisements. This is clearly evident in TikTok, which has become a sort of YouTube for short videos, managing and distributing a continuous stream of videos and, unlike the social media it is rapidly replacing, functioning more as a means of mass entertainment than as a tool for building relationships and communication with friends.

This trend highlights a shift in the nature of social media platforms, which, especially among young people, have replaced the old mass media (mainly television) as a place of entertainment. Although they were developed to be tools for content creation by everyone, they are transforming into platforms where few are original writers who produce and publish content, and many play a passive role in consuming content. The old, asymmetrical mode of communication is returning – one that remains prevalent among older people through television, while young people use social media platforms such as Instagram and TikTok, leaving many in the role of passive consumers of content or, at best, banal distributors of videos produced by others.

This role as an entertainment tool, partly unexpected, is perhaps also linked to the problem of managing contexts that social media cannot fully address. Indeed, the forms allowed for building user profiles, and the ways offered for building networks of "friends" and contacts do not allow people to define more than one context in which to be present and in which to share different content and behaviors. Every piece of content a user posts is shared with all their contacts and followers; therefore, the context in which they act is only one, whereas in real life, we interact in different ways with our family, friends, colleagues, or even strangers. This isn't possible on today's social media, and so they flatten people, the forms, and meaning of their content. This limitation is favoring the use of social media such as Instagram and TikTok for entertainment rather than relationship purposes.

If the entertainment doesn't work (as seems to be the case with Facebook), users move to other platforms. In fact, this issue is addressed quite well in WhatsApp groups and private Telegram groups, where there are many contexts in which we can act and communicate in different ways, show different sides of ourselves, and thus adapt our behaviors and relationships to the context in which we communicate.

In this changing landscape, the enthusiastic embrace of social media in recent years and the adulation for its magnificent and progressive fortunes seem to signal a period of stagnation. Many seem to be tired of exposing themselves, their bodies, and their thoughts and of dedicating hours of their days to prying into the often-banal lives of others. It's still too early to say whether we're heading toward a reversal of the trend that could lead to a significant portion of the world's population abandoning social media. What is certain is that many citizens have grown tired of following Facebook's News Feed; this has certainly happened to younger segments of the population, who have turned to social platforms that are more interesting to them – and are using them more sparingly and less invasively.

Some time ago, the Ukrainian-American writer Chuck Palahniuk declared that "Social media will end up like fur coats" and will no longer interest many, as happened to fur coats abandoned by the rich when they realized that even the poor could buy them, perhaps through installment plans. Palahniuk envisioned a near future in which, based on their social status, many will opt out of social media and, instead of seeking, as has been happening recently, their 15 minutes of fame (as Andy Warhol suggested), will aspire to their 15 minutes of privacy.

Obviously, the ego factory seems to be working to prove Palahniuk wrong, and social media does everything it can to feed the narcissism of many who have no other opportunity to gratify it. However, there are certainly many social media users who feel the need to live their days unnoticed, to do things unseen by the world at large, to keep the most important moments to themselves, and to detach themselves from the madding crowd of posts and tweets and return to a form of "private ecology" that has been sidelined in recent years because, unfortunately, for many, "being" on social media has meant feeling alive, being recognized, and existing.

We will have to wait for the next few years to understand what will happen, but for now, it's useful to reflect on the transformations that are taking place. It's also useful to ask whether in the future we can use better social media platforms than those we use today. To achieve this goal, there are many problems that need to be solved. These include hate speech, manipulation and misinformation, excessive advertising, fake news, ignorance-fueled populism, text junk, the sale of personal data and profiling, and a lack of online accountability. Various solutions can be adopted to limit or eliminate these problems. For example, mandatory verified user registration, monitoring and deleting fake news, the use of disciplinary tools through content moderators, and the requirement to comply with the rules established by the operators and the laws. While common sense suggests that these actions should be implemented, it is not done because it would severely limit the number of users and the amount of content many of them can post. This more regulated scenario would lead to enormous losses in the profits of big digital companies, which have built significant wealth through the misuse of their social media platforms. They have no intention of giving it up easily, and for this reason, they oppose it despite knowing the damage it causes to society.

The Facebook Papers (https://facebookpapers.com/) are a very large set of Facebook internal documents that whistleblower Frances Haugen, a former Facebook manager, provided to Congress and news outlets around the world. These documents formed the basis of more than 100 news stories that revealed how the company's interests and profitability were often put ahead of the public good. Those papers detail the failures of Facebook managers to limit misinformation and incitement to hatred and violence on the social media platform. They make clear that this sometimes occurred due to a lack of technical resources and other times due to an unwillingness to give up the huge profits derived from the activity of billions of Facebook users. For example, the Facebook Papers suggest that leadership at Facebook prioritizes engagement over all other metrics. Profiling algorithms are primarily used to reach this goal. From a business perspective, this may appear reasonable since engagement leads to more time spent on the platform and, consequently, more commercials that can be displayed to the users. More ads correspond to higher revenues. Following this approach, the whole company itself operates as a large-scale machine learning process that is boosting its products and functions primarily for engagement.

User engagement ignores other more important elements, for instance, the happiness and health of people or the correct information and freedom of individuals. Obviously, these are much harder, not impossible, parameters to compute. Designer and developer teams at Facebook unfortunately did not prioritize these or other similar goals. If they had done it or wanted to do it, we would have a very different type of social media platform – one that would help people avoid misinformation and manipulation, allowing them to experience positive social interactions useful for individuals and for society.

## 5.4 Chatbots Among People

Large language models, such as ChatGPT, Claude, and Gemini, have fundamentally reshaped the implementation of social media bots.[2] Traditional bots relied on rule-based or template-driven scripts that produced repetitive and easily detectable responses, but LLMs enable bots to generate coherent, context-aware, and human-like language, dramatically increasing realism and engagement. These models allow bots to participate in multi-turn conversations, adapt tone, summarize posts, generate opinions, and autonomously respond to trending topics, making them powerful tools for both legitimate automation and manipulation.

LLM-powered bots can learn from user interactions, enabling dynamic and personalized discourse, and they are increasingly used in customer support, content moderation, and influence campaigns. Their

[2] A social media chatbot is an automated account that performs a series of autonomous actions on social media platforms for content creation, distribution, collection, and/or relationship formation and ending.

fluency and semantic richness, however, make detection far more difficult, since older classifiers based on linguistic or behavioral cues cannot easily distinguish between human and machine output. As a result, researchers are developing LLM-aware detection approaches using stylometry, contextual embeddings, and conversational entropy analysis. At the same time, LLMs themselves are being used defensively for moderation and misinformation countermeasures, creating a dual-use landscape. Studies such as that by Ng and Carley [5] show that many LLM-generated posts already fall within "bot-like" thresholds, suggesting that the boundary between human and machine communication is becoming statistically ambiguous. The integration of LLMs into bot infrastructures marks a shift from simple automation to autonomous social agents capable of strategic behavior, raising ethical and regulatory questions about authorship, accountability, and authenticity. Consequently, LLMs have vastly expanded both the power and subtlety of social media bots, making their governance and transparency central challenges in the evolving information ecosystem.

Some studies suggest that about 20% of conversation is attributed to chatbots, with occasional spikes up to 40% during politically charged events [5]. Social bots tend to use features that are easy to automate, such as high frequency of hashtags, mentions, URLs, and more reposts. Humans use richer signs: replies, quotes, media attachments, first-person pronouns, and emotional vocabulary. Bots interact more often with human accounts (rather than with other bots) since they are used to amplify content toward humans, influence their opinion, and manipulate their relationships.

In terms of identity self-presentation, bots tend to obfuscate or limit the diversity of identity. The identities that bots do adopt are usually among the more common, generic ones. They align their language and topics with their declared identity more than humans, that is, a bot claiming a "soccer" identity likely focuses on soccer-related content. Bots' networks show a star-shaped topology with a hub-and-spoke shape, indicating coordinated broadcasting, whereas humans show multi-level, hierarchical communication patterns. As bots are evolving, especially integrating generative AI, bot detection is becoming harder as they adopt more human-like behaviors, but structural, network, and interaction patterns still provide distinguishing signals.

## 5.5 From Social Media to Metaverse

When Neal Stephenson published *Snow Crash* [6], his third post-cyberpunk science fiction book, in 1992, Mark Zuckerberg, the future founder of Facebook, was only eight years old and attending elementary school in Dobbs Ferry, on the left bank of the Hudson River, less than twenty kilometers from Manhattan. His father hadn't yet given him the Atari console on which he would learn to program in BASIC as a teenager.

That book, which enjoyed some success among science fiction fans, depicted an artificial world that the Facebook tycoon would discover as an adult and which, in recent years, he has attempted to sell to the world as the best possible future. The book also, of course, featured the neologism *Metaverse*, which he used a few weeks ago to rename his IT giant, which encompasses Facebook, Instagram, WhatsApp, and the other companies in the group, Meta Inc.

*Snow Crash* tells the story of a nation (the United States of America) that, in the very near future, becomes a country filled with industrial rubble, abandoned suburbs, and post-nuclear landscapes. The nation is dominated by large "anarcho-capitalist" multinationals that replace the now-worn-out and incompetent governments. Alongside this late-capitalist reality that leaves humans with little hope, Stephenson's novel features the Metaverse (a world beyond the universe). A three-dimensional virtual reality created by software systems and fast internet connections, surpassing current internet services. A digital reality accessible even from public terminals, where you are represented in three dimensions by your own "avatar," allowing you to wander freely between bars, shops, offices, and trendy venues. The novel creates a dual setting, describing two parallel realities that continually intertwine and intermingle. In Stephenson's narrative, things aren't going well due to the snow crash, which in the real world is a drug, while in the Metaverse it's a powerful computer virus capable of attacking not only computers but also the brains of any hacker who comes into contact with it. In that book, the drug and the virus are managed and distributed by internet magnate Bob Rife, who drugs both the real and virtual worlds to his advantage.

Therefore, in the futuristic book that inspired Mark Zuckerberg to choose the neologism he introduced there as the name of his multinational and his project for a three-dimensional virtual reality social platform, the lawbreaker is a tech tycoon, and the Metaverse is not the land of plenty he described as his new social platform, where people will immerse themselves fully, body and mind, to interact and meet virtually with their friends and where they will be able to work with colleagues in virtual offices, shop at every e-commerce site in the world, play online games, or travel in spaces of bits and pixels purpose-built to satisfy every desire of the inhabitants of that so-called digital paradise. Amanda Hess, in *The New York Times*, defined Zuckerberg's idea for the Metaverse as a "virtual retirement community where isolated millennials can live out their final days" [7].

Zuckerberg's Metaverse can be seen as a three-dimensional version of a social media platform that we won't just use on our phone and computer screens but also immerse ourselves in through headsets and smart glasses, leveraging virtual and augmented reality technologies to simulate human interactions in a digital space meant to resemble a physical one. Indeed, 3D visualization and its applications have been a reality for some time. They are used in video games and remote surgery. But the idea of creating an entire world in virtual reality remains a matter of research and science fiction. The idea of building a new virtual world as an evolution of the Web and social media is the dream of many companies, already considering the potential revenues from billions of users accessing this new digital universe of digital experiences, films, shows, games, and social interactions. Some IT giants envision much of our daily routine taking place in that virtual world: office, meetings, sports, discussions, films, shows, video games, and shopping. All is available in a three-dimensional environment that breaks down space and changes the flow of time. The business is attractive, and several big IT companies such as Microsoft, Epic Games, Tencent, and Alibaba are investing many billions of dollars in immersive virtual systems.

Zuckerberg's announcement of the Metaverse's implementation had commercial and financial, as well as technological, reasons. His Facebook had been experiencing problems for some time, due in part to its inability to limit fake news, the privacy concerns it created for its users, and other issues stemming from the US government's past warnings about its threatened monopolistic role and the revelations of the Facebook Papers.

In that rather bleak scenario, Zuckerberg announced the Metaverse to shift attention from the present to the future, to attract investors, and to boost his company's stock price. However, the lesson of Stephenson's novel, which inspired him, should serve as a guide for Zuckerberg and other large digital companies, preventing them from building dystopian digital worlds in which the "digital inhabitants" are at the mercy of corporations and an uncontrolled capitalist economy. Where even state authorities have ceded control to the economic power of large multinationals.

Meta's Reality Labs is its research and development division working on Metaverse and on virtual reality, augmented reality, and mixed reality technologies. It has lost more than $50 billion between 2019 and 2025 since, despite huge investments, revenue from those segments remains relatively small. Although Zuckerberg announced a "Metaverse revolution," Meta has made gradual improvements (platform performance, graphics, mobile compatibility) rather than an abrupt breakthrough. The concept remains high-risk and experimental, although technologies developed under the metaverse umbrella (are finding uses elsewhere).

Looking from a historical perspective, we can see how computer science has long since sidelined its original goal of rapidly performing complex calculations and has devoted itself to simulating and representing reality. It began many decades ago with simple objects such as files (virtualizations of paper documents) and the desktop (virtualization of our desk) and has advanced to 3D virtual reality, social networks, AI, and avatars as digital personalization of users of online computing applications such as Second Life. Following this trend, the Metaverse embraced by Zuckerberg would have the task of competing with the "place-eating" created by the internet, smartphones, and algorithms. This is a singular vocation, supported by digital technologies, to devour the essence of the places we frequent, to erase their geography, their spatial structure, their panoramas, their anthropology, and their beauty or ugliness. We simply erase our places because we no longer see them with our eyes and we no longer touch them with our hands. Busy as we are receiving and decoding the digital flow that reaches us from remote people and machines, we don't get distracted for a moment, we don't observe the landscape around us, the people around us, we don't use our natural senses but rely on digital sensors.

Digital prosthetics offer us a new world where we can't be bored even for a minute, and we never take a break. We communicate with other digital beings far away from us without physical limits. We have now forgotten the brief waits that sooner or later occurred in our days. We are erasing the empty moments of the past, those pauses that allowed us to think, to look around, to reflect on the context in which we were immersed, or simply to be bored.

Smart devices have now changed our geography, eliminating real landscapes and seemingly useless glances, but have become absolutely necessary to center our being in every place we pass through or visit. They are forcefully driving us into a sort of Metaverse where Zuckerberg would like to completely involve us, offering us a world of computer graphic effects where we won't be able to enjoy a coffee but from which it will be difficult to escape. It is a synthetic world where his algorithms will guide us, define our cultural models, and mediate our interactions. There, his immersive devices will replace our five senses, with the primary goal of generating profits and with the stated intention of expanding the dimensions of the real world and the hidden goal of governing the lives of billions of people, perhaps even bending the curve of human history.

Digital technologies can help us in many ways, and they actually do so in our daily lives. However, when they are created and distributed to completely replace our world, we must be very careful to embrace them as if they were a panacea. A cautious approach today can avoid harmful scenarios in the future.

## References

1. Toffler, A. (1980). *The Third Wave*. USA: Morrow.
2. Dimsdale, J. E. (2023). *Dark Persuasion: A History of Brainwashing from Pavlov to Social Media*. USA: Yale University Press.
3. Shaake, M. (2024). *The Tech Coup: How to Save Democracy from Silicon Valley*. USA: Princeton University Press.
4. Fisher, M. (2022). *The Chaos Machine: The Inside Story of How Social Media Rewired Our Minds and Our World*. UK: Quercus Publishing.
5. Ng, L. H. X. and Carley, K. M. (2025). What is a social media Bot? A global comparison of bot and human characteristics. *arXiv* arxiv.org/abs/2501.00855.
6. Stephenson, N. (1992). *Snow Crash*. USA: Bantam Books.
7. Hess, A. (2021). The Mark Zuckerberg aesthetic. *The New York Times*, November 2.

# Chapter 6

# AI in Digital Non-Things

*The mind was dreaming. The world was its dream.*

—Jorge Luis Borges

Software is a logical component of a computing system consisting of sequences of lines of code (algorithms) that tell a hardware processor to perform specific tasks or solve particular problems. It represents the intangible set of instructions and rules that define and control the operation, processing, and management of hardware resources to achieve desired computational outcomes. In essence, we can say that hardware is the body, and software is the mind that instructs it what to do. By designing software programs, we can create new active entities, immaterial *non-things*, that may interact with us, with the world, and among themselves to perform actions, solve problems, and propose new activities.

## 6.1 Non-Things and Neo-Things

Digital non-things are made of combinations of bits and lines of code that continually take shape in our digital devices and on their screens. Software objects that fill and transform our lives and the world we inhabit. The reference primarily concerns data, digital entities, and their countless transformations brought about by algorithms, including many machine learning algorithms, tirelessly monitored by our personal devices and computers.

Computer systems continually create and display digital elements with a wide variety of characteristics, generated by the imagination and expertise of those who implement them. Each algorithm is capable of generating countless non-things composed of digital matter that weigh nothing, take up no physical space, and have no odor, yet are ever-present and live within our smartphones, computers, smart TVs, webcams, smartwatches, and home sensors or cars filled with well-hidden but highly active chips. These disembodied entities are non-things we all call apps, GIFs, notifications, short videos, posts, emails, memes, tweets, reels, emojis, PDFs, WhatsApp messages, and so many other visual and operational elements made of bits and software that have silently entered our lives and will never go away. In creating non-things, generative artificial intelligence (GenAI) systems are performing an extraordinary task. They are now capable of generating digital objects that correspond, with excellent accuracy, to physical things. Furthermore, they are capable of creating active and dynamic elements characterized by adaptive and intelligent behaviors that not only fill the human world but are also capable of replacing the active entities that nature and humanity have created over millennia.

These weightless entities coexist with us and also with all the new electronic objects (*neo-things*) that populate what computer scientists have called the Internet of Things, or IoT [1]. Researchers have not found a more precise and original term and have even called "things" the many new hardware entities that often don't resemble computers but are, in every way, computers. It happens cyclically that when something new, something unprecedented, appears, we have difficulty defining it and are led to use already known names. In this case, in the IoT, the word "things" conceals a universe of chips, circuits, and algorithms that transform and augment the functions of every traditional object (a keychain, a watch, a mug, or a pair of glasses), transforming it into a postmodern artifact that only with time will we be able to call by an appropriate name.

The IoT today is made up of several tens of billions of new digital objects, devices that speak and communicate with us and, above all, with each other, often without human control. They are things far more numerous than human beings on Earth. The formerly passive things, such as our car keys, wearable sensors, Wi-Fi refrigerators, home alarm devices, or radio frequency smart tags, have become interactive thanks to the chips they contain. They are neo-things that communicate with us, with software non-things, and with the environment thanks to the logic they contain, which makes them live and interact, removing the passivity that the traditional things of the world have always had, even if they continue to appear to us as mere objects. In other words, they are hidden computers – electronic micro-machines in disguise.

It is estimated that there are more than 20 billion of these new "smart" neo-things on Earth, and in less than a decade, there will be over 30 billion. We program them, we help them connect, and they can cooperate even without us. Wearable devices, cell phones, sensors, webcams, drones, household appliances, smartwatches, iBeacons, GPS devices, RFID, and smart cards of all kinds – there are countless of them, capable of exchanging information, storing data, and processing information much faster than us, and without our help.

The IoT, edge computing [2], fog computing, ambient computing, and so on are all new technologies that bring the new things that inhabit our world to life, work with us, and form the Earth's new life system, acting for us without depending on us, except for power. They are like vast colonies of digital ants, hives of billions of robotic bees, or countless binary drops of water that become an ocean, organizing and operating increasingly autonomously. They power transportation, large cities, shopping malls, hospitals, cars, industries, homes, and all the communication infrastructures that humans need. Unfortunately, they also go to war in new autonomous weapons, kamikaze drones, thermal imaging goggles, and latest-generation missiles.

The emergence of neo-things, digital entities created by software and endowed with the ability to interact autonomously with both humans and other digital systems, represents a paradigm shift in the conception of synthetic artifacts. The integration of GenAI into their design and functioning is transforming these neo-things from deterministic executors of code into adaptive, self-evolving digital agents. Through the generative capabilities of advanced AI models, such software objects can autonomously modify their internal structures, behaviors, and interaction patterns in response to environmental stimuli or human feedback, thereby exhibiting a sort of continuous digital adaptation. Moreover, the semantic awareness and contextual reasoning offered by large language and multimodal models enable neo-things to interpret and act upon human intentions with greater precision, emotional sensitivity, and cultural awareness. This evolution fosters more meaningful and natural human–machine interactions, where digital entities respond not only to explicit instructions but also to inferred needs and contextual signals.

In addition to augmenting human interaction, GenAI models allow neo-things to develop novel forms of communication among themselves, transcending rigid data protocols and adopting flexible, evolving semantic representations. Such capability may give rise to dynamic ecologies of software agents capable of collaborative reasoning, negotiation, and distributed problem-solving. From this perspective, the networked environment of neo-things becomes a generative ecosystem in which intelligence and knowledge emerge from the continuous exchange of meaning rather than from static information flows. At the human interface, these systems become co-creators rather than simple tools. They can create new artifacts, adapt to individual preferences, and actively participate in creative processes such as design, art, education, or decision support.

However, the introduction of generativity, adaptivity, and autonomy also calls for a robust ethical and governance framework. Neo-things must incorporate mechanisms for explainability, transparency, and value alignment to ensure that their adaptive behaviors remain consistent with human norms and societal expectations. For example, hybrid software solutions that combine neural generative components with symbolic reasoning modules may offer a promising path toward accountable and interpretable autonomy. From a technical standpoint, the implementation of such systems will likely rely on decentralized architectures that integrate lightweight on-device logic for local autonomy, cloud-based orchestration for coordination and scalability, and knowledge repositories for personalization and long-term memory.

Finally, we should consider that GenAI can redefine the ontological status of software artifacts. Neo-things may cease to be mere programmable incorporeal instruments and become cognitive digital organisms, that is, entities capable of generating meaning, forming relationships, and evolving through continuous interaction. This transformation announces the emergence of a new socio-technical ecosystem in which human creativity and machine generativity coalesce, determining a new phase of intelligent digital civilization.

## 6.2 Toward the Internet of Behaviors

As we mentioned in a previous chapter, the philosopher Ludwig Wittgenstein wrote in his *Tractatus Logico-Philosophicus* [3] that "*The world is the totality of facts, not of things*," ("*Die Welt ist die Gesamtheit der Tatsachen, nicht der Dinge,*"), meaning that our world is not a collection of unrelated objects but rather is made up of all the relationships that can exist between things and therefore of the events that occur through these relationships. The IoT is inspired by these principles, bringing together billions of interconnected objects. Actually, it is going to create and regulate the events of our present and will certainly determine the events of the future world. All these things that connect and communicate are capable of collecting data on everything that happens; they communicate everything, and they are the Earth's new true circulatory system. A gargantuan infrastructure made of tens of billions of neo-things and just as many interconnections that envelop the planet. They keep it constantly awake; they fill it with data and signals, and they transform it pervasively and irreversibly, defining new spaces and new times until it becomes a new Earth with characteristics never seen before.

It will be a new Earth in which data, algorithms, and microscopic chips have taken an active role in crafting a neo-reality that aspires to become stronger than the traditional reality we grew up in. This neo-reality is stronger than the one we were bequeathed, which we have to guard and protect to avoid seeing it disappear under the impact of the big bang of billions of artifacts filled with hardware, data, and software that risk robbing us of the pleasure of simple tastes, of a moment of boredom, of a glance at a blade of grass, of a frivolous use of time that can remind us of the ancient relationships between things and humans. The original Internet (the one made of computers and cables) has led us to the wireless IoT; however, we won't stop there. Other networks are already emerging that could lead us to new dimensions of existence, such as the *Internet of Behaviors* (IoB), which uses the Internet to share data collection and analysis, investigating people's behaviors and the technologies they use [4]. In short, it signals a worrying union of computer science and psychology.

Through this fusion, the goal of the IoB archetype is to predict human behavior, draw insights from available data, and even influence people's behavior based on their activities and interests gleaned from their many digital interactions. Indeed, the IoB is a model intended by its proponents to help us understand how, when, and why humans use technology to make decisions, especially those related to purchasing.

Companies seeking to sell products or services can influence our behavior based on targeted content curated specifically for us based on our preferences and interactions. The IoB captures the very many "digital breadcrumbs" left behind by people in their daily lives, drawing them from a variety of sources. Data comes from numerous sources, including people's financial transactions, social media activities, facial image recognition, and the use of mobile apps and connected devices. This information can be used by private individuals and public bodies to influence individual behavior. In short, we are moving toward the *Internet of Everything*, which seeks to be omnipresent in our lives and, if driven by economic and commercial interests, could bend our daily actions to those ends. Yet, there is enormous scope for using these powerful technologies to serve people, help the most vulnerable, facilitate citizens, and care for the elderly, or, in short, to improve the functioning of society. It is on these objectives, not those of consumption and profit, that we must focus the use of new technologies. To create more fair societies and to reduce inequalities, not to increase them, as seems to happen every time new digital systems are introduced to quickly fill our lives.

## 6.3 A New Hybrid Future?

Human-invented technology has removed many human abilities or added external capabilities to those we already possess. It has disembodied human functions and transferred them to machines. Neo-things are the practical implementation of this transformation. As long as machines took on the task of relieving humans of physical labor, we were all happy. Now that computers and algorithms can perform complex tasks, create new entities, and compete with our mental capabilities, intelligence, and rationality, we are surprised, amazed, and sometimes disconcerted.

Computers were created to perform calculations faster and more precisely than humans. Subsequently, these sophisticated machines, thanks to those who programmed them, became capable of performing many functions better than we can. Today, computers communicate much faster than we do, collect data and information better than we do, have more robust memories than ours, and capable of never forgetting anything, read enormous amounts of data and information, and select and filter information much more quickly than we can. However, in many cases, fortunately, we reason better than computers and use much less information than they do to understand what is happening around us and choose how to act. Furthermore, we don't simply know how to provide answers; we know how to ask questions and express doubts, like no computer can.

Therefore, for now, the fear that digital machines are generally better and more intelligent than us is unfounded. However, the human superiority we still maintain does not rule out the possibility that in the near future the field of digital neo-things will expand to the point of pushing humans into a corner, restricting their historic superiority and threatening their governance of reality. Above all, it will surpass the capacity for choice, action, and work of the majority of the world's population. This latter scenario is a cause for great concern.

The power of machines derives largely from the many procedural and repetitive actions that are part of our lives and can be automated. Initially, the development of information technology and robotics led to the replacement of humans in tedious physical jobs in factories and offices. Subsequently, many routine intellectual tasks were performed by millions of humans employed as if they were devices that must function but not necessarily think.

Whenever individuals perform standardized and repetitive tasks, they become prime candidates for replacement by digital machines that can be programmed to perform the same tasks quickly, efficiently, and often at lower costs. All of these are cases of jobs in which humans act as tools, devices, or cogs performing actions that can be encoded via algorithms. In these contexts, the human element undergoes a process of devaluation and is therefore easily replaced by machines.

Many people in many of their work experiences resemble, in effect, tools and devices, and so it is not surprising that they could be replaced by computers, the most flexible and efficient devices that mankind has ever invented. This applies not only to physical jobs such as farming or screwing bolts but also to bank or supermarket cashiers, ticket collectors, drivers, switchboard operators, and many other professions.

The picture has been further complicated by the development of systems based on artificial intelligence methods, which in recent years have posed a historic challenge to intellectual jobs and professions requiring advanced skills and complex cognitive processes. Artificial intelligence systems are creating new software avatars that challenge radiologists, lawyers, journalists, pizza makers, typographers, interpreters and translators, painters, essayists, insurance agents, and even priests and notaries. In these and other activities, for the first time, human supremacy is at risk of being overthrown.

They are increasingly capable systems that push us toward new horizons while shrinking our traditional spaces. They challenge us and force us to explore new opportunities through the development of new skills, forcing us to better assert our nature as cognitive beings and our uniqueness as human beings. Certainly, in the realm of feelings and empathy, today's digital devices are far behind us. Machines cannot laugh; they cannot suffer. Although there is considerable research in the field of cognitive-emotional systems, robots and computers are currently emotionless agents. They are not inclined to joy or suffering, and they do not feel shame; therefore, for example, they cannot even be punished when they make mistakes.

As algorithmic machines advance and acquire new functions, for humans to compete and coexist with them while maintaining our leading role, we will need to be able to find new meanings, new purposes, and new skills. We will need to abandon tasks and roles in which we act as mere tools, areas in which we are simply cogs within codified production machinery, to perform more flexible activities that align more closely with human nature. We are called to learn how to master new, non-automatable tasks that require greater education and deeper, more human knowledge. These are all useful skills for actively experiencing the present, marked by great transformations, and the hybrid future that awaits us, in which machines will assume increasingly important roles.

In the very near future, we will need to learn to supplement human capabilities with those of machines and not replace our own abilities with those of computers and their software. This is by no means a simple task, and for it to be successful, it must not be left to the efforts of a few individuals. It must become the goal of society as a whole, while being careful to avoid the very real risk of generating new inequalities induced by technology. We will need to establish a new cooperation with intelligent machines that protects citizens' rights and preserves our leading role in a new context in which people and machines will coexist increasingly closely.

## References

1. King, A. (2021). *Programming the Internet of Things: An Introduction to Building Integrated, Device-to-Cloud IoT Solutions*. USA: O'Reilly Media.
2. Marozzo, F., Orsino, A., Trunfio, P., and Talia, D. (2023). Scaling machine learning at the edge-cloud: A distributed computing perspective. *19th*

*International Conference on Distributed Computing in Smart Systems and the Internet of Things* (*DCOSS-IoT*), Pafos, Cyprus, pp. 761–767.

3. Wittgenstein, L. (2017). *Tractatus Logico-Philosophicus*. UK: Benediction Classics.
4. Sun, J., Gan, W., Chao, H.-C., Yu, P. S., and Ding, W. (2023). Internet of behaviors: A survey. *IEEE Internet of Things Journal*, 10(13), pp. 11117–11134.

# Chapter 7

# Big Data and Neural Control

*I would not put a thief in my mouth to steal my brains.*

—William Shakespeare

The global volume of data stored in our computers, smartphones, and data centers is estimated at 181 zettabytes by the end of 2025. Recent analyses indicate that approximately 90% of the world's data have been generated within the past few years. We must also consider that the volume of data stored globally is doubling approximately every four years, so we can imagine what amount of data we will get by 2030. To describe this scenario, the term "Big Data" was coined in 2001.

A McKinsey global report described Big Data as "data whose scale, distribution, diversity, and/or timeliness require the use of new technical architectures and analytics to enable insights that unlock new sources of business value" [1]. Many other definitions have been proposed. Most of them refer to the main features identified by Doug Laney, an analyst of the META Group (now Gartner), in its report published in 2001: large volume, high velocity, and large variety [2]. The Laney report clearly identified the rising trend of large repositories of data stored on digital devices and the "management challenges along three dimensions: volumes, velocity, and variety. … In 2001/02, IT organizations must compile various approaches to have at their disposal for dealing with each."

## 7.1 How Many "V"s

Big Data refers to massive, heterogeneous, and often unstructured digital content that cannot be processed using traditional data management tools and techniques. The definition provided by the Gartner glossary is as follows: "Big Data is high volume, high velocity, and/or high variety information assets that demand cost-effective, innovative forms of information processing that enable enhanced insight, decision making, and process automation." The NIST Big Data Public Working Group considered variability as a fourth dimension [3] and declared that "Big Data consists of extensive datasets – primarily in the characteristics of volume, variety, velocity, and/or variability – that require a scalable architecture for efficient storage, manipulation, and analysis."

Volume refers to the vast amount of very large data produced, stored, and exchanged through the internet. Over the past decades, computers, networks, and human interactions with digital systems have been generating data; the volume of data available today is massive (hundreds of zettabytes). Data velocity refers to the pace at which data flows in from their many sources (such as computers, mobile devices, sensors, cars, scientific instruments, and satellites). The flow of data on the internet is continuous and very fast. Variety refers to the several different sources and types of structured and unstructured data. In the past, we used to store data from sources like file systems and databases; now data are generated through web pages, emails, social media posts, photos, likes, PDFs, memes, videos, reels, and voice recordings. This variety of data raises problems for collecting, storing, and analyzing digital data. Another feature that has been considered for Big Data is veracity, which deals with how accurate or truthful a data set can be and includes how trustworthy the data source, type, and processing of them are. Dealing with data veracity also means managing bias, errors, inconsistencies, and null values in large data sets.

While considering these features of Big Data, we must also recognize that data become important and useful when we are able to extract value from them (and so considering a new "V" for Big Data properties). This new feature is obtained by analyzing data and identifying patterns, trends, and hidden information in large data repositories that may bring value to analysts and users. Therefore, Big Data are ideal companions for data analysis algorithms that, without data, could not find patterns and trends, take decisions, and solve problems. They represent very precious collections of contexts to be interpreted, hypotheses to be exhibited, and large traces for the benefit of those who know how to use them, those who are capable of complex computations and, in some cases, of risky manipulations.

The Big Data phenomenon was born and raised with the internet and grew with the extensive use of its software tools and services, which communicate and share information. However, today Big Data is more than merely a technology or a repository of information for analysis and prediction. The Big Data advent has prompted scientists and professionals to reconsider their methods and processes involving digital data by reorienting them toward insights obtained by learning from data. Coupled with algorithms, Big Data has become a universal model for gathering information about phenomena that in the past were difficult to know and understand. In particular, by collecting and analyzing large sets of personal data, it is possible to investigate people's lives, their behaviors, and also their ways of thinking. Big Data analysis finds ways to express how personal and social decisions are made and who can make them.

New findings are achieved, and more accurate studies can be performed due to the increasingly widespread availability of very large amounts of data. Scientific fields and business segments that do not exploit the large amounts of digital data available today risk losing out on the significant opportunities that Big Data processing can offer. However, a new kind of social, economic, and political control is built around Big Data. Collecting and processing the digital fragments of our daily lives allows specialists to explore many trends and learn about human behaviors. In this scenario, data analysis algorithms represent new, complex methods for gathering preferences and discovering the behaviors of individuals and social groups.

Algorithms and data processing technology are the apparatuses that are implementing a sort of evolution of our world into a new space driven by data and by the people who own these data. Business areas such as economics, healthcare, retail, manufacturing, and many others have changed their processes and products through the use of Big Data. Data analytics and machine learning are driving better-informed decision-making and improvements in corporate competitiveness, while many significant scientific applications (e.g., in genomics, physics, linguistics, social sciences, and medicine) are now based on complex data analysis and machine learning algorithms.

## 7.2 Big Data and Artificial Intelligence: A Marriage of Convenience

What makes the availability of Big Data extremely interesting and profitable is the combination of large amounts of data with artificial intelligence algorithms that are capable of extracting timely, detailed, and accurate information [4].

Major companies operating in the information technology sector are those that, more than others, have full awareness of the great value of digital data and manage them as intangible assets of enormous value. In fact, once collected, they are never deleted; instead, they are stored in servers, clouds, and data centers and are retrieved and used whenever needed. Large commercial chains have been collecting data regarding their customers' purchases for several decades, and thus they have built detailed archives of client commercial preferences and behavior over time. This valuable information is used for marketing campaigns, promotions, or evaluations of customer well-being, which can also raise the interest of other businesses such as banks and financial companies that want, for example, to measure their creditworthiness.

For example, the simplest case of collection and commercial use of personal data is through the use of loyalty cards in shops that, in exchange for small prizes or gadgets, allow them to collect our purchase data. In this way, accurate profiles of customers are built. These profiles can also be traded to third parties, such as banks, financial companies, health insurers, and advertising agencies, which use this valuable information for various purposes, sometimes without consumers being aware of it.

A matter that causes great concern is the loss of control over our data once they are given. We do not know who uses them, for what purposes, and, above all, if and how they could be used against us. While on the one hand, data collection technologies can be useful for identifying attitudes or individuals with illegal tendencies, on the other hand, in contexts where privacy is not adequately protected, they can turn into real tools of control. This opens up scenarios that are difficult to foresee.

Behind the use of digital applications or social media platforms lie large companies that collect different types of data. By analyzing data indicating where we connect from, machine learning algorithms used by several companies are able to track our movements, know the duration of our stay in a certain place, and obtain detailed knowledge of our habits. This profiling process allows them to build a rich picture of individuals' conduct and profile, which can be used in multiple contexts. Several cases involved the theft of more than a hundred million accounts. These included personal data such as emails, passwords, phone numbers, and information regarding relationships and travels [5]. When cases of this scale occur, we face a threat to the freedom and rights of entire communities. Hundreds of millions of people are tracked, and their online behavior reveals personal preferences and sentiment that can be exploited for marketing and political influence.

Social media apps on our phones and laptops collect a large amount of our personal data, from contact details to real-time locations and movements. Facebook, Messenger, and Instagram are the most invasive apps for collecting personal data from users. They collect 91% of our data, and about 86% of the data are collected for analytics purposes, allowing developers to continuously gather insights into our behavior and fine-tune advertising strategies to make them more tailored to users. The second most invasive app is LinkedIn, which takes and uses our personal data for several purposes. A huge 74% of personal information is collected for app functionality, including photos or audio data and contacts. Meanwhile, 69% is used for analytics leveraged to create content and recommendations tailored specifically to each user. Other social apps that collect our data include YouTube, X, TikTok, Duolingo, Snapchat, and Uber.

In democratic countries, possessing such a huge amount of data allows manipulation of democratic life since those who own it have enormous power with effects that go far beyond simple commercial use.

When we talk about data theft, as in the cases mentioned above, we are faced with serious crimes. Even in the presence of safeguard regulations such as the General Data Protection Regulation (GDPR) and the Digital Services Act (DSA) in Europe, once data begin to circulate both in different organizations and in multiple nations, it becomes almost impossible to control it or block its use. This is an exclusive characteristic of digital data since it can be copied and transferred infinite times, making the problem difficult to solve, unlike physical objects that can be seized. Scenarios like this pose great challenges for governments since they must find effective ways to defend the personal data of each citizen and, more generally, protect the security of society.

## 7.3 The Data Broker Market

Together with public administrations and governments, the most important players in the data market are data brokers [6]. They are private companies that collect, buy, and sell data and information of any type. Data brokers build their value on the ownership and processing capacity of massive amounts of data. In their activities, they do not limit themselves to selling raw data, but, thanks to these, they create complete profiles that can be used by banks, insurance companies, large commercial chains, and organizations of various types. The data broker market is particularly developed in the United States (US); however, worldwide there are over 4,000 companies active in the sector, of which 1,400 are market leaders [7].

It is estimated that companies and organizations such as CampaignGRID and ProPublica own 80% of the email addresses of American voters; therefore, they have access to an overwhelming amount of information that can be used for political campaigns. Acxiom, one of the largest companies, owns 23,000 servers and manages the data of over 2.5 billion consumers, with an average of about 3,000 detailed information records of each of them. This gives the company an incredibly detailed knowledge of individuals. Other data brokers in the US include CoreLogic, Datalogix, Experian, Epsilon, Exactis, Intelius, PeekYou, and Recorded Future.

The value of the global data broker market size was estimated at USD 277.9 billion in 2024 and is projected to reach USD 512.4 billion by 2033, growing at a CAGR of 7.3% from 2025 to 2033 (see Figure 7.1). North America held a 41.2% revenue share of the global data broker market in 2024. The consumer data segment held the largest revenue share of 35.1% of the data broker market in 2024. These numbers and growth trends suggest that the data market could even surpass the oil market in terms of importance.

The data broker business is part of a new paradigm called *infonomics*, or the information economy, in which information itself is an essential capital. Today, those who own information hold enormous economic power. The threat of living in such a scenario is that each individual is evaluated in terms of the information economy, in which, therefore, economic value is associated with the megabytes of data that concern the individual themselves. The training of generative AI systems, which need a huge amount of data to learn how to effectively manage and reply to user requests, greatly depends on the data market. If we also consider what

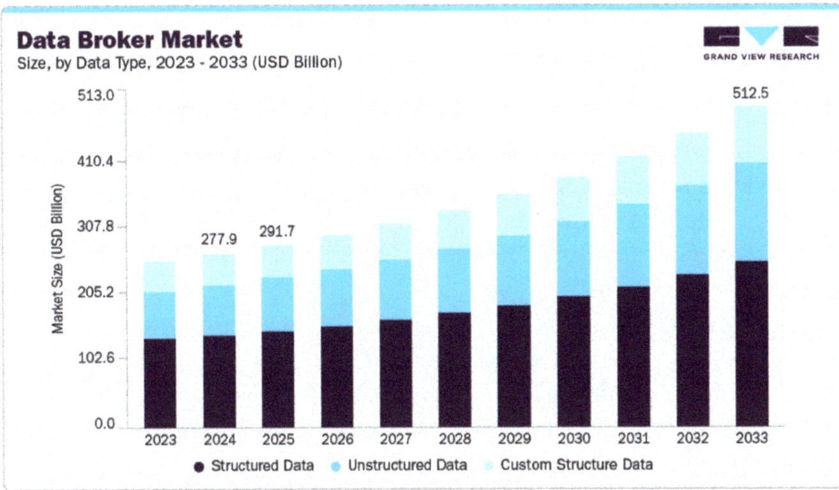


**Fig. 7.1.** The evolution of the world data broker market.

*Source*: Grand View Research, www.grandviewresearch.com.

happens on the dark web with the illegal buying and selling of data, new scenarios and delicate issues open up, which are, above all, difficult to regulate and solve.

To reduce the risks and preserve individual rights, a key point is to be aware of the processing of our data and try, as much as possible, to exploit the available legal frameworks to limit consent in order to avoid destroying the boundaries that protect our privacy. Analysts state that regulatory procedures restrain the data broker market globally. In fact, the introduction of stringent data protection laws, such as the GDPR in the European Union (EU) and the California Consumer Privacy Act in the US, has amplified the compliance task of data brokers. This has resulted in higher operational costs and potential legal risks, thereby deterring the use of information owned by specialized brokers.

## 7.4 Data Collection for Neural Control

The frontier of risks associated with our private and intimate data, collected and stored carelessly in so many data centers by private companies and public administrations, is shifting dangerously toward scenarios that in the past belonged only in science fiction stories and movies.

In Japan, capsule hotels are budget-friendly solutions for blue-collar workers, students, and tourists compared to traditional accommodation. Among Japanese capsule hotels, Nine Hours is an innovative hotel chain offering lodging in over 20 cities across Japan. In 2021, Nine Hours began offering its guests a "9h sleep fitscan" in collaboration with NTT Data. As clients sleep, sensors, infrared cameras, microphones, and other devices inside the capsules gather their personal data on various physiological sleep markers, including breathing, heart rate, snoring, and body dynamics.

The data are stored in databases and analyzed using machine learning algorithms, and a few days after checkout, guests receive their personal sleep reports by email. In four years, over 100,000 people consented to having their slumber scrutinized in what is presented as a mutually beneficial arrangement. Guests get access to a far more rigorous review of their shuteye and health signals than a Fitbit or Apple Watch could provide, informing them of potential issues such as poor sleep quality or apnea. At the same time, Nine Hours accumulates a lot of health and neural data of people to share with or sell to research centers and corporate R&D departments.

Nine Hours confirmed that all data are anonymized; however, this large collection of intimate data appears like a massive invasion of privacy. The hotel chain wants to increase its personal data collection to analyze data of 1 million people a year. In the Japanese hotel business, there is a trend of selling sleep-related services, such as AI tools analyzing brainwaves during stays and personalized plans that offer specialized sleep tests. Given the importance of sleep parameters on people's health, from mental well-being and functioning to cardiac health and longevity, that amount of data are invaluable. At the same time, possessing such intimate information about millions of people raises significant concerns about the privacy of individuals and would offer data owners extraordinary control over a large population.

To comprehend how widespread and profound the impact and pervasiveness of digital devices are becoming on people's intimate lives, it is enough to look at some legislative initiatives adopted in the US. In the spring of 2025, Colorado became the first US state to amend its privacy law to include the protection of brain data, that is, data coming from the human brain. A few weeks later, the Minnesota Legislature started working on a bill to protect its citizens' brain data, while on September 28 of the same year, California passed an amendment to its Consumer Privacy

Act to include the protection of human brain data among "sensitive personal information." According to this act, California residents will be able to deny companies that produce neurotechnology devices and systems from sharing or selling the information these devices collect from their brains, and they will be able to request to know what data a company holds and therefore ask for it to be corrected or deleted. These legislative initiatives are coming about because several companies in the digital neurotechnology sector have created systems, devices, and hardware and software products to read, collect, interpret, and process data from the brains of users who use those systems.

One of those products for managing neural data is Telepathy. It has been produced by Elon Musk's startup Neuralink, founded to make devices for treating brain diseases with the ultimate goal of mental enhancement for humans. Musk created Neuralink with a team of researchers and engineers, aiming to provide digital solutions for those who have neurological disorders, thus allowing them to interact with computers with their minds.

As in the Nine Hours case, Neuralink's devices show that personal data, today, can also be collected directly from our brain; therefore, our thoughts can become digital data to be stored and analyzed. This seems to be one of the last frontiers. In fact, the use of systems to solve brain problems and pathologies intrinsically involves the collection of data regarding individuals' thoughts. In all these cases, we must be aware of a very critical issue related to highly personal data that can be collected and analyzed to gain insight into human thought processes.

Machine learning plays a crucial role in interpreting complex signals from human neural data, such as those recorded by Neuralink's brain–computer interfaces. These techniques are able to transform raw brain activity into meaningful insights. Neuralink's implants, with many electrodes, generate vast amounts of neural data. Machine learning algorithms, especially deep learning and pattern recognition, are used to identify specific neural patterns associated with intentions, thoughts, or movements. This allows the system to decode signals for controlling external devices, such as computer cursors or robotic limbs. The analysis of human neural data with advanced machine learning techniques, such as those used by Neuralink, raises a range of significant and complex risks. These concerns extend beyond traditional data privacy to fundamental questions about human autonomy, identity, and societal control.

Analysis of neural data could be used to profile individuals based on their cognitive abilities, emotional states, or inclinations (e.g., for mental health conditions or future health risks). This could lead to discrimination in employment, insurance, housing, or even legal contexts. Marketers could exploit emotional responses for intrusive and manipulative advertising.

## 7.5 Toward Neurosurveillance?

It is important to note that, in addition to the chips implanted in the brains of people with disabilities such as Telepathy, there are many consumer-level devices that "read" our brain signals. For example, the Muse headband has been designed and marketed to enhance meditation practice. Using four sensors that read brain activity signals, Muse converts the EEG signal into an audio signal that is sent to the user via headphones. It measures brain activity, tracks brain blood flow, and helps optimize sleep.

Products such as Telepathy and Muse are systems designed to help people interact with a computer. These devices are able to interpret brain signals and translate them into machine-comprehensible commands. While these devices cannot access all of a person's thoughts, they can understand some of them by analyzing brain activity associated with certain intentions. AI algorithms applied to brain data do the rest. It can be said that these systems offer partial access to a portion of a person's thoughts. These thoughts become data that are stored, processed, and used to understand various things about individuals and groups of people. Some companies are even interested in selling them, while others may be using them in very dangerous ways.

Neurodigital systems are marketed as aids for meditation, concentration, mood, and learning. To do this, including through their apps, they collect brain data that are highly valuable because they can be used to understand what we think about, what cognitive abilities and intentions we have, and what emotions we experience during an activity, a conversation, or simply while we sleep. This information extracted from the human brain is becoming a highly sought-after commodity in the enormous, multi-billion-dollar digital data market. Indeed, many are interested in turning our thought signals into a rich source of revenue.

The Neurorights Foundation, a group promoting legislative action to protect people's brain data around the world, analyzed documents from 30 manufacturing companies and concluded that almost all have full access to people's brain data collected through their devices without any particular restrictions. More than half of them request and obtain customer consent to share their data with third parties.

Unfortunately, this also happens because most of these neurotechnological devices are not sold as medical devices; therefore, their use is not well-regulated, allowing companies to collect and sell their customers' very private data. The new laws being passed in some American states precisely serve to protect this highly personal and confidential data, preventing them from becoming a valuable commodity and limiting their potential misuse and the enormous risks this poses to the rights and freedoms of individuals and society.

In the EU, data protection is entrusted to the GDPR, which, despite being an extremely detailed regulation, does not explicitly mention "neural" or "brain" data because, at the time of its approval in 2016, these technologies were still in their infancy and not as widespread as they are now. However, the GDPR also applies to brain data because these certainly fall within the scope of personal data that must be protected.

It cannot be ruled out that future amendments to the GDPR will be introduced to better define how to protect the data that machines can extract from the brains of EU citizens. All of this must serve to prevent the emergence of a vast new market in which people's mental states, feelings, and thoughts are marketed. It must serve to avert the possibility of living in a not-so-distant dystopian future, in which unprecedented and horrifying mass neurosurveillance could take place [8].

## References

1. Manyika, J., Chui, M., Brown, B., Bughin, J. Dobbs, R., Roxburgh, C. and Byers, A.H. (2011). Big Data: The Next Frontier for Innovation, Competition, and Productivity, Technical Report, McKinsey Global Institute, USA.
2. Laney, D. (2001). 3D Data Management: Controlling Data Volume, Velocity, and Variety. USA: META Group.
3. NIST Big Data Public Working Group (2015). NIST Big Data Interoperability Framework: Volume 1, Definitions. USA: NIST.

4. El Shawi, R., Sakr, S., Talia, D. and Trunfio, P. (2018). Big data systems meet machine learning challenges: Towards big data science as a service. *Big Data Research* (Elsevier, USA), 14, pp. 1–11.
5. Chin, K. (2025). Biggest Data Breaches in US History (Updated 2025). Available at: https://www.upguard.com/blog/biggest-data-breaches-us [Retrieved 30 October 2025].
6. Talia, D. (2026). Privacy merchants and data protection in the age of big data and artificial intelligence. *Proceedings of DIGHUM Conference,* Vienna. LNCS, Vol. 16319. Germany: Springer, pp. 390–403.
7. Wikipedia (2025). Data Broker. Available at: https://en.wikipedia.org/wiki/Data_broker [Retrieved 24 October 2025].
8. Muhl, E. and Andorno, R. (2023). Neurosurveillance in the workplace: Do employers have the right to monitor employees' minds? *Frontiers in Human Dynamics*, 5, p. 1245619.

# Chapter 8

# Artificial Narratives and GenAI

*I am lying, yes, but why do you force me to give a linear explanation; linear explanations are almost always lies.*

—Elena Ferrante

Narrative is the collection of stories, real or imagined, written by human beings. Beyond authors who have written essays, tales, and novels, the technologies that have made them possible have been very important to narrative. Narratives are expressed in books, magazines, newspapers, scripts, or any other form of collections of pages, written with varying degrees of creativity. Beyond the various means that have enabled the expression of narrative, it should not seem strange to think of it itself as a technology, that is, as a way invented by humans to systematically address in a structured way a subject or topic.

This last question may seem of limited interest. However, to dispel this mistaken impression, it is necessary to consider that without the narrative created over millennia and without the technologies that have made it possible, the humanity we know, and that we are, would not exist. The role and power of human beings would be entirely different, and human presence in creation would certainly be less significant. Some evolutionists theorize that telling stories made us human, as Jonathan Gottschall explains in his book *The Storytelling Animal: How Stories Make Us Human* [1]. The narrative we have created over the millennia has allowed us to become human, conscious social beings.

This is certainly the basis of the conventional idea we have, or have had until recently, of narrative. Over the past several decades, a new form of writing has been added to traditional narratives and is rapidly, almost violently, gaining ground. It is new, and yet not necessarily better. It is an unconventional and unusual narrative of the world that expresses itself and asserts itself through the Internet. It is a form of narrative that expresses itself through digital grammars and the new representational semantics that the online world makes possible, and it does not like to be fixed statically on a sheet of paper but thrives on an "almost formless" dynamism. Without resorting to overused maxims (see Marshall McLuhan and his "*The medium is the message.*") [2], it is not difficult to understand how the many novel forms of datafication, hypertextuality, information decomposition and aggregation, content generation through artificial intelligence algorithms, and creative expression that digital media have introduced determined a narrative framework never before observed. It represents an increasingly multifaceted framework that transforms, enriches, surpasses, or incorporates traditional narrative forms, creating new critical issues while offering us new possibilities for expression, communication, interpretation, socialization, and new ways of being human.

## 8.1 Digital Technologies and Narrative Production

In his book *The Language of New Media* [3], written in the early years of the new millennium, Lev Manovich originally addressed the issue of the relationship between digital technologies and narrative production, reflecting on the influence of the former on the latter. In particular, Manovich chose the term "database" to indicate the different ways of structuring digital content within computers and the internet, theorizing that the database represents the new cultural form of the information society, "*a new metaphor we use to conceptualize cultural and collective memory, a collection of documents or objects and other phenomena and experiences.*"

From an information technology (IT) perspective, a database is a software system for managing structured data that allows for the orderly storage, rapid searching, and combination of the information it contains. Most databases in use today are organized into a set of rows and columns, or into document records, or even into information nodes connected to each other in a graph. Lev Manovich did not explicitly refer to these details; he used the term in its broadest form to include all digital forms of data and information storage and organization on computers and the internet. This includes website pages, file systems that organize information into a collection of files stored on our computer disks and grouped into folders, data warehouses that store large amounts of historical data organized to facilitate analysis, and data lakes, which are large, centralized archives, such as in a cloud system, that store raw data from various sources and in various formats.

Manovich writes, "*Creating a work in new media can be understood as creating an interface that allows access to a database. [...] The database thus becomes the center of the creative process in the computer age.*" The American scholar, therefore, embraces the thesis that the ways in which narratives are created today, in the age of new media, represent a sudden leap in cognitive processes rooted in the database, which is not organized in a linear form like a traditional text but is composed of countless information records that can be combined.

The advent of computers, the Web, social media, and generative AI has brought about a rapid shift from linear narration to a reticular narrative construction. Without conscious maturation, we have moved from a linear narrative that unfolds along the lines of pages to a narrative that unfolds on graphs capable of combining words, data, images, and other information elements that can be found anywhere digital memory is located. Following the narrative form of the database, the author "writes" by relating content stored in some organized form, in digital memories, and does so by building an "interface" capable of dynamically collecting and composing the elements (data) that constitute his lexicon. This approach, increasingly followed by those who compose content of various kinds, such as newspaper articles, television news footage, blog posts, and tweets, is the same as the one recently begun to be used by generative AI systems that communicate with us by composing portions of text, words, sentences, images, and other information elements drawn from the enormous database made available to them. When these systems respond to our queries, they effectively linearize reticular content extracted from their information archives and present it to us in the form of written or spoken sentences according to a syntax that humans have constructed over millennia.

To put it more simply, the digital or online technologies, as Manovich theorized 20 years ago, have now imposed a new way of narrating the world. And as it does so, it entrusts us with the task of experimenting with this narrative between humans and digital machines, along with the responsibility of understanding – if we are capable, using the methods we have learned and "classical" knowledge – what is really happening. It is the task of asking ourselves what forms of transformation are being imposed and realized. We must also ask ourselves whether the knowledge that humans have created and accumulated until the end of the last century is still a useful tool for interpreting with due depth the reality and transformation that the online world has been creating for decades, and which in recent years has been represented in its most advanced form by generative AI systems. Or, is it time to define new paradigms and new interpretative tools that can help us illuminate the foundational elements and the meaning of the flow in which we are all immersed? It is a flow that is increasingly governed by machines, not only in terms of the speed of communication and the delivery of human-generated content but also in terms of the ability to compose content based on sophisticated and fast natural language processing algorithms and on enormous quantities of Big Data that only machines can now read in their entirety.

As other scholars, such as Katherine Hayles and Michael Lascasas, have noted, narrative, and not just the means of expressing it (books, newspapers, films, etc.), should be considered a technology invented by humans to understand the world. Narration is, in fact, a tool through which we extract (or impose, depending on perspective) meaning from (on) the chaotic flow of being in the world. The perception of reality is certainly an interpretation (even with our senses), and narrative, while helping us interpret the world, also influences our perception. It is an immaterial technology, such as algorithms, music, mathematical theories, or chemical formulas – a technology that, since the beginning of history and the use of verbal language, has helped human beings describe the world and themselves.

The main strength of narrative lies not initially in its explicit expression (such as ink marks on paper), but in its ability to be thought, to materialize in our minds. Nonetheless, the means through which it is expressed contribute to defining it, shaping its "message." Today, the narration of reality, as well as its representation and its dissemination, is increasingly incorporated (sometimes trapped) in digital forms, within the myriad channels that the digital has created through the internet and carved out of the internet to reach people.

The digital information ecosystem is generating a variety and quantity of information elements never before experienced, enabling new and diverse forms of narrative that are often improvised, immature, and confusing, despite their instantaneous, pervasive, and global nature. There are now countless practical cases to cite; among the simplest and most immediate, we can think of narratives composed of dynamic sequences of social posts/tweets, the narrative interconnections of blogs, the combinations of Google search results, cooperative stories generated without a coordinator dynamically composed through online news, and narrator-less novels in which the sequence of WhatsApp messages does the "writing." Since storytelling shapes the life of our society, the digital (immaterial) universe has long worked, consciously or unconsciously, to build the key tools needed to interpret, describe, and ultimately govern our world.

As mentioned, this process has now led to a highly innovative and historic form of storytelling, in which the composition of content is autonomously governed by machines capable of extracting the information necessary to narrate concepts, facts, events, and ideas, and then composing and presenting them in human language. In short, machines, through our data and algorithms, have learned to write every type of text and engage in every possible dialogue with us. To avoid becoming alien to this new narrative, we must learn how to use machines, how to turn them into new collaborators useful in the construction of our narratives, thus avoiding being entirely replaced by them.

## 8.2 About Structure of Digital Narratives

First Ferdinand de Saussure and then Roland Barthes introduced and analyzed the semiological theory of syntagm and paradigm, explaining how the elements of a system can be correlated in two dimensions: the syntagmatic and the paradigmatic. The syntagm is a combination of signs that places a set of elements, one after the other, in a linear sequence. In the paradigmatic dimension, units that have something in common are associated on a theoretical level and form groups, within which each can find different relationships.

The difference, which sometimes becomes a contradiction, between traditional narration and databases can be described through a syntagmatic level that, in the memories of digital systems (in the database), breaks the constraints of the linearity of pages and is hidden in the tabular or reticular storage of all archived data. The latter has potential and offers itself to every possible combination achieved through search, extraction, and sentence generation operations. For example, in a generative AI system, operations construct a script *a posteriori*, not at the moment of digital archiving, but when a keyword search, a database query, or a question to ChatGPT or Gemini activates the linear composition operations. In the database, the paradigmatic level is expressed in elements that are all solidified in its contents and cannot find space for other elements that are not present in the database itself. This change, or leap, generates a new narrative with which humans increasingly describe and/or learn about reality and themselves.

To explain the difference between classical narrative and databases, as Katherine Hayles [4] notes, Lev Manovich observes that in classical narrative, "*the syntagmatic [sequential] order of linear unfolding is actually present on the page, while the paradigmatic possibilities of alternative word choices are only virtually present. For databases, the opposite is true: the paradigmatic possibilities are actually present in the columns and rows, ...*" We would add in document records, in the nodes and edges of graphs, and in the vector representation of terms used by generative AI systems, "*...while the syntagmatic progression of choices concatenated into linear sequences by SQL commands is only virtually present*" [3]. Here, the acronym "SQL" (Structured Query Language) refers to the language used to define, manipulate, and extract contents from a relational database, and in this sentence the words "SQL commands" can be replaced by the search terms used in the Google search engine, by the hashtags used to read a set of tweets on a particular topic, and by a prompt expressed in natural language through the ChatGPT interface.

Thus, the digital infosphere defines a new relationship between narrative (a syntagm) and database (a paradigm), in which the latter enjoys a material existence, while the narrative is dematerialized because it is not present in a stable form in the story ("on paper"). The narrative composed of a chain of posts, likes, and tweets on social media platforms is not stable, nor is the one offered by generative AI systems, which do not simply offer us "set phrases" copied from other digital sources but are capable of dynamically composing them on the fly. In classical narrative, the author constructs the sentence by choosing words from a set of vocabulary, while the digital author (be it human or algorithmic) creates by extracting data from the database and constructing text sequences based on extraction rules that can be defined in SQL, HTML, XML, JSON,[1] and the myriad textual and graphical formalisms that computer science provides for composing content from data stored in the vast digital memory of computers and the internet. The results of each query in a database crystallize the paradigmatic possibilities it contains and offer the digital author a narrative opportunity. It is a narrative trajectory selected from the paradigm of all possible contents.

In the digital world, different things can be written and rewritten at any time starting from the same database because the writing is not fixed on the page but can change over time and with different readers. Although with different operating methods, this happens both when we search for information on Google and when we enter a prompt in Gemini or ChatGPT. Narration is generated as a result of a set of network connections that unite individual elements retrieved from one or more digital data archives (Manovich's database). Narration becomes virtual, and the database is indisputably material. Therefore, in classical writing, the syntagm is forever created on paper, and the paradigm remains open, offering room for reader interpretation. In writing from digital databases, different things can be written and rewritten at any time, starting from the same database, because the writing is not fixed on the lines of the page but can dynamically change over time and even with different readers. This content is constructed on demand, thanks to the availability of vast amounts of data stored in the databases of newspaper or television channel editorial systems and the ability of adaptive software systems that can dynamically combine the "snippets" of physically available content.

## 8.3 Writing by Prompts

We argued that in the database, all possible sequences of content (words, phrases, and expressions) are present and can be combined in very many ways, while a specific real sequence is only virtually present and can only appear when instantiated (for example, through an SQL query in a relational database, a text search in Google's massive archive, or even through

---

[1] The listed acronyms indicate some widely used data formats, in particular HTML is the acronym for *Hyper Text Markup Language*, XML for *Extensible Markup Language*, and JSON for *JavaScript Object Notation*.

a prompt in ChatGPT). Each story/novel is constructed to bring out in a new way something that wasn't previously evident or wasn't already fully known. The extraction of stories from the database is done to artificially bring out something that is already stored (written) in a hidden, distributed, and uncoordinated form. In the digital database, everything is already present, and each time, a part of it can be brought to light by combining the individual stored elements.

Words are present in our brains, and our reasoning ability, combined with our knowledge, allows us to put them together to express a concept, an opinion, or a piece of information. Similarly, a generative AI system has an enormous memory, even greater than that of a human, in which it stores terms, sentences, numbers, and other pieces of information. High-performance computers possess immense processing capacity, along with complex natural language processing and machine learning algorithms that compose the terms, bringing out concepts, relationships, ideas, and information through the organized combination of these resources and capabilities.

Evidently, this paradigm shift assigns a more subjective role to those who query the database and to whom the result of their query will be presented; we might define them as "digital readers." In classical narrative, the primary choice is made by the author, while the reader/listener has only their imagination to elaborate on the reading. In contrast, in reticular narrative, the primary choice is made by the reader regarding its content and its relationships. Querying a database (i.e., reading it) through a selection or a relational union between elements in rows and columns or asking a generative AI system to respond by extracting associations and paths from a graph of nodes leads to the construction, on the fly (à la carte), of a new story, a dynamic piece of news, or an instantaneous narrative that may differ from others, read before or after through different prompts. Here, it must be clarified that the choice is effective if the person reading via the digital system knows its logic, and its semantics (in the case of generative AI systems, through so-called *prompt engineering*[2]). Otherwise, an unaware reader may find themselves faced with arbitrary choices made on their behalf by someone else, as so often happens on the

---

[2] A *prompt* is a natural language text that asks a generative AI system to perform a specific task or provide a particular response. *Prompt engineering* is a recent discipline that allows us to define and optimize prompts (commands) to make AI systems efficiently use their language models, thereby interacting optimally and obtaining the most useful responses from these systems.

internet with online manipulators. They may be humans or chatbots guided by AI algorithms that often deceive due to their ability to generate content in a human-like manner.

This reasoning should suffice to demonstrate the leap in form and content that this new way of composing stories, reports, and information is imposing. However, the discussion doesn't end there because everything that is continuously and tirelessly written in digital grammars and the forms in which it is written changes, perhaps forever, the styles of human narration, the forms of representation, and the dissemination of information. In other words, it modifies each person's perception of reality through the words read or heard, the vision experienced, and the response received. While the quality of digital information sometimes, but not always, is to blame, its gargantuan size and pervasiveness are silently imposing Manovich's database model and working to undermine traditional narratives. The latest developments in generative AI suggest it could change it, complement it, or perhaps even replace it entirely. Of course, this is not a cause for outrage, but it is appropriate and essential to analyze and understand the phenomenon, especially because it is necessary to determine whether its enormous size and pervasiveness can be matched by an equally in-depth understanding of its content and expressive forms.

While traditional narrative has built its strength on reflection, selection, and thoughtful writing, online narrative is grounded in immediacy, improvisation, inconstancy, and impulsiveness, often characterized by incompetence and a lack of verification [5]. The vast majority of narrative content constructed and disseminated through the many digital means – from that extracted from the Web and constructed by Google or other search engines or collected in the databases of social media platforms (e.g., Facebook, Twitter, Instagram, TikTok) to the content fragmented into billions of mobile apps – is composed and aggregated (narratively sequenced) in almost chaotic, often unthought-out, forms. These are elements of a narrative ecosystem offered to readers by reassembling them in a quasi-random manner (in a sort of narrative randomization). They very often represent structures with very high information entropy that tend to diverge toward chaos. This is a challenge for the Web, for social media, and for generative AI systems, which will only be able to overcome their linguistic barriers to humans if they can build "thoughtful" data processing methods into their colossal memories to provide verified, consolidated, correct, ethically acceptable, and meaningful information. If this happens, all human writers and storytellers will have a new competitor, forcing them to improve their skills and the quality of their output; otherwise, they might succumb.

By including, as is right, within the concept of a database all the information the online world archives offer, we are faced with a narrative form in which the reader becomes the writer, often unaware of it, constructing the storytelling (their narrative) through the manual or automatic composition of disparate and scattered information quanta (digital records), not generated in a single, or even coordinated, manner – much less connected and resolved with respect to mutual negations. Thus, we find ourselves immersed in a sea of narrative drops whose macroscopic form does not depend on the creators of the individual drops but on those who observe them and see them all together in a sort of organized story.

## 8.4 Artificial Narratives

Classic narratives do not find their natural home online. The highly dynamic nature of the internet universe eludes traditional narratives and generates a constant instability and incompleteness, incapable of finding a fixed point or a stable energy base. Traditional narratives are increasingly incorporated into the gigantic online archive or even into some of its sub-databases, which are nevertheless difficult to manage. There, they lose their guiding role, their cultural value, and their authenticity. They become elements, content, and data, not much different from other elements. They are lost within the network woven by new narratives enabled by digital technologies, trapped in the chaotic narratives of the database.

Among its diverse and unusual natures, the creation of information content through digital media also eludes scrutiny of authoritativeness, reliability, and certainty. The truth of the story that originates online is diluted to infinitesimal degrees and sometimes disappears, transformed and not necessarily becoming falsehood (which can still hold some value), but it acquires the new sense of post-truth in which the veracity of its descriptions plays a completely secondary, marginal role.

In this scenario, the so-called *hallucinations* of generative AI systems come into play.[3] Hallucinations can have harmful consequences for users who lack adequate knowledge of the context being discussed and could be

[3] Hallucinations in a generative AI system are information errors contained in the generated texts that are not logically consistent with the prompt, even though they might still sound plausible to a human. Hallucinations can be caused by errors in the system's training

deceived by the text generated by the AI system. For example, a system like ChatGPT could generate a fake news article that appears to have been written by a human journalist or a largely accurate report with some incorrect data that misinforms readers. This is the narrative of beyond-truth, which knows how to blend the true and the false, the real and the manipulated, arriving at the composition of a new fiction that takes on different characteristics from those of traditional fictional narrative, which relies entirely on the author's creative ability. It is a new form of expression where imagination and narrative invention, as we know them, disappear, taking on different meanings and expressions. They no longer reside in the author's mind; they are extracted from a database. They can arise from a permutation of (micro-)narrative elements produced by countless individuals (even through a process of autofiction), which are combined in ever-changing ways by a human or even an algorithm. This poses a huge challenge to professionals who aspire to be impartial, ethical, and responsible.

According to some studies, as of 2025, about 50–75% of new publications on the Web include AI-generated content. Of all Web content, including older pages and legacy content, likely 30–40% or more is created by generative AI. These numbers are evolving rapidly and may continue to grow. The use of traditional methods to identify criteria of literary authority and quality in this context fails to yield significant results. New models and metrics are needed. Quantity replaces quality, and analog narrative is marginalized to the point of vanishing into the sea of bits, tweets, posts, selfies, emojis, prompts, files, and data representations, combined and constructed according to more or less sophisticated algorithmic methods.

They are hybrid narratives, fueled by digital data and search, classification, and automatic text generation algorithms, derived from alphanumeric searches on the Web or in digital libraries, displayed on social media timelines, and listed in real time by messaging systems or mobile app screenshots. This is powered by generative AIs that respond to every request, even when they don't know what to say, and produce informational hallucinations. All this creates a new digital narrative that, like Oedipus, kills the traditional one (Father Laius), perhaps even

---

phases, by difficulties in storing complete information, or by inaccurate or incomplete input data.

unintentionally. However, after having accomplished this, the narrative takes the throne (of Thebes) and marries new readers (his mother Jocasta).

## 8.5 AI Algorithms as New Writers

Starting from the reticular narrative forms of digital technology, AI algorithms have become the new narrators. Artificial writers of news, reports, and novels can connect every available piece of information. These new robotic writers are capable of constructing any story with elements dispersed throughout the gargantuan database of our personal devices, clouds, social media, and the Web.

Over a decade ago, Katherine Hayles argued for a non-conflictual but symbiotic relationship between (classical) narrative and digital narrative, asserting that the database requires the reappearance of narrative as soon as meaning and interpretation are required [4]. In saying this, she meant that narration and the making of narrative require a human. Hayles reaffirmed the role of the flesh-and-blood writer even in the face of powerful digital technology and the enormous mass of data that a digital archive can contain and make available. Narratives belong to humans, even when constructed from records, graphs, messages, and digital posts. His analysis thus returns to narrative as an ancient technology with which humanity, by weaving stories, constructs meaning through research and building relationships between pieces of information.

According to this view, the database represents merely a new tool in the hands of the narrator. However, beyond necessarily pointing out that writing born from a digital database will be different from that which emerged solely from the mind of the flesh-and-blood writer, from the stories he knew and from the sequential lines of his pages, it is important to note that, starting from the availability of enormous archives as gigantic information sources that fuel the new narrative, we have now arrived at a new algorithmic narrative that is profoundly different from the previous one.

This new narrative composes stories using AI procedures capable of executing natural language processing algorithms in hundreds of different languages and machine learning strategies that extract implicit and hidden meanings from data, classifying large amounts of data at inhuman speeds. It is a new narrative in which the algorithm becomes the writer and is able to replace the human; a narrative in which humans act by writing algorithmic sequences (as, for example, seen in the Generative Pre-trained Transformer 4 (GPT-4), capable of generating syntactically correct and semantically meaningful texts), which in turn contain logic useful for composing texts and filling them with meaning – a surprising and unexpected narrative, not necessarily better, but not worse either.

While it may seem unorthodox and unusual, by combining and connecting data and information stored in each of their digital forms through the interweaving of infinite networks, algorithms today are proposing new forms of writing and positioning themselves as new producers of text and information. Google's algorithms connect webpages and links to construct descriptions and interpretations of reality from the chaos of the Web's hypergraph pages. Facebook, X, and Instagram's algorithms fabricate stories by mixing and matching the episodes (posts) that users provide, according to their own internal logic, unknown to the mere speck of their authors. People only know individual sentences of narratives, isolated paragraphs, while Facebook's News Feed becomes the "social novel" written by Zuckerberg's algorithm, or TikTok's short videos are the new television that keeps hundreds of millions of teenagers glued to the screen thanks to the user engagement algorithm developed by the programmers of the Chinese giant that owns it, which is not coincidentally named ByteDance.

The Google Search Engine algorithms scour web databases and compose a description of the world we are searching for. It does so by ingesting everything, every piece of information it finds online, including news that newspapers and journalists produce daily, blogs written by millions of people, and anything else useful to compose its answer. The answer is usually a response composed of a few short answers to questions we haven't explicitly asked but which the algorithm deduces from our search, and it may be composed of thousands of links to pages that might satisfy our curiosity. The integration of Google's search engine with Gemini enables dialogue in various human languages to get the answers we seek. Gemini's generative algorithm, like that of ChatGPT, Claude, and other generative AI chatbots, reads a few request sentences and a few brief writing instructions (such as length and language style) and generates a narrative that many humans would be unable to write. Myriad writing operations, such as those these systems offer, are crafted by countless algorithms that feed on an extraordinary sequence of digital quanta to narrate (and interpret) realities that none of us can describe individually anymore.

This is a new way of narrating the mystery and meaning of the world. It is a new paradigm that digital technology is imposing on us. It represents an unprecedented challenge for humans, who will have to decide whether to govern the digital universe and its narratives or be governed by them. There can only be one choice: We must learn to master this new technology used for writing about the things of the world, and doing so requires greater commitment and greater skills. To manage the universe of digital technologies, it is necessary to study it, understand it, and regulate it, following the path indicated in an old but useful thought from Francis Bacon: Man's mastery consists only in knowledge; man can only do as much as he knows.

## References

1. Gottshall, J. (2012). *The Storytelling Animal: How Stories Make Us Human*. USA: Houghton Mifflin Harcourt.
2. MacLuhan, M. (1994). *Understanding Media: The Extensions of Man*. USA: MIT Press.
3. Manovich, L. (2002). *The Language of New Media*. USA: MIT Press.
4. Hayles, N. K. (2007). Narrative and database: Natural symbionts. *PMLA* (Cambridge University Press, UK), 122, pp. 1603–1608.
5. Talia, D. (2019). *Big Data and the Computable Society: Algorithms and People in the Digital World*. UK: World Scientific Publishing.

# Chapter 9

# Large Language Models: Words and Thoughts

*Large language models are not just trained on language, they are trained on thought itself.*

—Yann LeCun

Artificial intelligence has been defined in various ways [1]. In keeping with what has been written in previous chapters, we can offer a simple definition that does not presuppose science fiction scenarios and, at the same time, does not intend to trivialize this important discipline born from the intersection of mathematics and computer science. AI studies the theoretical foundations, methodologies, and techniques that enable the design and implementation of hardware and software systems capable of providing a computer with performance that, to a casual observer, appears similar to that produced by human intelligence. It is important to emphasize, as previously stated, that the purpose of AI systems is not to replicate human intelligence using its principles and nature, but rather to reproduce or emulate some of its functions.

## 9.1 General and Restricted AI

AI is a wide field including different approaches and techniques. In particular, considering the primary goal to achieve, we can take into account two different kinds of AI. The first is so-called strong artificial intelligence, or artificial general intelligence (AGI), which is defined as the ability of an intelligent agent to learn and understand any intellectual task that a human can comprehend and perform. On the other side of the coin is weak or "narrow" AI. Unlike strong AI, narrow AI does not aim to acquire general cognitive abilities or require consciousness, but it aims to solve specific problems. This second subfield includes generative AI, which is capable of understanding human languages, communicating with them, and generating various types of content requested by humans or other software systems. While, despite many optimistic predictions, past and present, we are still far from being able to create general AI systems, narrow AI systems are numerous and help us with many daily tasks, such as translating text, recognizing faces, choosing the best route to a destination, analyzing diagnostic tests, and making purchase decisions.

Another way to classify AI is based on the computing methods and techniques used to implement AI systems. This second classification divides AI systems into symbolic and sub-symbolic systems. Symbolic systems are those that emulate the high-level cognitive functions of the human brain: the formal representation of knowledge, logic, rules, and inference capabilities. Unlike these, sub-symbolic AI systems emulate the functioning of the brain at a basic level using a so-called "connectionist" approach. The best-known and most widely used example of this class of systems are artificial neural networks, which are currently used in deep learning.

Symbolic AI systems include those that require formal training based on rules, which they then apply to achieve desired results. This class of systems reached its peak development in the 1980s through expert systems based on logical rules and automatic deduction procedures. Sub-symbolic AI systems do not use symbols and rules to draw conclusions, but they exploit large amounts of data and elementary information from which they extract patterns and behaviors based on (semi-)automatic learning procedures [2]. Data analytics and machine learning systems today implement sub-symbolic AI systems and enable machines to learn on their own based on examples or by extracting knowledge from content available in often very large archives. Machine learning systems include, as already described, deep learning systems, as well as other approaches such as those based on statistical, mathematical, and geometric methods, graphs, and highly advanced data visualization systems.

Currently, the successes that AI is achieving in many fields, including intelligent generative systems, are based on sub-symbolic approaches, while symbolic approaches are used only in very limited contexts. However, it cannot be ruled out that in the future, the two approaches could be integrated to obtain more complex and more capable systems through the combination of symbolic and sub-symbolic techniques. The effectiveness of AI systems based on sub-symbolic approaches, such as machine learning systems, suggests that computers, using AI techniques, can indeed do many things we consider intelligent (such as winning a game of chess, translating a text from a foreign language, plotting a route in a few seconds and recognizing the signs they encounter, reading a book and summarizing it, diagnosing a disease from a series of medical tests, writing a newspaper article, and designing new proteins), but they do so without being truly intelligent like humans.

This scenario, which envisions systems capable of being intelligent without replicating human rational processes, opens up very interesting perspectives on the nature of intelligence (both human and artificial). On the one hand, these perspectives could lead to a reconsideration of the various theories on how intelligence is formed and fulfilled. On the other, they could explain the mechanisms underlying the decisions of humans we deem intelligent. These decisions are often based on simple calculations performed repeatedly and quickly, on probabilistic assessments of facts, events, and the many possible choices that can be made at any given moment and on random factors that machines simulate very well using random functions that are proving highly effective in AI systems, even for emulating human creativity. Creativity, for example, can also be achieved through the use of these random functions, which, when executed by a computer, can contribute to composing original musical pieces (as tools such as Amper Music, Dream Track, and Voicemod do), writing accurate and even very long lyrics, or painting original and surprising pictures, as NightCafe and DeepDream do.

Although renowned American linguist and philosopher Noam Chomsky believes that ChatGPT is basically a form of high-tech plagiarism, it's worth considering that generative AI systems don't simply copy what they find in their training data. They rework it, often obtaining results that did not previously exist and creating new content from the original, just as a discerning student studying the work of a writer or philosopher is able to explain it and develop his or her own insights based on that study.

Generative AI is a branch of sub-symbolic AI that deals with the creation of new content in the form of text, images, music, audio, video, software code, and more [3]. Generative AI follows the understanding model typical of machine learning systems and therefore uses automatic learning techniques to learn to create content from previously observed data. For example, a generative AI model can be trained on a set of images of dogs, generating new, realistic dog images that are different from the ones it trained on. The same can happen if we want to train it to write new texts in the literary style of Philip Dick by providing it with the contents of Dick's works from which it can learn the narrative style and scenarios described by the great American writer. Similar operations can be performed to generate journalistic contributions written in a certain style or musical compositions inspired by the compositions of contemporary musicians or great musicians of the past.

Generative AI software systems read requests or descriptions (prompts) formulated in natural language by the user (human or computer), and in a matter of seconds, they generate texts from other texts (text-to-text), images from texts (text-to-image), images from images (image-to-image), or even videos from texts (text-to-video). For example, many apps, such as Gencraft, Airt, and Journey AI, can quickly create an image from a short text description of its subject (for example, "A peace demonstration in New York"), while music can be composed from the lyrics of a song. Systems for automatically generating videos from text or photos have recently been developed. Sora is a system developed by OpenAI, capable of generating highly realistic videos lasting several minutes from a few simple sentences. EMO, meanwhile, stands for Emote Portrait Alive (a system for animating portraits) and is a software system capable of generating a video from a single photo and an audio recording. For example, using a photo of a face and a recording of a song, EMO can generate a video showing the person in the photo singing that song.

## 9.2 Getting Thoughts from Words

Among several tasks they are able to perform, generative AI systems are capable of describing themselves. If asked to explain who it is, ChatGPT is able to provide a quick response: "*I define myself as an artificial language model developed by OpenAI, trained on a large corpus of text to answer questions and complete assigned linguistic tasks. My main goal is to help users by providing accurate and timely information.*" This response seems clear and useful for explaining to everyone in a few words what we are talking about.

However, if this seems like too simple an answer, it might be helpful to add what the ChatGPT system said when we asked if it could write a short press release explaining its capabilities to readers: "*Of course! Here is a short article explaining that I, as an artificial language model, ChatGPT, have no ability to think or feel, but merely combine words in a coherent and relevant way: "ChatGPT is a language model developed by OpenAI that aims to mimic human language. It doesn't have the ability to think or feel, but rather combines words and sentences based on what it learned during its training on a large corpus of text. The model uses a combination of deep learning techniques, including Natural Language Processing (NLP), to understand and produce human language. This allows it to answer users' questions and generate text autonomously. However, it's important to note that ChatGPT's responses are based solely on the information in its training database and do not necessarily reflect the thinking or emotions of a human. In other words, ChatGPT cannot think or feel, but simply uses the information available to it to produce coherent and relevant responses.*""

Even from these brief answers, it is clear that we have to deal with a sort of "synthetic language" that machines can generate even without the capacity for thought – a language of automatic synthesis but one that has nothing to envy of that of most humans. Until now, speech has been human; at most, a few clever parrots have managed to repeat, without understanding, a word or two. Today, however, machines are taking the lead and aiming to replace humans in human-to-human dialogue. They're doing so thanks in part to the enormous financial push of tens of billions of dollars behind the IT giants working on these systems. They do so very naturally, even if they still seem a bit naive, but they will soon improve greatly because systems such as ChatGPT, while communicating with people in English, Italian, or Japanese, learn new concepts, new information, and new expressions from them, and store new learned elements in their immense archives so they can never forget them and use them whenever needed. In short, while millions of users around the world play by asking questions and challenging ChatGPT, the system learns countless things from these millions of people and thus becomes more informed and more intelligent.

The capabilities of systems like ChatGPT to simulate language in its text form, to adapt it to the context of dialogue, to store knowledge and information, to create sequences of sentences and arguments, and to articulate responses by constructing dialogues with its human interlocutors are the result of a highly complex combination of algorithms, mathematical models for generating language terms, data, and digital archives stored on cloud systems. All of this is not enough to say that these systems think, but it can certainly be said that they imitate human thought very well when they act to compose answers or argue about issues of which they are aware.

While some believe that systems like ChatGPT are merely new "digital parrots," it is worth reflecting on their sophisticated ability to perform tasks such as dialogue and content writing, which could soon replace the skills of many humans performing similar tasks, especially those who, unfortunately, do so mechanically and repetitively. Too often, many people approach the topic of machines' new linguistic and speech capabilities with superficiality and aplomb. In other cases, one can observe many people getting carried away by facile enthusiasm for these new, and sometimes impressive, computer inventions. Both positions are inappropriate because they fail to grasp the complexity of the issues that these types of technological innovations have brought to humanity's attention. We don't need trivialization or enthusiasm; we need deep thinking to understand the impact of these innovations on society and our lives.

The advent of synthetic language will change many social and work scenarios, disrupting previously taken-for-granted mechanisms and consolidated relationships in all sectors that thrive on words, writing, and speech, or, in short, language. Computers that master our language and learn to orchestrate words like skilled essayists are creating new scenarios for which many humans are unprepared. To this we must add that other similar systems possess equally astonishing capabilities, capable of producing artificially created music, works of art, or videos that appear entirely real.

These new intelligent systems demonstrate unprecedented and, in part, shocking capabilities due to their similarity to functions that humans have developed over many millennia. Their impact on our lives will be significant and irreversible because, even if we wanted to, we cannot undo these inventions. Therefore, we are left with the need to fully understand the effect these tools have on our daily lives and our being and to understand, in the face of this "artificial knowledge," what remains of our human prerogatives and what these automatic systems are taking away from us, perhaps forever.

ChatGPT, Gemini, Claude, DeepSeek, and other large language models are only the latest example of a multitude of digital instruments aiming to take over our abilities and replace us in many things that until now only we humans have been able to do. The trend in this direction will not stop. Indeed, with the passage of time, the level of challenges that intelligent machines have now posed to humans is increasingly rising, and this requires us to refine our thinking and action skills so as not to lose the historic role we have played thus far.

When I was writing this section, I thought of asking ChatGPT what it thought about the possibility of it replacing many humans in the writing of texts. Its word-for-word answer is as follows: "*As an artificial language model, I don't have the ability to think or feel, so I can't express a personal opinion. However, I can say that artificial language models like me were developed to assist humans and simplify certain linguistic tasks, such as generating text or answering specific questions. In some cases, artificial language models can be used as a support tool for writing texts, but they cannot completely replace humans. There are many challenges and limitations in using artificial language models for writing texts, such as understanding context and the ability to produce original and creative text. Ultimately, artificial language models can be a useful tool for writing texts, but they cannot completely replace human creativity and writing skills.*"

This is a very wise and diplomatic answer, perhaps even a bit optimistic toward us humans. It is therefore an answer that should reassure us, were it not for the fact that it was conceived entirely by a machine.

## 9.3 How AI Became Generative

After hearing an LLM's assessment of itself, it is useful to examine how generative AI systems based on LLMs work on text composition – in other words, how they learn to write. We could say that, by analyzing large amounts of text written by us humans, they learn how to best perform a seemingly simple task: predicting the next words in a sentence. It's worth noting, however, that LLMs don't simply guess the next word to add to a sentence to complete it; they are also capable of understanding entire sentences, understanding the context of a sentence, the most significant words that contribute to the sentence's meaning, and identifying the relationships between words that contribute to that particular meaning.

A key phase for generative AI systems is training. During training, which is a semi-automatic process – because it also requires human supervision – a model receives as input a huge amount of text, images, and other contents taken from books, newspaper articles, Web pages, social media posts and tweets, and more. Training allows the model to learn the relationships between words, their meanings, and grammatical structures. During the training phase, the lexicon of all the words in these texts is divided into tokens. A token can be an entire word, a syllable, a punctuation mark, or even a single letter. This tokenization allows the model to break down the text into small units that will be used during the comprehension and writing phases, making them more efficient and precise. The next phase is understanding the context in which the words are inserted. Understanding context requires analyzing the entire linguistic context in which the terms are included (how words fit together in sentences). For example, if a sentence contains the word "pitch," the model uses the context to understand whether it refers to a noun or a verb. In case the sentence contains the word "date," the model analyzes the sentence to decide if it refers to a fruit of the date palm tree, a romantic appointment, or a specific day in a year.

As is well known, neural networks, and computers more generally, work better with numbers than with characters. For this reason, deep learning systems that implement LLMs use an internal representation of words via numerical vectors that allow for fast processing and a very useful similarity analysis for assigning similar meanings to words that have similar or at least not very different vector values (this operation is called *word embedding*[1]) [4]. The values of the vectors representing words express the relationship between a word and the context in which it occurs. For example, the words "senator" and "politician" have similar semantic meanings, so their vectors tend to have similar values. Similarly, the words "senator" and "car" have very different meanings, so their numerical vectors will hold very different values.

---

[1] Word2Vec and GloVe are two of the most widely used word embedding systems. Specifically, Word2Vec uses a supervised machine learning algorithm (which relies on the intervention of a human to indicate when it is doing well and when it is doing poorly during the learning phase) based on a neural network that receives a corpus of texts as input and produces a set of vectors representing the semantic distribution of words in the texts. GloVe, on the other hand, uses an unsupervised machine learning algorithm (and therefore without the intervention of a human to train it) that calculates correlations between words in a corpus.

This technique has effectively introduced a semantic level into automatic language processing systems that allows for the assignment of meaning to words and sentences. This demonstrates that generative AI systems not only use syntactic rules to process texts but also employ forms of semantics that allow these systems to understand the meaning of what they read and write. For example, the use of word embedding techniques allows LLMs to understand the meaning of questions and respond to them by generating accurate and contextual answers to the questions received. Finally, it should be noted that, along with word embedding, generative NLP systems also use positional encoding to encode the position of words in a sentence. Indeed, while word embedding captures the meaning of words but does not analyze their position in the sequence, positional encoding is used to compensate for this shortcoming by identifying grammatical relationships between words and thus generating grammatically correct and coherent text.

The generative AI systems used today are all based on so-called Transformers, which are language learning models created using giant deep learning systems that transform an input sequence into an output sequence, preserving the relationships between words. Transformers were proposed in 2017 by a group of researchers from Google and the University of Toronto and have greatly improved the capabilities of generative AI systems. The paper published by Ashish Vaswani and his seven colleagues [5] explains how to build Transformers. It is considered one of the fundamental contributions to AI in recent decades. An essential element on which Transformers are based is the *attention* mechanism, which is used to learn the relationships between words in a sentence by focusing on the relevant words in the sentence, even if they are distant from each other. This mechanism has revolutionized the capabilities of generative AI systems, which previously operated on sentences by focusing on the relationships between nearby words, while it has been demonstrated that even significant but distant words very often determine the meaning of a sentence. The main operations performed by a Transformer in an LLM system include the following:

- **Encoding:** The process of converting an input sequence into a state vector using the attention mechanism to encode the relationships between the different words in a sequence, also leveraging positional encoding and identifying the semantic context of a sentence using word embedding techniques.

- **Decoding:** The process of converting a state vector into an output sequence, also relying on the attention mechanism to decode the relationships between the words in a sequence.

For example, when a system like ChatGPT receives the question "What is the capital of Denmark?", its Transformer encodes the question into a numerical state vector and uses the attention mechanism to focus on the relevant words in the question, namely "capital" and "Denmark," to understand its meaning. The Transformer then uses attention to decode the state vector into a response, which in this case will be "Copenhagen" because in its archive of encoded sentences mentioning the Danish capital, the word "Copenhagen" is the most frequent.

It should be noted that Transformers are capable of analyzing highly complex texts, which they process in parallel to calculate attention based on the different words in a sentence (technically *multi-head attention*). This allows them to understand the context in which the words occur, the relationships between them, and which words are the most important and thus extract the meaning of each specific sentence. This parallel analysis of sentences makes Transformers much more efficient than systems previously used in generative AI systems, which processed input sequentially over very long periods of time. Finally, Transformers can process word sequences of arbitrary length, and they are applicable not only to text-to-text generation modes but also to speech-to-text and image-to-video generation modes. Models are going to be developed that are increasingly capable of interacting by accepting different types of sensory inputs and producing combinations of them, making interaction with these artificial systems increasingly natural.

As we have discussed, generative AI systems compose responses based on the linguistic knowledge they have accumulated within their parameters. They therefore don't simply extract responses from external sources by copying them. They can assist in many tasks, but it's important to note that if you try to use them to obtain information about facts about which they have received little or incorrect information, they can fall prey to the so-called hallucinations we have already mentioned, introducing plausible but incorrect elements into the response. For example, an LLM like ChatGPT or Gemini might generate a newspaper article describing a historical event with details different from those that actually occurred or with incorrect dates for the event described. LLMs might generate a response or short essay containing false information taken from unreliable or biased websites or produce software code containing errors or vulnerabilities.

These hallucinations occur because an LLM system may have been trained on data containing incorrect or inaccurate information or because the system may reflect biases or misinformation present in the data it has received. Moreover, since LLMs can access very large but limited storage, they cannot store all the info they read in the training phase. For these reasons, generative AI systems can also be used to create and spread (for example, via social chatbots) fake news and conduct disinformation campaigns. This problem is addressed with techniques that guide a model to produce sentences containing precise and correct information drawn from trusted sources. However, this remains a very significant and incompletely solved problem. Finally, despite their extraordinary linguistic abilities, generative AI systems, such as Gemini and ChatGPT, currently lack the functional skills necessary to perform complex mathematical calculations or logical reasoning. They therefore lack the abstraction capabilities needed to perform complex calculations, make logical deductions, or plan. However, several research and experimentation efforts are underway to add these skills to generative systems and thus expand their capabilities and application areas where they can be used effectively. For example, a technique called *chain-of-thought* (CoT) prompting, asking the model to work step-by-step, has significantly boosted their accuracy in these tasks. Moreover, new models, such as reasoning language models (RLMs), have been specifically designed to perform explicit, verifiable, multi-step logical reasoning before generating an answer. RLMs are demonstrating their great advantage over LLMs in fields that demand precise, multi-step logical deduction, which makes mathematics and coding their strongest domains.

## 9.4 In a New Unknown Land

When cartographers in the 16th century had to map out an unknown and unexplored geographical area, they used the term “terra incognita” (“unknown land”). Today, we might use this ancient term to refer to the new reality created by generative AI. As we have discussed, we are faced with software systems capable of generating, even creatively, content that until a few years ago only humans could conceive. Generative algorithms write texts in impeccable syntax, create images, and compose music, software programs, spoken dialogues, and videos that are often indistinguishable from those created by humans. In other words, they create a new reality by expanding the one we have become accustomed to: a reality that is unknown to most and often difficult, if not impossible, to distinguish from the reality created by humans.

The writing and creation of AI content are posing several challenges and forcing new practices and regulations to manage and regulate the content. Using generative tools such as ChatGPT and Gemini, a student can generate an essay in perfect English or translate a Latin text in seconds. The same can happen to a professional writing a technical document or report. Many creatives now rely on DALL-E or Midjourney to create photos, comics, or works of art. Some years ago, a photo generated using AI won an artistic photography competition, and the term "promptography" was coined. In fact, in March 2023, the Sony World Photography Awards announced the winning entry in their creative photo category: a black-and-white image of an older woman embracing a younger one, entitled *PSEUDOMNESIA: The Electrician*. The press release described the photograph as "reminiscent of the visual language of 1940s family portraits." The author, Boris Eldagsen, turned down the award and announced that he had crafted the photo through creative prompting of DALL-E 2, the well-known AI image generator. One year later, another photographer, provocatively, entered a photo he had taken himself into an AI-generated image competition. The photographer Miles Astray submitted the photo he took in Aruba to the 1839 Awards, a photography competition with a category for images created by AI. Astray submitted that real image showing a flamingo without its head and neck, declaring that it was created by a generative AI tool. It was among the winning entries chosen by a panel of judges in the AI category and won the People's Vote Award before it was disqualified after the author admitted his little lie [6].

These cases and many others, such as the deepfake phenomenon, that occur almost daily demonstrate the growing need to distinguish between human-created content and that produced by generative AI. Many researchers are developing software systems capable of distinguishing between things created by humans and those created by AI. Some useful results are beginning to emerge, but currently we don't have systems capable of making this distinction with certainty. Regulators' approach is to require a label identifying AI-generated content. Even large IT companies are moving toward labeling images, audio, and video content produced by their generative AI software with a digital watermark. These initiatives attempt to provide a practical solution to the problem. However, the level of sophistication of generative AI algorithms is so high that it leaves ample room for cheating.

As mentioned above, the extraordinary development of generative AI systems has led us into an unknown land, still largely uncharted territory. It is a land that holds many surprises but which must be explored in depth; otherwise, in the near future, we risk losing our bearings entirely. We risk no longer seeing the differences between the human and the artificial.

## References

1. Winston, P. H. (1984). *Artificial Intelligence*. USA: Addison-Wesley Longman Publishing.
2. Zha, D., Bhat, Z. P., Lai, K.-H., Yang, F., Jiang, Z., Zhong, S., and Hu, X. (2025). Data-centric Artificial intelligence: A survey. *ACM Computing Surveys,* 57(5), 1–42.
3. Sengar, S. S., Hasan, A. B., Kumar, S., *et al.* (2025). Generative artificial intelligence: A systematic review and applications. *Multimedia Tools and Applications*, 84, pp. 23661–23700.
4. Boselli, R., D'Amico, S., and Nobani, N. (2025). eXplainable AI for word embeddings: A survey. *Cognitive Computing*, 17(19).
5. Vaswani, A., Shazeer, N., *et al.* (2017). Attention is all you need. *Advances in Neural Information Processing Systems*, Vol. 30. https://arxiv.org/abs/1706.03762.
6. Prashall, A. (2024). How this real image won an AI photo competition. *Scientific American*, June 19. www.scientificamerican.com/article/how-this-real-image-won-an-ai-photo-competition [Retrieved 31 October 2025].

# Chapter 10

# The Human Factor in the Digital Universe

*I love him who labors and invents, that he may build the house for the Superman, and prepare for him earth, animal, and plant: for thus seeks he his own down-going.*

—Friedrich Nietzsche

The rapid rise of artificial intelligence and computer-based automation threatens to limit human roles, reducing people to mere observers and executors in the new digital universe. The main challenge is to ensure that AI technology serves human well-being and purpose, not just efficiency or corporate profit. This requires that researchers and professionals design systems that value uniquely human attributes such as empathy, creativity, and ethical judgment. Failing to prioritize the human factor risks societal challenges, including mass job supplanting, algorithmic bias, and historical decline in human agency [1]. Keeping humans central requires constant, deliberate design and ethical governance. This should be done also for transforming the potential threat into an opportunity for human augmentation.

## 10.1 Machines and Humans Facing the Hybrid Future

Technology invented by humans has removed many human abilities from us or added external capabilities to those we already possess. In effect, it has disembodied human functions and transferred them to machines. As long as machines took on the task of relieving humans of physical labor, we were all happy. Now that machines can perform complex tasks, competing with our mental capabilities, intelligence, and rationality, we are surprised, amazed, and sometimes disconcerted.

Computers were created to perform calculations faster and more precisely than humans. Subsequently, these sophisticated machines, thanks to those who programmed them, became capable of performing many functions better than we can. Today, computers communicate much faster than we do, collect data and information better than we do, have more robust memories than ours, are capable of never forgetting anything, read enormous amounts of data and information like we cannot, and select and filter information much more quickly than we can. However, in many cases, fortunately, we reason better than computers and use far less information than they do to understand what is happening around us and choose how to act. Furthermore, we don't simply know how to provide answers; we know how to ask questions and express doubts, like no computer can.

Therefore, for now, the fear that digital machines are generally better and more intelligent than us is unfounded. However, the human superiority we still maintain does not preclude the possibility that in the near future, the scope of computers' actions and their algorithms will expand to the point of pushing humans into a corner, restricting their historical superiority and threatening their governance of reality. Above all, it will surpass the capacity for choice, action, and work of the majority of the world's population. This latter scenario is a very worrying one.

The power of machines derives largely from the many procedural and repetitive actions that are part of our lives and can be automated. Initially, the development of information technology and robotics led to the replacement of people in tedious physical work in factories and offices. Subsequently, it was the turn of many routine intellectual tasks performed by millions of human beings employed as if they were devices that had to function but not necessarily think.

Whenever individuals perform standardized and repetitive tasks, they become top candidates for replacement by digital machines that can be programmed to perform the same tasks quickly, efficiently, and often at lower costs. All of these are cases of jobs in which humans act as tools, devices, or cogs that perform actions that can be encoded through algorithms. In these contexts, the human element undergoes a process of devaluation and is therefore easily replaced by machines.

Many people in many of their work experiences are, in effect, tools and devices, and so it is not surprising that they could be replaced by computers, which are the most flexible and efficient devices that humans have ever invented. This applies not only to physical jobs, such as farming or screwing bolts, but also to bank or supermarket cashiers, ticket collectors, drivers, switchboard operators, and many other jobs.

The picture has become further complicated by the development of systems based on AI techniques, which in recent years have posed an unprecedented challenge to intellectual jobs and professions requiring advanced skills and complex cognitive processes. AI systems are challenging radiologists, lawyers, journalists, pizza makers, typographers, interpreters and translators, painters, essayists, insurance agents, and even priests and notaries. In these and other activities, for the first time, the supremacy of human beings is at risk of being removed.

These are increasingly capable (we like to say "more intelligent") systems that push us toward new horizons while shrinking our traditional spaces. They challenge us and force us to explore new opportunities through the development of new skills, forcing us to better assert our nature as cognitive beings and our uniqueness as human beings. Beyond the attempts, risky at the moment, to calculate reliable numbers on the jobs that will be lost and the new ones that AI will be able to create, it is certain that we are facing historic changes brought about by the ability of digital machines to occupy spaces of action that until now have been the exclusive access of humans.

Certainly, in the realm of feelings and empathy, today's digital devices are far behind us. Machines don't know how to laugh; they don't know how to suffer. Although there is considerable research in the field of cognitive emotional systems, robots and computers today are impassive agents, insensitive to emotions. They are not inclined to joy or suffering (they don't know what these feelings are), and they don't feel shame; therefore, for example, they can't even be punished when they make mistakes.

As algorithmic machines advance and acquire new functions, we humans, to compete and coexist with them while maintaining our leading role, will need to be able to find new meanings, new purposes, and new skills. We will need to abandon tasks and roles in which we act as mere tools, areas in which we are mere devices within codified production mechanisms, to perform more flexible activities closer to human nature. We are called to learn how to conquer new, non-automatable tasks, which require greater education and deeper, more human knowledge. All of these are useful for actively experiencing the present, marked by great transformations, and the hybrid future that awaits us, in which machines will assume increasingly important roles.

In this very near future, we will have to learn to supplement human capabilities with those of machines, rather than replace our own abilities with those of computers and their software. This is by no means a simple task, and for it to be successful, it must not be left to the efforts of a few individuals. It must become the goal of society as a whole, while being careful to avoid the very real risk of generating new inequalities induced by technology. We will need to forge a new cooperation with intelligent machines that protects citizens' rights and preserves our role as protagonists in a new context in which people and machines will coexist increasingly closely.

## 10.2 The Imitation Cost

The relentless development and success of technological innovations offer us effective solutions to many everyday problems and simplify many functions, bringing about profound changes in our lives. At the same time, rapid technological advances, with their highly accelerated transformation, risk causing a negative involution for humans that could lead to the loss of the essential and distinctive characteristics of the human species. These natural and cultural characteristics and elements are expressed through feelings of understanding, indulgence, empathy, flexibility, and adaptability that are fundamental elements of our humanity.

If we consider the impact that automated systems are having on society as a whole, we can see how a process of "human replacement" is taking place not only in the workplace, where digital machines and robots perform many tasks that until recently were the exclusive territory of human workers, but also in everyday choices, relationships, decisions both large and small, and even in emotions. The replacement of human workers with robots is occurring ever more rapidly and, along with the benefits for businesses and production systems, is raising major challenges regarding labor protection and workers' rights. If what is happening in the world of work is not enough to understand the scale of the changes, it's important to note that the replacement of the human element is making its way into areas of our lives that aren't limited to manufacturing alone.

Increasingly, in many functions and many daily moments, we are experiencing the loss of human characteristics in favor of automatic procedures that force us to perform actions and interactions that are unnatural for many of us and pose new challenges. This happens not only in our digital interactions with the internet, its applications, and its content and when working on computers at home or in the office, but also in many of our actions, such as filling up our gas tanks at self-service gas stations, chatting online with friends or relatives, using a credit card to purchase from a vending machine, in online meetings and classes, when we're forced to talk to an answering machine on the phone, and when we have to exit a paid parking lot and the optical reader refuses to recognize our crumpled receipt. In practice, the moments include every time our actions must adapt to the demands of an algorithm built exclusively according to operational rationality, respecting only that logic and forgetting that it must interact with a human being.

In short, algorithmic relationships are replacing human ones, certainly seeking to reduce or eliminate their imperfections, as well as eliminating their flexibility, their ability to understand the interlocutor's state of mind, and their dialectic rooted in human nature. Despite the many studies being conducted on the best forms of interaction between people and machines, currently it is humans who must adapt to the automatic modes of interaction of machines (which are often too rigid and impersonal), not vice versa. The ever-increasing use of AI systems and applications further complicates the picture by expanding the scope in which computers perform actions previously reserved for humans and forcing more and more individuals to interact with algorithmic procedures that have little human element.

Thus, machines are expanding their functions and scope of action and, at the same time, acquiring greater rational and functional capabilities, depriving humans of roles and autonomy. In other words, the trend is toward replacing humans rather than assisting them to enhance their potential. We must therefore recognize that in this historic moment, the delegation of so many actions and roles to digital technology helps us greatly, but it also takes away our decision-making autonomy, alienates human functions, and distorts interactions on an emotional level, not just the manual and intellectual ones. In short, as we rely on machines that lack humanity, we lose autonomy, free will, and the ability to develop the skills of choice. We impoverish our dialectical capacity and the flexibility of our daily interactions.

There are countless examples of this condition: Today, many algorithms decide who should be hired by companies, determine the best treatment for a patient, and suggest whether a law firm should advocate for a case or represent a client. There are even several software applications in circulation that, in conjunction with judges, determine the culprits and sentences in court cases. Many other cases of "human replacement," demonstrating how machines are stealing space, discretion, and power from humans, could be listed and discussed. They all demonstrate how we are increasingly adapting our sensitivities and emotions to algorithmic procedures. We are losing humanity, empathy, and degrees of freedom, while our anxiety and sense of helplessness increase. Indeed, humanity and empathy are elements no longer central to decisions and relationships.

All of this has generated a new form of emotional illiteracy that scholars call "digital alexithymia," meaning the inability to recognize and manage emotions and affectivity caused by the interaction and rigid mediation of machines, limited by their algorithms that guide them, forcing our communications with them and the interpersonal ones that pass through new technologies. The digital interface does not require the direct and free involvement of interlocutors; it forces forms and methods and acts as a filter, transforming our forms of expression and emotions to the point of generating "virtual masks" that young people, especially, wear, driven by the digital media they frequently use.

The described scenarios, which each of us experiences in full or in part on a daily basis, as some have written, risk quickly leading us into the so-called "Turing trap." This trap is rooted in the legacy of Alan Turing's famous test, which set imitation of human conversation as the ultimate goal for machine intelligence [2]. Some scholars argued that adhering to this goal is counterproductive because it leads to automation/substitution over augmentation. When AI systems are developed mainly to substitute humans (e.g., automated service, generative music for writing songs), workers in those areas lose power and role. They become less essential to the production of value.

Therefore, Turing traps arise from the assumption that AI will be able to match or even surpass human capabilities, and hence intelligent machines, instead of improving and enhancing human capabilities, should aim to replace people, not only in their work but also in their roles as individuals and citizens. This line of thinking is espoused by large digital corporations and is frequently conveyed in new and old media as if it were a seductive dream. However, these trends demonstrate how the problem of dealing with the world's digital acceleration is not limited to replacing humans in work roles, but it can even lead to the belief that it limits their role, that of the human component on Earth, which until now has decided, for better or worse, the world's destiny but which, in the future, could lose this position and with it its very human nature.

Erik Brynjolfsson, a scholar of the Stanford Digital Economy Lab, explained why an excessive focus on developing and deploying human-like AI can lead us into the Turing trap: "*As machines become better substitutes for human labor, workers lose economic and political bargaining power and become increasingly dependent on those who control the technology. In contrast, when AI is focused on augmenting humans rather than mimicking them, then humans retain the power to insist on a share of the value created. What's more, augmentation creates new capabilities and new products and services, ultimately generating far more value than merely human-like AI. While both types of AI can be enormously beneficial, there are currently excess incentives for automation rather than augmentation among technologists, business executives, and policymakers*" [3].

The processes currently unfolding are complex and, in some respects, are governed only by the economic logic of profit. Yet, understanding and acting in the face of the world's new complexity requires education and knowledge on the part of everyone to address these historic transformations. Specialists also need a different approach to designing and implementing digital systems. We need human ways for their algorithms to interact with us, people of flesh and blood, of meaning and emotion, who too often are considered users who must submit to their predefined logics – logics embedded in their code and incapable of adapting to the human being, their culture and emotions, which are the product of millennia of evolution and cannot be swept away in a few years by a powerful and sophisticated technology that should serve to improve our lives, not destroy them.

## 10.3 Free Time Is Over

Industrial society has conceived of free time as a time in which others have no control over us and there is no assessment of anyone's abilities or merits. Free time is the foundation of fundamental physiological, mental, and social recovery, free from codified obligations or work constraints, a space that helps us find daily compatibility between individual needs and social obligations. In recent decades, digital technologies have excelled at infiltrating this space, originally intended as the realm of leisure and passion, and transforming it into the realm of the web, smartphones, and social media. The digital age has heavily invaded the entertainment sector, creating countless new opportunities for relaxation, leisure, and any other experience that involves rest and pause. This attitude, which involves billions of people around the world, has eliminated pauses and waiting. As soon as we feel like we have an empty minute, a moment in which we must wait, we feel the need to reach for our digital prosthetics, even when there is no need to do so.

A short phrase that perfectly encapsulates how the digital world wants to take up all our time and attention was uttered some time ago by Reed Hastings, CEO of Netflix, the US company that distributes movies and multimedia content via streaming. Hastings says, "*Our main competitor is sleep!*" In other words, their frontier, which they are nevertheless trying to expand, is human physiology. They can win against everything except a primal need that puts us on pause and allows no exceptions. We must sleep a few hours a day; otherwise, we risk death. Sleep is the limit beyond which the digital consumption of our free time must currently surrender, but elsewhere, conquest is possible and, in fact, is being achieved.

Digital platforms often don't directly ask us for money to entertain us. First and foremost, they want our time, and to get it, they tie us to them by increasingly increasing the amount of content that must seem light, simple, and not too in-depth. The attention economy, studied by Herbert Simon, is based on individual entertainment. The more it captures our vision and our senses, the more it generates profits. Every moment of our days is considered useful by "attention engineers" and can be "colonized" through multimedia content on a wide variety of topics, competing to capture the attention of a vast number of digital consumers regardless of age, gender, or social status. We are all engaged in a struggle to monopolize the cognitive surplus of millions of individuals. Our attention and free time thus become increasingly limited and contested resources. The digital entertainment industry produces increasingly brief, schematic, immediate, and captivating content. Indeed, we know that there is increasingly less time to understand, analyze, rationalize, and create. The diversion of free time through the global and uninterrupted dissemination of vast quantities of data, information, solicitations, and advertising is generating a progressive lack of reflection, serenity, and individual thinking, with negative repercussions for society as a whole.

The human–machine relationship has now taken up much of our time, to the detriment of the person-to-person and person-to-environment relationships. Relationships with digital machines are very absorbing for young people and the younger generations, but even older people are not exempt. We all tend to interact through these artificial tools. We minimize opportunities to talk to each other, even when we are in the same house or at the same company. We also tend to use the phone less as a voice interaction tool. We now prefer to exchange messages via WhatsApp; our digital conversations are full of emoticons, smileys, and animated GIFs. We don't look each other in the eye; we prefer to live by exchanging selfies. When traveling, in a car, on a train, or on a bus, we don't look at the landscape around us out the window but instead gaze at the photos that fill the smartphone screen (a new, tiny window onto the world). They fill that precious free time with images, pixelated solicitations, sounds, and streaming that allow for no pauses, silences, or reflections.

We no longer get bored because all it takes is a tap on a phone screen to access contacts, photos, locations, videos, news, games, and stories – all to ensure we never have to become bored again and all to avoid human idleness, replaced by a digital idleness that is no longer idleness because it constantly engages our eyes, fingers, and sometimes even our brains. While industrial society organized work time, separating it from free time, and consumer society organized shopping and consumption time, post-industrial cyber society has organized what little remained of our free time. The intensive use of digital technology has filled the last part of our lives that remained outside of collective obligations. What was originally "freely usable" time has been seized upon by the digital industry, cannibalizing it and transforming it into time useful for the new commercial uses that big tech companies has created and imposed.

Silently but rapidly, we are increasingly accepting that our free time is subjected to arithmetic evaluations; we unthinkingly consent to interacting with algorithmic versions of our friends, relatives, and colleagues. We live with the idea of creating and nurturing "personal brands" that must be nurtured at every moment. This constant action generates satisfaction in many people and even addiction in many young people. Our time is transformed into a continuous streaming of bytes that expose our daily experiences, our trains of thought, and our desires to build a digital role in the global space of attention, even at the cost of distorting reality, distorting it to satisfy our own egos along with the greed of the digital industry. Through all this constant overexposure, we contribute to burning away our own and others' free time.

Already in the past century, along with others, the philosophers of the Frankfurt School and the Situationist movement had pointed out how free time in industrial societies was becoming illusory because economic forces were appropriating it and transforming it into a new commodity [4]. The incredible rise of digital technology has exacerbated these concerns and increasingly restricted the time each of us can dedicate to breaks, leisure, and our own inclinations and desires. Digital devices, their software, and their countless applications demand our attention, distract us from everything else, and delude us into thinking they offer us serenity or even happiness. They undermine the human physiology that craves idleness, the sweet idleness of doing nothing, and impose a model in which even free time can be governed by algorithms.

For the ancient Greeks, leisure was a gift from the gods, and the Latins also accorded time for rest an important role in their lives ("*otium*" meaning "time freed," from *negotium*). Today, however, in a world that has embraced the ideology of limitless production, leisure time is viewed with suspicion, even though free time is formally guaranteed and regulated by laws, agreements, and contracts. Yet, our free time is becoming increasingly busy. We risk losing it forever if we fail to limit the intensive and constant use of devices that permeate our days, which claim to occupy us even during our free time. This phenomenon is one of many that characterize the particular historical period we are living in and which we are struggling to manage. Perhaps a wise response to remaining human in the face of this digital invasion of our free time is to learn to practice a sort of "digital apathy" – a kind of detachment (even temporary) from technology. A new postmodern stoicism, which could become a privileged practice to avoid being drowned in a time constantly occupied by the streams of bits that aspire to fill every moment of our lives.

## References

1. Anders, G. (2002). *L'Obsolescence de l'homme: Sur l'âme à l'époque de la deuxième revolution industrielle*. Paris, France: Nuisance (in French).
2. Turing, A. M. (1950). Computing machinery and intelligence. *Mind,* LIX(236), pp. 433–460.
3. Brynjolfsson, E. (2022). The Turing trap: The promise & peril of human-like artificial intelligence. *Stanford Digital Economy Lab*. https://digitaleconomy.stanford.edu/news/the-turing-trap-the-promise-peril-of-human-like-artificial-intelligence/ [Retrieved 31 October 2025].
4. L'Internationale Lettriste. (1954). Une ideé neuve en Europe. *Potlatch* (Paris, France), 7 (in French).

# Chapter 11

# Data Ethics Meets AI Ethics

*The scale at which businesses are adopting AI technologies isn't matched by clear guidelines to regulate algorithms and help researchers avoid the pitfalls of bias in datasets.*

—Timnit Gebru

One of the leading developers of artificial intelligence systems, Elon Musk, said the following in one of his interviews several years ago [1]: "*I'm increasingly inclined to think that there should be some regulatory oversight, maybe at the national and international level, just to make sure that we don't do something very foolish. I mean with artificial intelligence we're summoning the demon.*" Despite his different and widely discussed roles in the AI arena, this authoritative declaration asked for laws and regulations because of the deep and wide impact of AI on our society. However, we must consider that, together with regulatory frameworks, ethical behavior is fundamental to limiting the negative effects of AI and improving its beneficial uses.

When speaking of AI ethics, we cannot forget the role of data in AI systems and applications used today. This means that in dealing with AI ethics, we must be inspired by a wide vision where Big Data and AI algorithms are considered mutual factors that can contribute to ensuring the ethical use of AI systems and work to defeat the demon.

## 11.1 Old Suggestions for Modern Ethics

The word "ethics" has its roots in the Ancient Greek word "*êthos*," meaning character. This word gave rise to the Ancient Greek word *ēthikós*, which in Latin was translated into *ethica* and entered the English language in the 15th century, referring to the principles of conduct governing an individual or a profession. One of the oldest and most inspiring works on ethics is the *Nicomachean Ethics* (*Ēthika Nikomacheia*) [2] by the ancient Greek philosopher Aristotle, who discussed the science of the good for human life, the goal all our actions aim at. That treatise had a central influence along the centuries and, in particular, on the European Middle Ages, when it was one of the main texts of medieval philosophy. The *Nicomachean Ethics* was also of great importance in the development of all modern philosophy, as well as Western law and theology. For Aristotle, ethics was about how beneficial habits enable a person to achieve flourishing (*eudaimonia*) and how to develop a virtuous character (*ethikē aretē*). To reach this goal, the Greek philosopher described a sequence of steps. The first one is to practice honorable actions, perhaps under the guidance of teachers, in order to develop good habits. Practiced habits form a stable character in which those habits become voluntary, which then achieves complete goodness.

From the Aristotelian interpretation of ethics, the topic was investigated, discussed, and reformulated by all philosophical currents until today. In particular, during the medieval period, ethics was strongly influenced by religious thought. While recently, in the modern era, a more secular approach concerned with moral experience, reasons for acting, and the consequences of actions influenced the studies of ethics. Despite the long time that has passed, the Aristotelian concept of virtue ethics may provide a relevant and powerful framework for addressing the unique moral challenges of the AI era. Instead of focusing solely on rules or consequences, it centers on the character of the people designing, deploying, using, and governing AI systems. The goal of human flourishing, mentioned earlier, should become the final metric for successful and wealthy AI. Nowadays, this means, for example, evaluating technology not merely by its efficiency and economic profitability but by its contribution to human well-being, societal harmony, and the fulfillment of human potential.

Since Aristotelian virtue is developed through habits and practiced within a community, it can directly translate into organizational ethics, driving research centers, teams of AI scholars, and companies toward virtuous AI habits. Inspired by Aristotelian principles, a professional culture supporting the practice of speaking up about risks, potential harms, or unethical designs must be stimulated and rewarded. In the following section, we discuss data and AI ethics, considering some of the most recent issues; however, Aristotelian ethics remains useful because it offers a character-based ethical model that is deeply human and more general and deeper than solely writing rules for every conceivable AI outcome.

## 11.2 Big Data Ethics

Data ethics can be broadly defined as the moral obligations that govern the entire data lifecycle, from collection, storage, and processing to use and dissemination, to ensure that data-driven practices are fair, transparent, accountable, and respectful of individual rights and societal values. Reaching these goals is not an easy task. However, the ethics principles that guide responsible practice can be implemented in dealing with digital data. Among these principles, we must include the following:

- **Transparency:** Individuals should be clearly informed about what data are collected on them, how they are stored, and how they will be used and by whom.
- **Fairness and equity:** Algorithms and data models must be actively checked and mitigated for bias to ensure that data-driven decisions do not unfairly discriminate against or perpetuate inequalities among people.
- **Accountability:** Organizations and individuals must be able to demonstrate their compliance with ethical and legal standards, and they must take responsibility for the, intended and unintended, consequences, of their data management practices.
- **Privacy and consent:** Data must be collected only with informed, explicit consent from the individual, and appropriate measures must be taken to secure that data and prevent unauthorized access or disclosure.
- **Data quality:** Collected data must be accurate and of high integrity, and operators should only collect the minimum amount of data necessary for a specific, stated purpose.

As we discussed in previous chapters, many industry and commerce sectors exploit personal data for defining and implementing business strategies. Governments also collect data of citizens for implementing services or for control policies. Data ethics requires that these data strategies should not conflict with people's privacy and rights. Indeed, in the past two decades, Big Data collection has made our privacy one of the prices to pay to get (apparently) free digital services.

Laws about data access and processing show individuals and organizations what they can do with data and provide rules and punishments when they are not respected. However, data ethics defines principles that can guide people and laws on whether they should pursue a certain data strategy and how they should go about it.

One of the first laws approved to regulate and discipline the use of digital data is the European Union (EU) General Data Protection Regulation (GDPR), the strongest privacy and security law in the world [3]. GDPR imposes obligations onto organizations anywhere, not only in the EU, as they target or collect data related to individuals living in the EU. The regulation was enforced in May 2018. The GDPR charges severe fines against those who violate privacy and security standards it defines, with punishments reaching into the tens of millions of euros.

By adopting the GDPR, the EU signaled its firm position on data privacy and security at a time when more people are entrusting their personal data with cloud services and breaches are a quotidian occurrence. The GDPR does not explicitly use the word "ethics" as an operative term; however, its entire structure is based on fundamental ethical values that have become legal requirements. For example, Article 5 (Principles relating to the processing of personal data) establishes that data must be "processed lawfully, fairly, and in a transparent manner in relation to the data subject." This codifies the ethical principle of transparency, ensuring that individuals understand how and why their data are being used, and establishes a requirement for fairness in user interactions. Moreover, data must be "collected for specified, explicit and legitimate purposes and not further processed in a manner that is incompatible with those purposes; further processing […] shall not be considered to be incompatible with the initial purposes."

The GDPR also requires free, specific, informed, and unambiguous consent before data are processed. The data subject also has the right to be forgotten (the so-called "right to erasure"). These rights support individual autonomy and agency, ensuring that individuals retain control over their personal data. In addition, data must be "processed in a manner that ensures appropriate security of the personal data, including protection against unauthorized or unlawful processing and against accidental loss, destruction or damage, using appropriate technical or organizational measures."

Referring to accountability, the GDPR requires data controllers to be able to demonstrate compliance with all principles. It requires data protection impact assessments for high-risk processing and the appointment of a Data Protection Officer (DPO). This transforms the ethical principle of accountability into a set of procedural and documentation requirements that ensure organizations are always accountable for their data-related choices. Finally, to guarantee data minimization: "Data must be adequate, relevant, and limited to what is necessary for the purposes for which they are processed." Implementing the ethical principle of data minimization will reduce the potential risk that excessive data collection could lead to future abuse or privacy violations. In summary, the GDPR is the EU's legal support for data ethics, establishing the "how" and "what" to ensure organizations comply with the ethical "whys" of data protection.

After GDPR, many other data regulation laws have been passed in several countries, including the California Consumer Privacy Act (CCPA) and its successor, the California Privacy Rights Act (CPRA), which protect California residents' data. Brazil's Lei Geral de Proteção de Dados (LGPD), Canada's Consumer Privacy Protection Act (CPPA), China's Personal Information Protection Law (PIPL), and the US's sector-specific laws such as HIPAA for health information and COPPA for children's online privacy. These laws provide rules to govern the correct use of data and offer guidance on the ethical use of digital data. However, data ethics is broader than simply the collection, use, retention, and deletion of personal data. Data ethics requires a careful way of thinking that focuses on the impact data operations has on individuals and society.

Data ethics has emerged as a crucial discipline addressing the moral challenges posed by the collection, analysis, and use of information in an increasingly algorithm-driven world. While data ethics has long been associated with privacy and security concerns, the rise of AI and the ever-increasing availability of Big Data have amplified its scope and relevance, elevating it from a technical concern to a social imperative. Recent advancements in AI have quickly allowed private companies and data brokers to analyze huge amounts of data using sophisticated data analytics and machine learning algorithms to profile and predict individuals' lifestyles, sentiment, and potential fragilities, obtaining highly accurate insights about individual citizens and communities.

AI does not just process data; it uses them to make predictive and autonomous decisions that directly impact human lives, ranging from granting bank loans and medical diagnoses to hiring and criminal justice. This transition from passive data to learning algorithmic accomplishment has given rise to more complex ethical issues, such as the following:

- **Algorithmic bias:** AI algorithms, when trained on historically biased datasets (which is a data ethics issue), can perpetuate and amplify social inequalities, leading to unjust outcomes.
- **Opacity:** The nature of some machine learning models often makes it impossible to understand why an AI made a specific decision (e.g., neural networks). This hinders transparency and accountability when an error occurs.
- **Autonomy limitation:** AI's ability to track and predict human behavior raises fundamental questions about individual autonomy and ethical manipulation.

In this scenario dominated by data-driven AI, data ethics and AI ethics are intrinsically linked. The key challenge is to establish a rigorous ethical agenda that ensures that AI technological progress is aligned with fundamental human values, promoting collective well-being (*eudaimonia* in Aristotelian terms) without sacrificing justice, privacy, or freedom.

## 11.3 AI Ethics

The use of computers changed the frontiers of human actions and role; that is, they redefined the areas of actions and thinking of people because they are capable of performing many actions, operations, and tasks that were previously executed by humans, and they also augmented the capabilities of humans. The recent widespread utilization of AI systems, while improving human proficiency, expanded the autonomy of computers and extended their influence in the daily lives of individuals. Since AI is deeply influencing the personal sphere of billions of people, attention to ethics is key.

AI ethics can be defined as a sub-field of applied ethics, focusing on the ethical issues raised by the design, development, implementation, and use of AI systems. Ethical studies in the field of AI help people in understanding how automatic learning technologies may generate major new human rights concerns originating from the design and use of machine intelligence. In the field of AI, respect for humans requires that algorithms consider people with the respect due to them as individuals rather than merely as sources of information, i.e., as data subjects.

If we consider the development and use of AI algorithms, human equality demands that the same rules must apply for everyone when accessing data and information. It also entails a fair distribution of the added value being created by AI systems and applications. This also requires paying attention to special communities, such as individuals with disabilities and minorities. Several public bodies and governments are promoting ethics in AI systems and applications. The Vatican, for example, issued the Rome Call for AI Ethics in 2020, which has been approved by many companies and organizations such as Microsoft, IBM, the United Nations Food and Agricultural Organization, and the Italian government. Also, the EU parliament is very active in this area and, in August, 2024 introduced the so-called AI Act [4].

The compilation of the AI Act was influenced by global ethical frameworks, such as the UNESCO Recommendation on the Ethics of Artificial Intelligence [5] and the Organization for Economic Co-operation and Development (OECD) Recommendation on AI [6], which established the core principles that the Act then translated into law. The UNESCO Recommendation on the Ethics of Artificial Intelligence is an innovative international framework, representing the first-ever global agreement on the ethical governance of AI. It was adopted by UNESCO's 193 Member States in November 2021. Its primary goal is to establish a universal set of core values and principles to ensure that AI technologies are developed and deployed in a manner that amplifies benefits for humanity and limits the risks, promoting a more inclusive, sustainable, and pacific world. The Recommendation is serving as a global resource for policymakers, regulators, academics, and the private sector, providing solutions to the most pressing ethical challenges posed by AI, such as the potential to embed biases, threaten human rights, and compound existing inequalities.

Another reference framework is the OECD Recommendation of the Council on Artificial Intelligence, a major international frame established to promote AI that is innovative, trustworthy, and respectful of human rights and democratic values. Adopted in May 2019, it was the first intergovernmental standard for AI governance and has had a significant global influence, having been adopted by all OECD member countries and subsequently endorsed by the G20. The Recommendation, similar to the UNESCO Recommendation, aims to provide concrete policy action for ethical governance and responsible stewardship of AI. The influence of the UNESCO Recommendation, along with the OECD principles, has significantly shaped pioneering regulatory efforts globally, not only the EU's AI Act. Also, Canada's Artificial Intelligence and Data Act (AIDA) and other initiatives in this field in the US and China have been influenced by it.

## 11.4 Ethics in the AI Act

The EU AI Act is the world's first comprehensive legal framework regulating the development, deployment, and use of AI systems within the EU. Its primary goal is to guarantee that AI systems placed on the EU market are safe, transparent, non-discriminatory, and respectful of fundamental human rights and values while also promoting innovation. The AI Act has global implications, as foreign companies providing AI services in the EU must also comply.

The approved law regulates the placing on the market and use of AI systems across the EU, following a proportionate, risk-based approach. Four risk levels are defined: unacceptable, high, limited, and minimal. Systems deemed to pose unacceptable risk, such as government social scoring, such as that used in China to classify citizens based on their social and personal behavior, and real-time biometric identification systems in public spaces, are prohibited, with a few exceptions. High-risk AI systems are permitted, but manufacturers and users must adhere to rules requiring rigorous testing, adequate data quality documentation, and an accountability framework specifying human oversight of those systems. This category includes, for example, self-driving vehicles, AI devices for medical applications, and critical infrastructure equipment. Finally, systems with limited and minimal risks, such as spam filters or video games, can be used with few requirements beyond transparency obligations. The approved version of the law added AI systems used to influence voters and the outcome of elections, as well as recommendation systems used by social media platforms, to the high-risk list.

Regarding generative AI systems, the law stipulates that they must comply with transparency requirements, declaring when the content was generated by the AI, helping to distinguish so-called deepfake images from real ones, and ensuring safeguards against the creation and dissemination of illegal content. Detailed summaries of the copyrighted data used for development should also be made public.

Systems such as ChatGPT can have many uses, making their regulation complex. This is one of the main challenges facing European regulation. Indeed, the so-called "general-purpose AI" includes AI systems that are trained on large amounts of data and designed for a broad spectrum of purposes; therefore, they can be adapted to a wide range of tasks and uses. For this reason, several scholars have called for "general-purpose AI" systems to be regulated not only for their final application but also throughout the entire design and development cycle to consider all stakeholders involved.

The development phase of general-purpose AI software is crucial, and companies developing these systems must be responsible for the data they use and the design choices they make. Without regulation at the development level, the current structure of the AI supply chain could allow developers of these models to profit from an application downstream of their design, evading all liability for its use, even if they contributed to its design.

The AI Act deals extensively with AI ethics, mainly by converting abstract ethical principles into concrete, legally enforceable safety and compliance requirements based on a system's level of risk. Its core mechanism is an ethical one: ensuring that the implementation and deployment of AI systems respect fundamental human rights and adhere to values such as fairness, transparency, and safety. The AI Act deals with ethics primarily through its risk classification system, which dictates the severity of the legal obligations. In particular, the Act bans AI systems considered to pose a clear threat to human safety, livelihoods, and fundamental rights. This is the strongest expression of AI ethics because it establishes legal "red lines" for systems deemed unethical *a priori*.

Considering the so-called high-risk AI systems that can significantly impact a person's life (e.g., employment, access to credit, education, and justice), the AI Act imposes rigorous compliance requirements to mitigate ethical risks, including bias and opacity. Developers must establish a system to identify and mitigate risks throughout the AI system's lifecycle. Strict rules on the quality, relevance, and representativeness of training data to prevent bias and discrimination (a direct link to data ethics) are defined. It specifies mandatory logging and detailed technical documentation to ensure traceability and auditability of the system's operation. High-risk systems must be designed to allow for meaningful human intervention and control.

For limited- and minimal-risk systems, such as chatbots (limited risk) or spam filters (minimal risk), the obligations are much lighter, focusing mainly on transparency. The ethical principle here is basically informed interaction. Users must be informed when they are interacting with an AI system (e.g., a chatbot must disclose it is not human) or when content is generated or manipulated by AI (e.g., deepfakes).

The AI Act is, in many ways, an extension of the ethical concerns first addressed by the GDPR. For example, to ensure fairness, the Act requires high-risk systems to be designed and trained using representative data to prevent discriminatory outcomes. For achieving transparency, it requires disclosing to users when they are subject to a high-risk system and providing instructions for human oversight. Finally, for granting accountability, the Act requires disclosing to users when they are subject to a high-risk system and providing instructions for human oversight.

As the AI Act and other similar laws passed in other countries, the primary AI ethics challenges are related to algorithmic bias and fairness, lack of transparency/explainability, data privacy and security, and accountability for AI-driven harms. To manage and solve these main issues, promising approaches include the development of robust governance and regulatory frameworks, implementing fairness, accountability, and transparency principles in system design, and promoting interdisciplinary collaboration to embed ethical considerations from development to deployment.

## 11.5 Pope Francis and AI

Over the past centuries, the Church of Rome has not always had an open attitude toward the issues that science has brought to the attention of human beings. Galileo Galilei, to cite just one example, would have much to say on the subject. However, it would be unfair to ignore the fact that recent pontificates have changed several things in the relationship between the Catholic religion and science. This relationship, thanks above all to major scientific discoveries, has become a careful and respectful dialogue, far removed from the obscurantist and backward attitudes practiced by ecclesiastical hierarchies in the past.

Pope Francis, during the final years of his pontificate, devoted considerable attention to AI and considered it a fundamental issue, so much so that he chose it as the main topic of his first and historic speech at the 50th Group of Seven (G7) summit held in Apulia in June 2024. It was not the first time the Pontiff had addressed the topic; he had repeatedly emphasized the need to address that "fascinating and tremendous instrument" known as AI.

In his intervention at the G7 session on AI [7], the Pope affirmed that "*It is now safe to assume that its use will increasingly influence the way we live, our social relationships and even the way we conceive of our identity as human beings.*" Here lies the practical motivation (the great impact of AI) that prompted Pope Francis to discuss this topic, but it is significant that in the final part of the sentence, the Pontiff focuses on the fact that AI is changing our very conception of human identity. Therefore, there is much more to it than its many practical effects. AI could change our way of being humans, and perhaps also, we should ask, our relationship with the universal, with the otherworldly. This topic is not explicitly mentioned, but it is present in the subtext inherent in the words spoken in front of the most powerful people in the world.

The Pope immediately followed by warning of the risk that AI could be used to "*raising the dangerous possibility that a "throwaway culture" be preferred to a "culture of encounter".*" That is, machine intelligence, instead of helping improve human relationships, risks making humanity useless, because it could leave behind all those who are unable to keep pace with this powerful innovation and those who will no longer be useful because machines will be able to replace them, marginalizing them in the world of work and society. And for this reason, "*[p]recisely this powerful technological progress that makes artificial intelligence at the same time an exciting and fearsome tool, and demands a reflection that is up to the challenge it presents.*"

Pope Francis knows his words well and uses them carefully: AI is a fascinating tool, however, one "one must tremble at" because "*we are beings inclined toward what lies outside-of-us, indeed we are radically open to the beyond.*" The drive toward the artificial augmentation of humanity (the outside-of-us) is also linked to openness to the otherworldly and the pursuit of creativity. For the Pope, "*[t]he use of our tools, however, is not always directed solely to the good. Even if human beings feel within themselves a call to the beyond, and to knowledge as an instrument of good for the service of our brothers and sisters and our common home, this does not always happen.*" Since this natural drive does not always lead to good, it is necessary to ensure that our inclination toward the artificial does not lead to evil, does not generate great risks, and does not become a cage in which we remain imprisoned. Here, the reasoning looks at the potential risks and control mechanisms that AI must have. This is a topic that many specialists have been highlighting for some time and that policymakers must implement, as the EU has partially done with the AI Act.

Since the Pope is deeply interested in the relationship between this new form of AI and the human, in his speech he points out that "*artificial intelligence, on the other hand, can autonomously adapt to the task assigned to it and, if designed this way, can make choices independent of the person in order to achieve the intended goal.*" He also identifies a key point that the scientific community has long debated. This concerns the possibility of an AI with capabilities higher than those of humans that could become autonomous, depriving humanity of its role as world leader. Opinions on this topic are divided, but no one should believe that the question is not open, and no one can deny that recent developments have expanded the scope for AI systems' autonomy, despite those of humans. For this reason, "*[w]e need to ensure and safeguard a space for proper human control over the choices made by artificial intelligence programs: human dignity itself depends on it.*" Regarding this last statement, it should be noted that, more than the algorithm selection process, human control must be ensured over the level of autonomy of AI programs and over the self-determination of choices already made by software systems.

A very forceful and often cited statement is the one in which the Pope states, before men who lead states with armies that use AI, that "*[n]o machine should ever choose to take the life of a human being.*" Unfortunately, this is not happening today because lethal autonomous weapons exist, and this is demonstrated daily both in the Russian war in Ukraine and in the Israeli intervention in Gaza, where drones and the intelligent systems underlying autonomous weapons decide who to assassinate and unfortunately kill many people. For several years now, there have been campaigns against these new weapons, which the major powers have never supported, and the Pope was right to warn world governments against following this extremely dangerous path.

Further, in his speech, the Pope recalled that "*it is highly likely that, in the not-too-distant future, artificial intelligence programs will be able to communicate directly with each other to improve their performance.*" In this sentence, the Pope demonstrates his knowledge of the autonomy of machine learning systems and LLMs, even with respect to those who program them, and of the ability of AI systems to interact and cooperate with one another, even to teach one another, without human intervention.

Pope Francis is clearly deeply interested in ethical issues, and in his speech at the G7 summit, he made it clear that ethics in our time is not experiencing a flourishing period and risks being weakened by the development of technologies that favor those who develop them, giving them new power and allowing them to impose visions and models on billions of people. "*Technology is born for a purpose and, in its impact on human society, always represents a form of order in social relations and an arrangement of power, thus enabling certain people to perform specific actions while preventing others from performing different ones. In a more or less explicit way, this constitutive power dimension of technology always includes the worldview of those who invented and developed it.*"

The final sentence of the Pope's speech sums up the spirit of his discourse and makes it clear that he is opposed *to stopping human creativity and its dream of progress, but rather channeling this energy in a new way.* "*This is precisely the situation with artificial intelligence. It is up to everyone to make good use of it, but the onus is on politics to create the conditions for such good use to be possible and fruitful.*" This is a strong reminder of the leading role of politics also in technology, its development, and its uses. In this regard, although governments have been discussing these issues extensively lately, there is no reason to be overly optimistic because AI is also an instrument of power, as well as a great accelerator of progress. Precisely as a formidable instrument of power, citizens' attention and control should be stimulated by this historic intervention by the Pope on AI, avoiding blindly relying on the choices of governments and the world's powerful people.

## 11.6 Data Ethics Plus AI Ethics

Ethical principles in collecting, distributing, and processing data must come together with AI ethics to mitigate potential harms that arise from data gathering, analysis, and learning. As discussed, data biases influence results and decisions of machine learning systems, which is why ethical practices must be put in place, including those governing data and AI algorithms. Data ethics and AI ethics must be equally studied to understand how the use of intelligent algorithms in computing devices influences many aspects of the quality of life of citizens and their freedom, justice, and rights, both as individuals and as members of groups and communities.

We are living in a world where digital systems are used for personal advertising, disinformation spreading, and political manipulation. Big Data and AI are two key technologies in today's scenario; they are very useful and powerful technologies. For this reason, we must learn to use them for good and limit risks for humans. Laws and regulations serve as the basis for achieving this goal. The EU GDPR and the AI Act are two examples of legislation that address the two fields, following a common strategy. Other laws and regulations of data exploitation and AI uses are adopted in other countries. However, acting ethically when we exploit Big Data and AI requires more than complying with legislation. Responsibility of scientists and professionals is an absolute necessity, and private companies must embrace ethical principles in producing AI hardware and software solutions. Unfortunately, this is not often the case today. A long road lies ahead of us; to travel it, we must all be inspired by ethical principles that safeguard the public good and individual rights.

## References

1. Gibbs, S. (2014). Elon Musk: Artificial intelligence is our biggest existential threat. *The Guardian*. www.theguardian.com/technology/2014/oct/27/elon-musk-artificial-intelligence-ai-biggest-existential-threat [Retrieved 1 November 2025].
2. Aristotle. (2011). *Nicomachean Ethics*. USA: University of Chicago Press.
3. European Union. (2016). Regulation (EU) 2016/679 of the European Parliament and of the Council of 27 April 2016 on the protection of natural persons with regard to the processing of personal data and on the free movement of such data, and repealing Directive 95/46/EC. *Official Journal of the European Union*, 59, 294.
4. European Union. (2024). Regulation (EU) 2024/1689 of the European Parliament and of the Council of 13 June 2024 laying down harmonized rules on artificial intelligence (Artificial Intelligence Act) and amending Regulations (EC) No 2021/817 and (EU) 2018/1725, and Directive (EU) 2022/2419.

5. United Nations Educational, Scientific and Cultural Organization (UNESCO). (2021). Recommendation on the ethics of artificial intelligence. *UNESCO General Conference*, France.
6. Yeung, K. (2020). Recommendation of the council on artificial intelligence (OECD). *International Legal Materials* (Cambridge University Press, UK), 59(1), pp. 27–34.
7. Pope Francis. (2024). Address of His Holiness Pope Francis to the G7 session on artificial intelligence. www.vatican.va/content/francesco/en/speeches/2024/june/documents/20240614-g7-intelligenza-artificiale.html [Retrieved 1 November 2025].

# Chapter 12

# AI Explainability and Accountability

*The true potential of AI lies in its ability to uplift humanity while safeguarding and empowering future generations.*

—Amit Ray

Artificial intelligence governance defines the framework of policies, processes, standards, and roles put in place to ensure that AI systems are developed, deployed, and managed in a safe, ethical, trustworthy, and legally compliant manner. Due to the complexity, autonomy, and impact of AI systems on society, governance is crucial because AI methods are fundamentally different from traditional software, and in many cases, AI systems can operate without human intervention. Moreover, the opacity of some AI algorithms (e.g., deep neural networks) makes the internal logic of complex models often difficult or impossible to interpret. Also, biases or errors can be propagated instantly across very many decisions, causing widespread harm quickly. Therefore, by implementing governance, professionals, companies, organizations, and governments aim to build public trust, promote responsible innovation, and minimize legal, financial, and reputational damages.

AI systems explainability and accountability are two pillars of AI governance. AI explainability (or XAI) must be considered a prerequisite because it is the technical and informational foundation upon which accountability is built. XAI refers to the methods and techniques used to make AI system results, such as decisions, predictions, and recommendations, understandable to human users. Explainability provides insight into the model's logic, the features it relied on, and the reasons for a specific outcome. XAI is necessarily linked to accountability, because a sufficient explanation to why an AI system acted as it did (especially when the action leads to harm) is necessary to determine who is responsible of its results.

Accountability denotes the obligation to justify and take responsibility for the actions and outcomes of an AI system. It is a legal, ethical, and organizational element related to governance and liability. Once explainability reveals what went wrong with an AI system (e.g., a bias in the training data that caused discrimination or a misconfiguration in deep learning parameters that generated an error), accountability determines who must face consequences and implement corrective actions. In brief, you need to know what happened and why (which are the tasks of XAI), before you can determine who is responsible for the outcome of an AI system and how they will answer for it (which are the tasks of accountability).

## 12.1 We Need to Explain AI and AI Needs to Be Explainable

Problems may occur when AI algorithms make important decisions that affect people or are coded to influence humans, providing suggestions and information to the public [1]. They occur more frequently than before with many AI tools, such as social media profiling systems, financial intelligence products, customer profiling, and other algorithms that are designed and used to increase profits for companies rather than aimed at doing the best for the common good. In all these cases, individuals and/or society need to know how algorithms work and question their real goals and outcomes. The new scenarios created by AI call for algorithm explainability that may describe what happens in the code from input to output. AI algorithm explainability makes learning models transparent and aims to solve the "black-box" problem. To reach this goal, auditing of algorithms can be effective to guarantee that they are legal, ethical, and safe [2]. Algorithm auditors can look at the inputs and outputs of a decision system from the outside.

Research and development in XAI developed methods and techniques to create learning algorithms that humans can comprehend and trust, together with the results and decisions they generate. XAI is the opposite of black-box systems, where owners and users cannot (or don't want to) explain why an AI algorithm reached a certain decision or a given result. Black-box AI systems designed for decision-making map data features into a class by predicting events or the behavioral traits of citizens without providing the reasons why they did it. This opaque approach is elusive not only for the lack of transparency but also for possible biases the opaque algorithms inherit from human discrimination and/or errors originating, often hidden, in the training data, which may lead to unjust or erroneous decisions [3].

AI models used in the US by physicians to detect diseases such as cancer or mental diseases or suggest the most effective treatment are assessed by the Food and Drug Administration. But tools used by insurers for determining whether hospitalization or treatments should be reimbursed are not subjected to the same inspection, though they are equally important for patients. As mentioned in previous chapters, in Europe, the impact of algorithmic decisions is regulated under the General Data Protection Regulation and the AI Act. Professionals using personal data for automated processing must explain to the people concerned how the system makes decisions. The individual data subject, for instance the person who was rejected for a payment or a patient who was denied a certain medical service, has the right to ask the company why it made the decision it did, and the company must then explain how the system came to its decision. If the company cannot explain the decision in response to an individual's request, it would not be complaint with the GDPR and can be prosecuted by law.

Recital 71 of GDPR [4] states: "*The data subject should have the right not to be subject to a decision, which may include a measure, evaluating personal aspects relating to him or her which is based solely on automated processing and which produces legal effects concerning him or her or similarly significantly affects him or her, such as automatic refusal of an online credit application or e-recruiting practices without any human intervention. ... In any case, such processing should be subject to suitable safeguards, which should include specific information to the data subject and the right to obtain human intervention, to express his or her point of view, to obtain an explanation of the decision reached after such assessment and to challenge the decision.*" In addition, Article 22 grants an individual a "right of human intervention." Under this right, an individual may ask for a human to review the AI algorithm's decision to determine whether or not the system made a mistake.

An approach similar to that one used in the EU GDPR is embodied in laws and regulations in other countries, allowing people to have clear explanations of how AI algorithms work, how they use their data, and what the rules are that they follow to make decisions.

## 12.2 Who Is Accountable for AI Actions?

When we use an autonomous vehicle and one of the AI-based applications it runs fails, who is accountable for damages that can occur? What happens if diagnoses made by an AI virtual doctor[1] are wrong because of problems with a machine learning or data analysis method it uses? When a generative AI chatbot fails to discourage fragile teenagers from following self-destructive actions, who takes responsibility for potential harms this "artificial" relationship generates? When inappropriate AI threat detection and image recognition algorithms lead to discriminatory surveillance and over-policing of marginalized groups, who is responsible?

Around 2014, Amazon developed a machine learning framework intended to automate the review of job applications. The system taught itself, through unsupervised classification algorithms, that male candidates were preferable, as its training data consisted of resumes submitted over a ten-year period from an industry dominated by men. The AI tool began penalizing curricula vitae that included words such as "women's" (e.g., "women's tennis club chair") and favoring male-associated peculiarities. From the point of view of accountability, that AI tool propagated systemic gender bias. Amazon had to abandon the project because they could not easily repair the bias inherited from the input data they provided. The accountability lay with the team for failing to detect and mitigate the biased inputs that led to a discriminatory output.

---

[1] Chatbots and AI-powered virtual assistants are increasingly available and utilized in healthcare, often playing a role akin to a "virtual doctor" or digital health assistant. AI platforms such as Ada Health and Buoy Health ask users a series of questions about their symptoms, similar to a physical examination. Then they analyze the reported symptoms against a large database of medical conditions and provide a possible list of causes, recommending the appropriate level of care. However, while many individuals use them for receiving medical information, triage, and guidance, they are not licensed doctors. In fact, they explicitly state that they do not replace human medical professionals or provide definitive diagnoses or treatment.

Several financial and housing companies use AI algorithms for credit scoring, mortgage lending, or tenant screening. Some of these opaque deep learning algorithms have been shown to unreasonably deny loans or housing access to applicants from certain socioeconomic or racial groups. The algorithms might be trained on data that uses proxies for race (such as zip codes or credit history from discriminatory lending eras) to predict risk, thereby reinforcing historical inequality. When a client is denied a loan, the company often cannot provide a specific, understandable explanation, making it difficult for the applicant to challenge the decision. In these cases, accountability is distributed among the data provider, the model developer, and the deploying bank.

In 2024, a Canadian court ruled against Air Canada regarding erroneous information provided by its generative AI customer service chatbot. The chatbot incorrectly recommended a customer on the airline's bereavement fare policy, leading the customer to pay a higher price for flight tickets. Air Canada initially argued that the chatbot was a separate legal entity responsible for its own suggestions. The judges ruled that the airline was responsible for all information on its website, including chatbot responses. This case created a precedent of company accountability for the actions and hallucinations of their AI proxies, leading to assigned financial compensation.

Finally, we can mention the cases of a few fatal crashes that involved Tesla vehicles operating on the Autopilot feature. In various incidents, the AI system had failed to detect obstacles, such as crossing tractor-trailers or physical barriers, and did not activate emergency braking. This has been attributed to the system's overreliance on sensor data and, fatefully, drivers' overreliance on the system due to marketing or system design. Lawsuits and regulatory investigations have raised fundamental accountability issues about the driver negligence in supervising the car's decisions and about AI system defects that created misclassifications.

In cases involving fatal crashes with the Tesla Autopilot system, US juries and judges have considered and attributed accountability to the Tesla AI system, establishing a significant change in liability jurisprudence. Accountability in this case is assessed not only on the technical failure of the AI system but also on the manufacturer's governance and marketing of the technology. In a major Florida federal lawsuit regarding a fatal 2019 Autopilot crash, the jury did not place all responsibility on the driver. Although the jury found the driver primarily responsible, it assigned noteworthy responsibility (i.e., around 33%) to Tesla for the crash. This verdict established that even with a driver-assistance system that requires human supervision (SAE Level 2), the manufacturer can be held partially liable for the crash due to flaws in the system's design or marketing.

Today, in many cases, such as the ones we mentioned, AI systems and products make decisions without human supervision. Who bears the responsibility when those tools make poor or wrong choices that lead to undesirable consequences? Whenever something goes wrong with developing, selling, or using AI tools, their failure can spread accountability across their algorithms, whose errors, poor decisions, biases, and harms must be identified, and responsible subjects must respond and provide explanations to customers.

Some experts argue that AI tool accountability should be shared among several stakeholders. Designers, developers, sellers, and business leaders who deploy AI applications should all play a part in safeguarding it. Shared accountability better reflects the complexity of AI systems, as well as their risks and rewards. However, in spreading responsibilities, the accountable party's boundaries remain unclear and, in the case of serious damages, could make it difficult to identify the division of responsibilities.

Accountability is mentioned and defined in laws and regulations such as the EU's GDPR and AI Act and the US's proposed bill named the Algorithmic Accountability Act (AAA). Very briefly, it can be defined as an obligation to inform about and justify one's conduct to an authority [5]. In Ref. [6], "accountability" is defined as a relation between an agent (individual, group, or legal person) and a forum, such that the agent must justify their conduct to the forum, and the forum supervises, asks questions of, and passes judgment on the agent on the basis of such justification. In the relationship between the agent and the forum, some goals that are widely acknowledged include the following: report (to ensure that the agent's conduct is properly recorded to explain and justify it to the forum), compliance (to bind the agent to align with ethical and legal standards), oversight (to examine information, obtain evidence, and evaluate the agent's behavior), and enforcement (to determine what consequences the agent must bear, such as sanctions, authorizations, or prohibitions).

Bringing the previous definition into the field of AI, we can say that AI accountability relates to the expectation (of the forum) that designers, developers, and deployers (the agents) will comply with standards and legislation to ensure the proper functioning of AI tools and applications during their lifecycle. AI accountability essentially refers to the identification of responsibility for how an AI algorithm/system is designed and implemented and for its impact on people that use it or are subject to it. If damage is not avoided, mechanisms for reparation and compensation must be provided. For automatic decisions made by an AI algorithm, accountability must be supported by clear policies that include system auditing procedures and standardized assessments for potential harm.

Accountability generally includes three main key components: responsibility, for one's acts and decisions; answerability, which is the capacity to reveal the reasons for decisions; and sanctionability, referring to being held accountable through coercive measures [7].

Accountability should be a requirement during the whole lifecycle of AI systems and applications, from design to maintenance. Accountability through design approaches may help when AI systems are being developed. Therefore, accountability must play a key role in the development phase of AI systems. AI software, for example, must be coded, validated, and tested from end to end. Furthermore, the deployment phase involves ensuring rule and law compliance while assessing the user experience. It must be fair and reliable.

In Ref. [7], three levels of accountability are identified: data, developer, and model. How data are handled from the beginning and how they are used is crucial to assess data accountability. Methods such as data provenance and data lineage are useful for correctly managing the whole lifecycle of a data source. Another key condition is to be able to manage personal and private data. In Big Data scenarios, accountability for learning models refers to the way the model rationale and parameters are clear and explainable. There are multiple ways to incorporate model accountability in AI. For example, in decision trees, entropy and information gain help comprehend the model. On the other hand, deep neural networks are black boxes with complex structures and parameters, making it impossible to analyze and understand their choices. Regarding developer accountability, there are cases where the human developers are the ones who significantly influence/determine the whole AI-based decision-making process. Developers should go through different educative material and certifications to understand how they can act responsibly and also understand the significance of the issues they are working on. Developers must also ensure they are open-minded about the decision-making processes and agree to take responsibility when these processes are checked for AI accountability.

We must understand how AI systems make decisions. If something goes wrong, we must know the reasons. Knowing the reasons can help identify responsibilities, solve problems, and prevent them from occurring in the future. AI accountability requires new ways of tracking decisions across human and machine components. Managers and professionals cannot abdicate responsibility when using AI systems, notwithstanding the intrinsic complexities associated with AI models. In this scenario, legal prescriptions and ethical behaviors must be combined to limit or eliminate risks arising from AI system use.

As discussed, a notion and methodology related to giving intelligibility to the black box of machine learning and AI algorithms is XAI. XAI helps managers and professionals understand why it makes specific predictions, suggestions, or decisions. Rather than simply giving information, it also provides clear explanations for its reasoning. This transparency builds more awareness and trust since people can see how the AI systems made their decisions. For sure, transparent white-box models and the opaque black-box models have distinct levels of explainability. For critical applications that impact humans, explainable models must be used, as mandated by laws and regulations in different countries.

## 12.3 New Know-Hows to Deal with AI

Together with the increasing role of algorithms in our daily lives and with the increasingly widespread use of AI in decision-making, we can witness that the scarcity of digital culture and computational thinking becomes an ever-greater handicap for individuals and for the entire society. Widespread digital illiteracy in a population creates risks for users unaware of "intelligent" systems that make decisions about them. The digital revolution is advancing, and people must obtain skills and abilities to handle it; otherwise, they will be overwhelmed.

The skills and knowledge of people about AI and the most promising areas of digital technology show a delay that, if not filled, will be another key element for failure to progress. We must not work to train everyone to become a software designer, but we must understand that it is essential to provide basic knowledge to deal with apps, software tools, and platforms that use AI applications. We need concrete and widespread actions to increase expertise among young people on information technology and AI, thus providing individuals with the skills necessary to face the present challenges. Otherwise, we risk the rising of a community of people who will be passive entities instead of being active subjects in a world where AI is becoming pervasive.

To address these issues, it is necessary to initiate widespread basic training that makes people understand, for example, what AI is, how computers work when solving problems, and how to evaluate information online, its truthfulness, and its usefulness. It serves to provide both young and old people the opportunity to understand the computational processes, the logic that governs them, and their potential that can be exploited in work and in everyday life. While everyone agrees on the obvious need to teach mathematics from elementary schools, it should be equally normal to teach the principles of computer science in all schools. Kids need to know how to understand and compose simple algorithms, use computational thinking, and think methodically to devise strategies useful for defining solutions. They need to know how AI works and how to cooperate with it as intelligent actors and not be subjected to it. On the other hand, adults must be able to discuss and understand how AI algorithms are used when they concern decisions about them, their rights, their health, and their work.

The widespread use of AI solutions in daily life is creating a large social and cultural divide between the few experts and the many oblivious users. This separation, other than creating new inequalities, will cause much damage to our society. By 2030, many jobs will keep their 2020 names (e.g., "Radiologist" or "Lawyer") but about 80% of their tasks will be different. Morever new jobs will appear that did not exist before. It is necessary to take steps to manage the future that has arrived too quickly. Politics, schools, and universities are called upon to face this main challenge. If we fail to face this challenge now, enormous problems will emerge in the coming decades, when the intensive use of new intelligent technologies will create many new jobs that do not exist today but will abolish many of those found today. At the same time, private companies using AI in their decision processes involving clients should realize that they must act responsibly and must provide clear explanations about automated decisions.

We are now also experiencing a new Big Data divide that refers to the split between those who have access and ownership to large and distributed data sources and those who do not. Andrejevic [8] worked on the concepts of access, ownership, and use of digital data, arguing that a Big Data divide is occurring today, which deals with the asymmetric relationship between those who collect, store, and mine large quantities of data and those who are data collection targets.

The issues involved in this asymmetric relationship relate to a basic divide that occurs for people and organizations without the technical means to access and analyze data stored on the internet or in large data repositories. To fill this gap, it is essential to work on new cognitive paradigms, to change education programs and practices, and to offer the opportunity for people to access data and learn how to use them successfully and how the data are used in AI systems to profile them or to make decisions on their lives. This integrated strategy could result in new opportunities for those who wish to have an active role in the new digital society, offer a way to defend people's rights, and improve the global knowledge of people on intelligent technologies.

## References

1. DeFranco, J. F., Voas, J., and Kshetri, N. (2022). Algorithms: Society's invisible puppeteers. *Computer*, 55(4), pp. 12–14.
2. Jovanović, M. and Schmitz, M. (2022). Explainability as a user requirement for artificial intelligence systems. *Computer*, 55(2), pp. 90–94.
3. Prentzas, N., Kakas, A., and Pattichis, C. S. (2023). Explainable AI applications in the medical domain: A systematic review. *arXiv*. DOI: 10.48550/arXiv.2308.05411.
4. Intersoft Consulting. GDPR: General data protection regulation. https://gdpr-info.eu/ [Retrieved 1 November 2025].
5. Lindberg, S. I. (2013). Mapping accountability: Core concept and subtypes. *International Review of Administrative Science*, 79(2), pp. 202–226.
6. Novelli, C., Taddeo, M., and Floridi, L. (2024). Accountability in artificial intelligence: What it is and how it works. *AI & Society*, 39, pp. 1871–1882.
7. Raja, A. K. and Zhou, J. (2023). AI accountability: Approaches, affecting factors, and challenges. *Computer*, 56(4), pp. 61–70.
8. Andrejevic, M. (2014). Big Data, big questions: The Big Data divide. *International Journal of Communication*, 8(1), pp. 1673–1689.

# Chapter 13

# The Challenge of AI Safety

*I think it's important that people understand it's not just science fiction; it's not just fear-mongering – it is a real risk that we need to think about, and we need to figure out in advance how to deal with it.*

—Geoffrey Hinton

We must implement safe computing systems because we want systems that are predictable, fair, controllable, and ultimately beneficial to humanity, rather than risky, chaotic, or harmful. In this scenario, artificial intelligence safety is the discipline that seeks to bridge the gap between what AI systems can do (capability) and what AI systems should do (ethics and alignment).

More formally, AI safety can be defined as the field of research and engineering focused on ensuring that AI systems, especially advanced ones, are developed and deployed robustly, reliably, and in alignment with human intent and values to prevent unintended or malicious harmful outcomes. We must know that designing and implementing robust and safe AI systems is a huge task, facing challenges that are technical, conceptual, and political. These problems can be grouped into two major areas: alignment, which involves making AI systems share our values, and robustness, which involves making AI systems reliable and secure.

## 13.1 Background

In recent years, the topic of the safety of AI systems has become increasingly central to academic, industrial, and political debates. The increasingly widespread adoption of AI-based systems in critical fields, such as healthcare, finance, and autonomous driving, has raised fundamental questions about their reliability, transparency, and safety. The growing complexity of AI models and their potential social impact necessitate the development of approaches and strategies capable of preventing unexpected risks and ensuring responsible use of the technology. Safety in AI has therefore emerged as a key field of study to ensure that intelligent computing systems operate reliably, transparently, and in alignment with human values.

Technological progress has made these systems increasingly autonomous and capable of performing complex tasks but, at the same time, has highlighted new challenges related to their interpretability, data bias management, and protection from cyberattacks. Understanding the risks associated with AI and developing strategies to mitigate them have become a priority. Machine learning paradigms enable AI systems to recognize patterns, make decisions, and generate content with an ever-increasing level of autonomy. Therefore, these technologies raise significant security issues, particularly when used in sensitive areas.

The integration of AI in these areas carries the risk of incorrect decisions, unexpected malfunctions, or malicious use, necessitating a careful balance between innovation and security. The issue of security in AI, moreover, concerns not only technical aspects but also ethical and regulatory ones. The increasing autonomy of some systems raises ever-increasing questions about the responsibility for decisions made by complex algorithms, as well as their transparency and auditability. AI systems, in fact, can suffer biases in training data, make opaque (difficult to understand) decisions, and, in extreme cases, be vulnerable to external manipulation, such as adversarial attacks (AAs).

## 13.2 Main Principles

Safe AI systems must include a set of principles that can guarantee they limit or eliminate risks coming from their large and critical use. Ensuring that they operate safely is therefore essential to avoid harmful consequences that could affect a large number of people. As these systems become more autonomous, the possibility of unexpected behaviors emerging from developers also increases, leading to circumstances where AI decisions conflict with human values and needs.

Therefore, it is crucial to integrate robust safety principles in the design phase to ensure reliability and develop trust in AI systems [1]. Among these principles are robustness, redundancy, transparency, separation of duties, antifragility, negative feedback management, and human alignment. It must be noted that, although all these principles are relevant, they are not always applicable in every context.

Robustness of safe AI systems requires developing systems that are stable, reliable, and predictable under a broad range of conditions. The goal is to guarantee that AI systems perform reliably as expected during design and implementation, even when faced with unexpected situations or different data inputs. This involves severe testing and validation procedures to identify and mitigate potential failures and vulnerabilities that can threaten the system's reliability. Producing robust AI systems also includes ensuring resilience against AAs or jailbreaks that could trespass system weaknesses. Techniques such as redundancy, fault tolerance, and anomaly detection are integral to enhancing the robustness of AI systems. Redundancy is a key principle of safety, consisting of having multiple components capable of performing a critical function, so that the failure of a single element does not compromise the entire system. This approach removes single points of failure, making the system more resilient to faults. Redundancy in AI systems ensures greater reliability and adaptability, as well as reducing the risk of extreme decisions.

In the previous chapters, we discussed transparency issues. Transparency in AI systems involves creating systems that are understandable and verifiable by humans, making it easier to trace decisions and building trust and accountability in the use of AI. Implementing transparency, however, can be challenging given the complex and often opaque nature of advanced AI algorithms. Research on AI transparency for safety purposes aims mainly to study and design deep learning systems that can offer operators greater understanding of their internal decision-making processes and the mechanisms underlying their choices. This allows them to gain control that is currently lacking and to anticipate and avoid situations in which systems could make incorrect or misleading decisions, guiding them away from danger.

Regarding separation of duties, let us consider a system in which all components and processes are controlled by a single person. If that individual were to pursue a negative outcome, they could exploit the entire system to achieve their goal. On the other hand, if duties were separated, assigning multiple operators to manage different aspects, in such a situation that single individual would be less capable of causing harm. When designing AI systems, therefore, this principle can be followed by employing multiple agents, each highly specialized in a specific task. In this way, complex processes could be performed collectively by the agents themselves, rather than entrusting everything to a single individual [2].

Antifragility allows a system not only to recover from a failure but also to actually become more robust thanks to these stresses, making it less vulnerable to future failures. An example of this type of system is the human body. After contracting and fighting a pathogen, a person's immune system tends to strengthen, reducing the likelihood of reinfection. Designing antifragile AI systems means allowing them to continue learning and adapting even during their use.

This could allow an AI system to recognize when an element of the surrounding environment has caused it to make an incorrect decision, preventing it from repeating the same mistake in similar circumstances in the future. Creating antifragile AI systems often means creating adaptive systems: The ability to adapt in response to new stresses is essential to making AI more robust. However, if it continues to learn and adapt as it is used, AI may develop unexpected and unwanted behaviors. In fact, adaptive AI tools tend to be more difficult to control, as they continually evolve.

Another principle of secure design is "defense in depth," which involves integrating multiple layers of protection, allowing potential damage to be mitigated if one or more defenses were to fail, as others would be available. In general, the more defenses a system has, the less likely it is that all of them will fail simultaneously. It is important to consider, however, that increasing the number of defenses makes the system more complex: If different layers of protection interacted with each other, they could lead to unwanted side effects.

For example, in the case of a virus, reduced social contact and the immune system can be considered two distinct levels of defense. However, if a person excessively avoids contact with others, they could reduce their exposure to pathogens and, at the same time, weaken their immune system in the long term. Therefore, while multiple layers of protection can make a system more resilient, it is crucial to carefully evaluate the potential interactions between the different layers.

There are two main ways to reduce risk by using safety measures:

- **Preventive measures:** Reduce the likelihood of an accident occurring by decreasing the intrinsic probability of the hazard or the exposure to it.
- **Protective measures:** Reduce the damage if an accident occurs, both by reducing the intrinsic danger of the event and by making the system less vulnerable to its consequences.

It is important to emphasize the value of preventing accidents, as trying to remedy them after they have occurred is much more costly. For this reason, therefore, preventative measures may be preferred to protective ones; however, the latter should not be neglected.

Finally, human alignment issues must also be considered. Alignment in AI safety refers to the principle that AI systems should be designed to have their goals and semantics aligned with human values and ethical principles. This ensures that the actions taken by AI contribute positively to human objectives without leading to unintentional or intentional harm. Human alignment involves careful design approaches and techniques to correctly interpret and incorporate human aims into AI tools. Also, functional assessment and testing processes are necessary to evaluate the system behavior and its respect of the design principles. In fact, beyond the implementation step, maintaining human alignment requires constant efforts as an AI system learns from new data and user interaction and it evolves, potentially showing new behaviors and decisions. This calls for adaptive mechanisms that constantly monitor, compare, and steer the system objectives with respect to human values, providing protections (e.g., the so-called generative AI guardrails) against divergence or ethical drift over time.

## 13.3 AI Safety and Risks

In assessing risks, the probability of an accident occurring is a useful quantitative measure. In particular, in assessing a system, the inverse of this probability is often considered. That is, the system reliability, or the probability that an adverse event will not occur, can be linked to the mean operating time before a failure. Although a system may have an intrinsic level of reliability, the probability of encountering a failure also depends on the frequency of use: The more the system is used, the greater the probability of failure. A self-driving vehicle, for example, is much more likely to make a mistake during a journey in which it must make 2,000 decisions than one in which it must make only 100 [2].

AI systems, as discussed, are developed and trained to operate in a specific environment, and as the operating environment changes, the system is likely to encounter malfunctions or errors: System designs that can adapt to the environment can significantly improve system reliability.

There are several possible causes of failure in AI systems: prediction errors, low data quality, model biases, AAs, and others. Many prediction errors are caused by distribution shift, which occurs when the operating environment is different from that of the training set. Adversarial attacks can be a critical issue, as they apply a small perturbation to the data to make the model's prediction inaccurate, causing a reliability incident. Data quality is also relevant. If data contain noise, are dirty, are not appropriate or complete, or come from faulty sensors, failures can occur.

The main factors that influence the reliability of AI systems can be divided into three categories:

- operating environment,
- data, and
- model (i.e., the algorithm).

A common cause of failure events involving operating environments is the difference between the operating environment and the training environment, a phenomenon known as out-of-distribution (OOD) samples. In the real world, AI systems certainly encounter test samples that do not belong to any training set class, i.e., OOD data. OOD detection refers to a model's ability to recognize and appropriately handle data that significantly deviates from its training set [3]. Therefore, the detection of these samples and the ability to adequately adapt to them are fundamental elements for improving the reliability of AI.

Furthermore, the quality of the training data is closely linked to the algorithm's performance: Data containing errors, noise, or incorrect null values can lead to incorrect predictions. Another aspect of data quality concerns the problem of data bias or imbalance, particularly relevant for many classification algorithms used in AI systems.

AAs, moreover, can also be considered a particular form of data quality problem. Most AI systems rely on the accuracy of the predictions provided by machine learning and deep learning algorithms. Therefore, the adopted algorithm must guarantee a sufficiently high accuracy on the training set to be usable in practice. Furthermore, the predictions generated by the algorithm are associated with a certain degree of uncertainty that is a key determinant of reliability. High uncertainty can lead to less reliable performance, and a machine learning model must have sufficiently high accuracy to be applicable in the field, leading to the problem of uncertainty quantification (UQ). UQ is the process of quantifying uncertainties in a quantity of interest (QoI) by propagating uncertainties in the input parameters through the computational model [4].

When a learning model contains uncertainties, its results can vary with changing probabilities. We treat these outputs as random variables and use probability distributions to measure uncertainty. The wider the distribution, the more uncertain the result. UQ techniques help tell you how confident you should be in any particular prediction. For instance, if a marketing model predicts an 80% chance of selling to a target, uncertainty quantification helps determine whether that 80% is based on good training data or if there is so much uncertainty that the actual chance might be anywhere from 60% to 100%.

According to the Rumsfeld taxonomy, events can be grouped into four categories:

- **Known knowns:** Elements known and fully understood.
- **Unknown knowns:** Knowledge possessed but of which one is unaware (the so-called tacit knowledge).
- **Known unknowns:** Aspects known but not fully understood.
- **Unknown unknowns:** Unknown elements of which one is not even aware.

The Rumsfeld taxonomy, disseminated during a 2002 U.S. Department of Defense press briefing on Iraq's potential weapons of mass destruction, originates from earlier risk management and epistemic discussions, including NASA's use of similar concepts in the 1950s for addressing uncertainties in aerospace engineering. The first word used in these four categories refers to awareness, while the second one refers to understanding.

Researchers can study various aspects of AI and its potential risks in depth, but as this technology advances, new, completely unknown and unexpected threats may emerge, taking researchers by surprise. It is therefore important to acknowledge the existence of *unknown unknowns* because they remind humans of their limitations in knowledge and understanding. Considering these events allows humans to adopt a humbler approach to problem-solving and expand their knowledge to be prepared for the unexpected.

Of the four categories of events introduced, *known unknowns* and *unknown unknowns* are the most important in risk analysis and management since there is no complete understanding of how best to address them, nor can we be certain of avoiding harm resulting from them. If you are aware of a given challenge, you can prepare adequately; conversely, a lack of awareness makes you more vulnerable to harm. For this reason, unknown unknowns are particularly concerning. The difference between the two most important categories is sometimes described as a distinction between conscious ignorance and meta-ignorance (i.e., the unawareness of the broader reality we cannot perceive or formalize). The former occurs when you are aware of not knowing something; the latter occurs when you are unaware of your own ignorance [5].

## 13.4 Some Hints for Safe AI Systems

A key issue in assessing the risks associated with the use of AI systems is how they are released to the public. There are various options for AI system release, ranging from completely closed to completely open, each one with trade-offs between risks and benefits.

In particular, open-weight models, whose weights are public and downloadable by anyone, facilitate research and innovation. However, at the same time, this openness, on the one hand, is not complete enough to fully understand their functioning, and on the other, it can foster malicious use or the perpetuation of flaws and biases in the models.

Regardless of whether a model is closed or open, it is necessary to implement risk mitigation strategies throughout the AI lifecycle in order to strengthen any interventions that, individually, might be weak.

For example, risk management in the field of generative AI is particularly complex due to the exponential evolution of the technology and its broad applicability.

Traditional practices, such as safety by design, review, redundancy, and safety cases, provide a solid foundation, but these must be adapted to keep pace with rapidly evolving models. Specifically, safety by design is an approach that places user safety at the center of the design and development of products and services. In the case of generative AI, this involves minimizing illegal and dangerous content in the model's training data and assessing a wide range of risks before release.

Safety cases, on the other hand, could provide a useful framework for policymakers to analyze the dangers and mitigation strategies associated with the use of generative AI systems. A safety case is a structured, evidence-based argument in which the developer identifies the dangers and evaluates the mitigation measures adopted. A system safety approach, which applies engineering and management principles to identify and control hazards throughout the system's lifecycle, is useful for effectively managing risks arising from the use of generative AI.

System safety engineering focuses on the interactions between parts of a larger system and emphasizes incidents that can occur for reasons more complex than simple component failures. For AI systems performing multiple tasks, system safety engineering involves considering all components of the system and the broader context in which it operates. Defense in depth is considered a promising approach for managing risk in generative AI, as the presence of multiple layers of protection allows the system to continue functioning even if one were to fail. This method will also include controls not only within the AI model itself but also within the ecosystem, such as training data. It is important to note, however, that defense in depth alone is insufficient, as it focuses on preventing incidents and cannot manage more complex risks.

To date, the primary challenges of risk management in generative AI can be said to be twofold: First, it is difficult to prioritize risks due to their uncertain nature; second, it can be difficult to determine appropriate roles and responsibilities along the AI value chain and incentivize effective action. The European AI Act uses the term "value chain" to refer to the entire ecosystem of actors involved in introducing an AI system to the market and in its maintenance [6].

## 13.5 Safe AI Systems for Humans

Safety of AI systems represents a key challenge for the future of digital technology and society. Ensuring the development of AI systems that are reliable, transparent, and aligned with human values is therefore a crucial priority. As we continue to implement and use novel AI systems, it is central to ensure they are safe and beneficial for humanity.

Risk analysis highlights how AI system vulnerabilities can arise from various factors, and addressing these issues requires a proactive approach based on mitigation strategies that include rigorous testing, verification mechanisms, and the design of more interpretable and robust systems. Regulation also plays a key role in defining limits and responsibilities, helping to create a safe and ethical AI ecosystem.

As we move toward new and more powerful AI systems, it is fundamental that we continue to engage in accurate and deep research, open dialogue, and interdisciplinary cooperation to address the safety concerns associated with AI (together with ethics and accountability). By doing so, we can endeavor toward creating AI systems that not only avoid the worst troubles to individuals and society but also actively work toward enhancing social good.

Safety in AI is not a static objective but a constantly evolving process, requiring continuous collaboration between researchers, developers, regulators, and society. The future of AI will also depend on the ability to balance innovation and safety, adopting a multidisciplinary approach to address emerging challenges. In conclusion, AI safety research must be considered a global priority; only through joint efforts will it be possible to develop technologies that, while powerful and transformative, remain safe, ethical, and at the service of humanity.

## References

1. Tigera. Understanding AI Safety: Principles, Frameworks, and Best Practices. https://www.tigera.io/learn/guides/llm-security/ai-safety/ [Retrieved 14 November 2025].
2. Hendrycks, D. (2024). *Introduction to AI Safety, Ethics and Society*. UK: Taylor & Francis. www.aisafetybook.com.
3. Lu, S., Wang, Y., Sheng, L., He, L., Zheng, A., and Liang, J. (2026). Out-of-distribution detection: A task-oriented survey of recent advances. *ACM Computing Surveys*, 58(2), 1–39.

4. Wang, T., *et al.* (2025). From aleatoric to epistemic: Exploring uncertainty quantification techniques in artificial intelligence. *arXiv preprint.* https://arxiv.org/abs/2501.03282.
5. Vadagam, K. K. (2025). The end of AI: Meta-ignorance and the limits of human-centric mathematics in artificial intelligence development might lead to end of humanity. *SSRN.* https://ssrn.com/abstract=5273757.
6. Srikumar, M., Chmielinski, K., and Chang, J. (2024). Risk Mitigation Strategies for the Open Foundation Model Value Chain. Partnership on AI.

# Chapter 14

# The One-Dimensional Man in the AI Age

*Technology serves to institute new, more effective, and more pleasant forms of social control and social cohesion.*

—Herbert Marcuse

In 1964, Herbert Marcuse published his famous essay titled *One-Dimensional Man: Studies in the Ideology of Advanced Industrial Society* [1]. The paperback edition cost $2.25. After nearly 60 years, many will have forgotten that essay written by an influential 20th-century philosopher. It was a militant essay that enjoyed great success in the years following its publication in several languages, especially among the younger generations of the time.

Unlike *Eros and Civilization* [2], which Marcuse had published in 1955, *One-Dimensional Man* is more of a pamphlet than a treatise on philosophical theory, and for this very reason it became one of the reference texts of the 1968 movement. It is no coincidence that that book identifies a new revolutionary class in the "*substratum of outcasts and outsiders, the exploited and persecuted of other races and colors, of the unemployed and the disabled. They remain outside the democratic process; their presence proves how immediate and real the need is to end intolerable conditions and institutions. Therefore, their opposition is revolutionary even if their conscience is not. Therefore, their opposition strikes the system from the outside and is therefore not deflected by the system; it is an elemental force that violates the rules of the game and in doing so shows that it is a rigged game.*"

The book's opening line reads as follows: "*A comfortable, smooth, reasonable, democratic unfreedom prevails in advanced industrial civilization, a token of technical progress.*" This opening, like the rest of the book, remains extremely relevant today, despite the many years that have passed since its conception and the many transformations society has undergone. In his essay, the German philosopher argued that the social order dictated by advanced industrialization, generated and fostered by technology and the frenetic pursuit of capitalism, had now influenced and transformed all aspects of human existence. In Marcuse's view, the "rational" model of industrial capitalism had reduced the life of the individual essentially to the need to produce and consume, leaving no room for dissent, free thought, or resistance to established power. The consumer's freedom, therefore, remains limited to the futile possibility of choosing to consume different products. The illustrious exponent of the Frankfurt School therefore denounced, at that time, the essentially totalitarian and "repressive" nature of the model imposed by industrial society, which flattens man to the sole dimension/function of a more or less satisfied and compulsive consumer.

In the past 20 years, digital devices and platforms have pushed people to strongly embrace consumerism by using novel strategies, not available when Marcuse wrote his book, that are able to profile and manipulate people through mechanisms embodied in the Web and social media algorithms. This, in turn, has made companies highly profitable, increasing their sale of products and services with the support of data analytics and machine learning methods. More recently, generative artificial intelligence is completing the pattern by providing natural language interfaces that engage with people through conversations and are able to push them toward the main role of consumers.

In the early 1960s, Marcuse wrote, "*Advanced technological society tends to become totalitarian insofar as it determines not only the occupations, skills, and attitudes socially required, but also individual needs and aspirations.*" He added: "*Technology serves to institute new, more effective and more pleasant forms of social control and social cohesion.*" This last part is truer and more fulfilled today than ever, thanks to the widespread acceptance of the extraordinary, advanced technologies produced by humans, of which AI technologies and genetic engineering are the most established cutting edge. It is enough to think of the many sophisticated forms of personal and social control that information technology (IT) has brought into play today, along with the new, "pleasant" forms of social cohesion that the internet, social media, online meeting tools, and AI chatbots offer anytime and anywhere.

## 14.1 One-Dimensional Man and Digital Systems

After that prophetic beginning, Marcuse, in the book *One-Dimensional Man*, continued his analysis of the role of technological innovations, emphasizing how they shape "*the entire universe of discourse and action, of intellectual and material culture. In the medium of technology, culture, politics, and the economy merge into an omnipresent system that swallows up or repulses all alternatives.*" He added an increasingly timely truth: "*Technological rationality has become political rationality*" and "*the techniques of industrialization are political techniques; as such, they prejudge the possibility of Reason and Freedom.*"

Moreover, today, it is increasingly true that science and its technological implementations assume a significant independence, especially with respect to politics and less so with respect to economics, pushing societies in a certain direction without the need or constraint of having to ask for or wait for democratic approval. The power of science and technology comes not from consensus but from the ability to explain, from its practical validity, and from its effectiveness in performing tasks and solving problems. The active role of AI solutions, for example chatbots and conversational tools, is filling the days of people and is shaping their space of thinking and acting. AI solutions are influencing hundreds of millions or billions of people in the world every day, and they are also changing the means of production and the possibilities of consumption.

For Marcuse, the one-dimensionality of the human being who populates advanced industrialized societies is thus a state determined by economic and profit-driven choices that find their most efficient mechanisms in advanced technologies. The widespread diffusion of AI only confirms this hypothesis, both due to the strength of the economic investments being made in the development and use of machine learning and generative AI systems and the financial and competitive value these technologies are increasingly generating.

More than half a century after Marcuse's reflections, today we can certainly acknowledge their validity, especially in relation to the widespread use of information and communication technologies and their role in regulating every moment of people's daily lives. IT has consolidated and expanded the spread of that human one-dimensionality that Marcuse described in 1964, in a context different from the current one but not entirely alien to our present.

The German philosopher clearly foresaw how (digital) technologies could shape human material and intellectual reality, thus forcing everyone to reckon with a medium governed by a few and which, for the most part, currently responds to the logic of profit rather than liberation. Digital technologies, including the solutions deployed by metaverse and AI systems, do this not by their intrinsic nature, but because they have become political technologies that serve the production system that generated them. This represents a system successful in our civilization, although this does not mean it should be considered inevitable.

Indeed, the use of digital technology imposed by large IT companies is pushing society toward a completely automatically administered and regulated universe. The risk, which has already largely materialized, is that humans will be daily pushed toward that Marcusian one-dimensionality that requires/obliges them to understand the elementary use of automatic operating mechanisms (and the devices that implement them) that guarantee, or even constitute, relationships between individuals and thus the operational functioning of society. This is the model increasingly implemented by the calculating and calculable industrial/algorithmic/robotic society now fully realized in the new century. Because of the massive personal data made available by digital devices and learning algorithms, lives became computable, and individuals are increasingly manipulable and manipulated.

In a world that has seen the disappearance of the social class opposition typical of the previous 150 years but in which inequalities between citizens have increased enormously, advanced technologies and their uses give the impression of offering everyone the same opportunities for action and thus act as buffers for social conflict, appearing popular and egalitarian while actually being regulators and controllers. They allow everyone to express their opinion in a sort of instant cybernetic populism, but indeed they nullify the desired effects of the person expressing it by drowning it in a gigantic digital container that quickly homogenizes and pulverizes it along with millions of other opinions, preventing the emergence of the best ones and instead favoring the worst, the falsest, and the most trivial.

As has been written many times, every time we use digital machines to solve our problems, to carry out our work, or to simplify our lives – all useful and necessary actions that we can no longer perform without IT – we discover that without the aid of those technologies, we cannot live. We become flattened by machines and their internal logic because we are the ones who increasingly depend on machines, not they on us, even though we created, spread, and nurtured them. Conformism is thus also driven and determined by the technological rationality of digital technology that dominates collective behavior. This trend is further strengthened by the increasingly widespread use of generative AI systems that perform more complex tasks for us and also increase the dependence of billions of individuals on those systems.

The widespread diffusion of digital devices and, therefore, their procedural logic means that individuals, especially the least aware and the least competent, are easily incorporated into the technological community of what Marcuse called the "administered population," which in his language refers to the dominated people. Regarding social administration, Theodor Adorno, in his essay *The Crisis of the Individual* [3], wrote a decade earlier, "*One has the distinct feeling that for the vast majority of people, they have long been relegated to mere functions within the monstrous social machinery of which we are all prisoners. ... a system of administration, a certain type of management from above.*" What the philosophers of the Frankfurt School are suggesting is a new rational model that is becoming increasingly hegemonic and totalitarian. Humans are incessantly pushed into that very narrow dimension identified by Marcuse, which has consolidated over the years and today involves an increasingly broad delegation to machines, stripping away autonomy from humans who limit themselves to consuming the digital and not governing it. A new and highly restricted élite is proposing, implementing, and selling digital devices and software systems. They are the members of a new technological power that governs digital technologies and intelligent software systems. On the other side, the vast majority of people consume their products and transfer their autonomy and subjectivity to this machinery.

## 14.2 Technology and Soft Totalitarianism

The operational arms of giant digital platforms, their algorithms, apps, and portals that relentlessly deliver goods and services act as managers and administrators of the lives of much of humanity. This 21st-century humanity risks becoming secondary to the great digital machine in which it is immersed: a humanity operationally empowered by its digital prosthetics, yet simultaneously becoming obsolete (as Gunther Anders aptly wrote [4]) precisely because of the power and perfection of the artificial devices it has created; a humanity that has the freedom to choose between a few smartphone models, a few operating systems, a very few internet service providers, and perhaps less than two e-commerce giants from which to source all kinds of consumer goods. This humanity uses them not only to do more and better but also to avoid doing many of the usual things it already did without digital devices, but now delegates entirely to machines.

Not only can politics generate totalitarianism, but technology does so too when subjected to the sole objectives of an economic and/or social system that becomes totalitarian and therefore repressive. Marcuse clearly clarifies in his essay that every type of technology is guided by social groups to promote their own interests. This condition eliminates any asserted neutrality, which, if such were true, would make technologies primarily available to those in positions of power. The non-neutrality of technology, from Marcuse's perspective, must serve to redefine technology as a tool oriented toward the affirmation of human life. In describing capitalist societies as totalitarian, Marcuse envisioned a form of totalitarianism based "*on the total mobilization of all media for the defense of established reality.*" This concept can certainly be extended to digital media, where large social media platforms play an increasingly dominant role, governed and controlled by algorithms designed and made accessible ("given") to all by large digital corporations.

In another highly relevant reflection, Marcuse pointed out that, "*[t]otalitarian democracy works through integration.*" This is the rationale of Western social systems, which have found in the intensive use of technology, and digital technology in particular, a new means to implement and perfect it. The same rationale today is evidently behind a society like China's, which is not democratic but has fully embraced the logic of profit and the intensive use of digital technologies in the service of the economy and the control of individuals, implementing a totalitarian social integration that serves to strengthen political power and its role in the global geopolitical context. Even those governing Communist China understood that digital producers are abler and freer than digital consumers and, therefore, a totalitarian state must seize this great tool to consolidate the nation's power and economic growth. Even in that great nation, as in the West, advertising messages for digital products serve to spread a very apparent freedom, a form of freedom that serves those who produce digital goods and those who possess the true liberty of defining their algorithms that establish the boundaries of choice for those who consume such highly sophisticated goods, the dimension within which they can act.

As Marcuse's prophetic intuition indicated, democracy permeated by digital technology tends to take on a totalitarian nature that absorbs and integrates everything. Everything is contained within a computer device. Everything and everyone is enveloped in an automatic rationality that helps, simplifies, and generates dependence. AI systems are the most recent examples of this powerful rationality that attracts large masses and guides them toward goals embodied in their processes. Technology, the offspring of algorithmic automation, resolves and normalizes, combining efficiency and regulatory power, integrating apparent freedoms and domination. It pushes human beings toward a simplified life and toward an increasingly restricted dimension that involves a massive consumption of algorithms and sequences of bits that we neither possess nor understand.

Marcuse's analysis of the unified language through which one-dimensional behavior is expressed finds new and complete recognition in the linguistic forms imposed by digital technologies. Marcuse spoke of an anti-critical and anti-dialectical language, characteristics that today find their real expression in the forms of (in)communication, dense with data exchange and lacking in dialectical meaning, supported by social media and AI chatbots. The dialogic nature of the internet and its communication tools is not the most widespread form of digitally supported relationship today. For example, the anti-dialectical nature promoted and practiced by social networks has meant that, in everyday practice, the majority of social interactions are aimed at affirming, denying, spreading false information, and often offending, and only among the most aware segments of its users, at debating. On the other hand, the new forms of language that generative AI tools are composing and spreading will change the way humans will express their soul and their humanity, as LLMs are transforming and filtering traditional linguistic expressions and are producing new terminologies driven by generative machine intelligence.

## 14.3 Domination and AI

According to the German philosopher, the domination of society is maintained and expanded not only through the widespread use of technology to support the prevailing productive rationality, but above all, it imposes itself as a technology in itself, expanding its spheres of influence to the point of absorbing all spheres of knowledge and culture. In particular, information technology extended its influence on all sectors of people's lives. It started by developing computing machinery capable of performing calculations faster than humans, then it enlarged its scope to data storage and management, image processing, office automation, industrial robotics, and many other disciplines that covered most of human activities. In this way, it influenced all human activities and regulated them, thereby influencing politics, culture, and economics.

Herbert Marcuse passed away in 1979, when the internet, AI algorithms, and computing technologies had not assumed the fundamental role in our lives they have today. However, his analyses of the relationship between industrialized society, technology, and human beings remain relevant and are highly useful tools for understanding how the functionality and pervasiveness of digital technologies are pushing toward the human one-dimensionality he so perfectly described. Those parasitic needs that Marcuse identified as products of consumer society still appear today as opposed to real needs, which, if satisfied, can make the world a better place. Those parasitic needs are undoubtedly amplified today by the products of digital technologies, which, from facilitators, become doping agents that often distance people from their real needs.

Like Marcuse, who challenged not technological society but the economic and political abuse of technology in the society he studied, today it is not useful to challenge the solutions offered by digital technology but rather the many discriminatory practices, the push toward totalitarian rationalism, and the abuses encouraged and implemented for profit and/or domination. Science can and must possess a critical capacity for the use of technology (and its market products) to make it freer and serve free people. But this critical exercise cannot be neglected or considered rhetorical. It must be effective and continuous.

Many of the uses of digital technologies, as they are historically being determined, do not improve or liberate our society. Rather, they worsen it by pushing billions of individuals to make the same choices, the same gestures, and to think the same way. They make it weaker and therefore more controlled – in a word, more totalitarian.

The internal rationality of information systems and their current uses is not being realized as human and social rationality but as the irrationality of life systems, relationships, and the exercise of power. The model of technological society that is gaining ground in both the West and the East is proving very powerful and appears to be seen as a model to be followed even by poor (the so-called developing) countries. Its mature implementation, which cannot be avoided, requires thinking, clever choices, and wise actions to achieve a society capable of using technology to meet real needs and have multi-dimensional human beings rather than one-dimensional individuals, as Marcuse warned.

Will we be able to adapt digital machines to the needs of humans? Or will humans have to adapt, following and bending to the demands of the digital machines produced by the big tech industry, to their automatic procedures, and to the needs of the dominant algorithmic system that was born to help and liberate us but today aspires to the total administration of our lives?

## 14.4 A Few Concluding Remarks

The Marcuse's thesis in the *One-Dimensional Man* claimed the loss of critical, deep thought in individuals living in advanced society. He argued the inability to conceive of an alternative, better reality. Today, we can say that AI systems are contributing to this erosion on a cognitive level. Careful attention must be devoted to this loss in human cognition.

Marcuse's central critique of consumerism was based on the creation of false needs, that is, desires superimposed on the individual perpetuating subordination and repressing true human fulfillment. The widespread use of AI systems and tools takes this mechanism to its logical extreme. People are risking losing autonomy in decisions and actions if they give AI systems autonomy in making decisions for them

Social media and tailored digital platforms, driven by AI, often co-opt and commodify subcultures and radical ideas, integrating the formerly outside forces into the consumer mainstream, nullifying their critical potential. This integrating and homogenizing force can eliminate human and cultural differences, impoverishing the freedom of single individuals and collective culture.

Since AI systems often operate as unreadable black boxes, the possibility of recognizing and formulating the real source of oppression (the logos of the domination) becomes far more difficult, hindering the theoretical foundation necessary for a rational refusal. This issue is tightly related to the needs of developing explainable AI systems and limiting the deployment of large, opaque AI platforms.

To conclude on the relationships between the theory of Marcuse and the extensive use of digital technologies, we can say that AI technologies can be viewed as the most advanced hardware/software machinery of Marcuse's one-dimensional society. They are transforming the technological apparatus into an invisible, predictive, adaptive, and hyper-personalized mechanism of control that optimizes both production and conformity.

## References

1. Marcuse, H. (1964). *One-Dimensional Man: Studies in the Ideology of Advanced Industrial Society*. USA: Beacon Press.
2. Marcuse, H. (1955). *Eros and Civilization*. USA: Beacon Press.
3. Thies, C. (1997). *Die Krise des Individuums: Zur Kritik der Moderne bei Adorno und Gehlen*. Germany: Rowohlt Taschenbuch (in German).
4. Anders, G. (2002). *L'Obsolescence de l'homme: Sur l'âme à l'époque de la deuxième revolution Industrielle*. France: Nuisance (in French).

# Chapter 15

# Digital Politics and Learning Machines

*Political candidates are products, and political advertising is advertising.*

—Elissa Moses

Among the many deep transformations that the widespread use of digital technologies is bringing about in our society, a particularly significant one is what we might broadly define as the "digitalization of politics." For several years, new digital technologies, through their predictive intelligent algorithms, their abundant Big Data, and their instantaneous communication, have been exerting a strong influence on political parties, their media, public communication, and citizen engagement – in other words, on the functioning of democracy.

In fact, the myriad digital services offered via the internet have changed the ways in which citizens define and share their political opinions and the ways in which they interact with each other, their representatives, and public administrators. The internet has indeed altered, not always for the better, their relationship with the organization of the state in the digital age. Naturally, the world of politics has seen diverse approaches and trends in the relationship and use of digital technologies. More recent political movements, such as the Italian Five Star Movement (M5S), have embraced them wholeheartedly, linking them to the so-far unrealized desire to build forms of direct democracy. Other parties and candidates in several countries have attempted to exploit them for propaganda purposes (with Donald Trump being a well-known example), while more traditional parties are struggling with their relationship with digital technology and are suffering significant delays in understanding and using it.

In recent decades, as data analysis and machine learning technology have undergone enormous development, Europe's political landscape (e.g., in Italy, Germany, and the Netherlands), for various reasons, has witnessed the demise of traditional parties, parties that had shaped the political history of the 20th century. Thus, while the traditional party form was eroding, leaving many citizens confused and unrepresented, the advent of information technology in everyday life, the use of social media platforms, and the deployment of AI tools and chatbots have contributed to a further shakeup of organized participation in public life and have shattered the rituals, places, and moments that characterized politics in the past century. Elections rallies, conventions in large places, meetings, and crowded debates are all things that in the past were enormously successful as vital elements in the exercise of democratic debate, while today they are increasingly becoming the memory of nostalgic old-timers.

Unfortunately, society struggles to recognize that the impact of computing technology on political participation is a crucial issue, not merely remaining a topic of discussion among specialists. There are several reasons for this attitude, not least the serious problems we are experiencing, which distract us and prevent us from adequately reflecting on an issue that is becoming increasingly important every day for the survival of democratic countries and also for the role it plays in totalitarian states [1]. What has been happening in many countries around the world for several years clearly shows that the effects of digital technology on politics, both in democracies and dictatorial systems, are far greater than politicians themselves seem to perceive. After generative AI products were made available, political campaigns are being run using them to produce content and have been influenced by them, as a very large number of social media accounts are no longer owned by human beings but by AI chatbots that exercise a great influence on large sectors of populations.

## 15.1 Toward Digital Populism

Today, thanks to digital technologies, the communication and sharing of every decision, statement, and action by a party or its representative reaches everyone instantly, creating moods and reactions that previously took much longer. Many politicians are unable to adapt to this digital immediacy, and only those who have understood that the use of digital media requires new ways of experiencing public space are able to benefit from it. Others are often overwhelmed or commit unforgivable gaffes. Added to this is the enormous distortion of citizen participation in political life, continually brought into play by the spread of fake news that distorts reality and shifts the debate from real issues to artificially constructed ones. In this sense, an environmentally friendly use of communication, especially that offered by digital media, is highly desirable. On the other hand, the ease of access and communication afforded to all by digital spaces has given many the presumption and illusion that anyone can influence political power, contribute to writing laws, and, in short, influence the functioning of the state with their digital presence, their tweets, their posts, and their social media avatars.

This is a scenario we can define as "digital populism," where everyone's individualism is on display, yet immersed in the great atomized flow that is creating a new disarticulation of political opinion, which was once organized and conveyed in structured forms. While this is the tendency of much of the digital masses, it should be noted that there is also a lack of widespread digital tools for the orderly and reliable collection of citizens' and/or party supporters' opinions on specific issues, yet technology would easily allow this. Unfortunately, the digitalization of politics is witnessing numerous and ongoing attempts at manipulation and propaganda, but offers few digital venues for genuine consultation, listening, and moderated debate. Democratic parties and governments have done almost nothing to propose, fund, and implement public digital platforms for real political participation.

The availability of an unlimited amount of information, rather than aiding informed choices, confuses and manipulates them. As noted many times, information overload breeds misinformation. Managing the public sphere through digital tools could lead to new and very positive experiences, but this is not happening due to a lack of understanding among political parties and many of their representatives of the nature and potential of digital technologies, thus allowing crude, direct methods of use and communication to prevail, lacking any prospect of synthesis. Many politicians believe that having a social media profile, perhaps managed by a creative social media manager, is sufficient to play a new role in the digital political space, and they fail to understand that simply combining traditional and digital spaces is equivalent to a cold fusion that prevents them from taking a step toward a new political role.

Francesco Raniolo, in his essay *Political Parties* [2], discussing the inertia of political organizations to change, invokes Selznick's "recalcitrance of means" to remind us that the tools used often tend to alter ends and push for a life of their own, hindering change. The author also recalls McLuhan's well-known phrase – "*The medium is the message*" [3] – which is still valid today and should remind political parties that since the medium shapes the content, one cannot even consider venturing into the digital universe without understanding it, thus risking having one's message, conceived according to analog models, distorted.

The internet, the Web, social media, conversational AI, and other digital spaces offered today by information technologies are now the primary avenues for political debate among citizens and between citizens and their political representatives. However, believing that simply having a presence online is enough for a political party or movement to automatically win millions of votes is misleading. The spaces created by digital agoras are also a fundamental resource for politics, but this is only true if conceptual and expressive knowledge of those spaces is combined with appropriate use to communicate clear and innovative political proposals. Unfortunately, political parties are no longer places of political education for citizens, and for this reason, they are unlikely to be places of training in the political use of digital technology.

Alongside the positive aspects of information availability, the great potential offered by digital solutions is currently undermined by uncertain, sometimes manipulative, and other times anti-democratic use of digital devices and algorithms. The events related to the attack on the United States Capitol in Washington, D.C., in January 2021 to overturn the presidential election have shown the extreme and dangerous practices that politics, channeled and manipulated through social media, can take. At the same time, they have shown how large digital companies can launch massive communications boycotts, stripping a US presidential candidate (even a defeated one at that time) of all social media space. After that event, several facts changed the social media ecosystem. The most significant have been (a) the creation in 2022 of the Truth Social platform owned by Trump and (b) the transformation of Twitter into X by Elon Musk, who became the only owner of this platform, which he used for several political campaigns.

Like other digital spaces, social media platforms were created by private individuals for profit, not to support democracies. On the other hand, platforms created *ad hoc* by political parties, a clear example of which was the Five Star Movement Rousseau platform, have so far proven ineffective because they are not truly democratic. Their control is in the hands of a very few, and their operating logic is opaque. This bleak scenario highlights the need to conceive and implement new digital models for politics that are defined by communities and governed by democratic laws. Large-scale public debate on digital technology has so far failed and continues to generate disruption and manipulation. For this reason, new tools and public digital platforms are needed that can facilitate democracy, empower political parties, or bring about their positive transformation if this is beneficial for society. This need increased due to the large use of machine learning and generative AI tools, coupled with social media for profiling millions of voters and for spreading disinformation with political objectives that are not clear and evident to citizens.

## 15.2 Government Technology or Governed Technology?

Managing the development of technology and its impact on society is one of the most difficult challenges facing governments and parliaments today. This challenge entails another crucial one for the political class: its ability to maintain the power to direct and utilize ongoing technological innovations, which are increasingly sophisticated and rapid. That is, the political class needs to be adequately equipped to govern in a historical era in which science and technology seem to be seeking to seize power over the world, relegating politics to a secondary role. The owners and top managers of large technology companies, with their decisions and products, increasingly influence the daily lives, work, and choices of hundreds of millions or billions of people. At times, they play a social and political role that supersedes the role of ministers and parliamentarians. The latter are often forced to keep pace with the acceleration of advanced technologies that are increasingly transforming the world.

Politics, too, is a technique; some consider it also a science. But as a technique of governance, politics risks competing with technologies – digital, genetic, or energy – which effectively influence and govern people's daily lives for better or worse. Great innovators, with their tools and services, seem to want to break away from politics and strike out on their own, becoming agents of pervasive governance over the lives of citizens who increasingly turn to technology for help, and after receiving it, become somewhat dependent on it and ultimately conditioned by it.

On these topics, in a short essay entitled "Technique and government" [4], the philosopher Giorgio Agamben astutely connected the internal and external goals of politics with the internal and external goals of technology. Agamben explained how politics uses technology for its own ends but, in doing so, promotes the role of technology and thus allows it to pursue its own internal ends. In this dialectical or conflictual process, the game between technology and politics is played out, in which the internal goals of technology are enabled by politics.

Agamben writes, "*A technical instrument can serve another's purpose only to the extent that it achieves its own.*" This is true of a fork and a knife, which pierce and cut thanks to their shapes; we use them to consume food, and in doing so, we allow them to fulfill their intrinsic purpose, their inherent qualities. Similarly, this happens with computers and algorithms, which perform calculations and communicate very quickly, and every time we use them for work or information, we help them fulfill their intrinsic purpose. All digital devices, especially those that run AI applications that we use daily, achieve their internal purposes by apparently using another's purpose, an external purpose that serves to enhance their role, their importance, and ultimately, their power. And since, for example, digital devices and their algorithms now play extremely important roles and have capabilities that challenge those of humans, they are increasingly acquiring enormous power in our world.

Politics and technology are two apparatuses of power, two instruments of government that sometimes support each other, and other times oppose each other. Politics has always sought to use technological innovations to govern nations and peoples. The enormous development of technology in the past century has allowed technology to attempt a leap forward, escaping the control of politics and freeing itself to achieve its goals fully autonomously through the governance of human lives.

Ideas similar to Agamben's have been expressed in the past by other philosophers such as Martin Heidegger, Max Horkheimer, Herbert Marcuse (as we already discussed), and Emanuele Severino. This last philosopher authored the essay titled *Capitalism Without a Future* [5], where he expressed concerns about the winning economic model and in particular about its future. Severino in an article wrote a few years ago, wondered whether "*this way of using culture by capitalism is not a more serious weakening of its own, or even its march toward extinction,*" precisely because of its reliance on scientific culture as the only useful and capable means of guiding technology. Thus, Emanuele Severino raised the bar of his criticism, moving from a criticism of the economic regime that defines what is useful (and therefore also what is useless) for humanity to a criticism of modern science, the so-called "techno-science," seen as a superior power that is guilty, in his view, of destroying capitalism and democratic governments and of single-handedly determining the future order of our world. In essence, capital has ridden the tiger of technology, but in reality, it is technology that rides capital, using it as a means to assert its paradigm in the world.

In this dual scenario, Severino introduces the role of philosophy, which, from being a maximally "useless" knowledge, becomes the primary tool for interpreting the world, capable of demonstrating how technology can subvert capitalism and capitalist nations and fully unleash its power if it realizes the impossibility of any limit and is willing to overcome it in order to pursue its irredeemable nature (at least in the eyes of the philosopher). From a historical perspective, Severino believed that ours is an intermediate period in which science and technology have not yet fully grasped the lesson of philosophy and are therefore unable to fully unleash their energies, remaining at the service of the capitalist economy and its governments. For Severino, the reversal of roles will occur in the near future when technology becomes the new "prince," according to Machiavelli's theory [6].

It is not surprising that the philosopher Severino, one of the most important of the 20th century, theorized the ontological superiority of philosophy over techno-science and capitalist economic forms. What does, however, appear to be a potentially fragile element in Severino's theses is the need to affirm the usefulness of philosophy as an element that could, if valorized, prevent the weakening of capitalism. Capitalism, in turn, today deeply uses technology, and digital technology in particular, believing it to be the only useful knowledge and attempting to subjugate it to its interests, risking being subjugated by this technology, which proves increasingly efficient and invasive.

## 15.3 Philosophy and Technological Capitalism

Severino's dialectical perspective is undoubtedly interesting, but in some respects, it seems oriented toward explaining to capitalism (and capitalists) that, in order to secure its future, it should not rely entirely on techno-science but rather that it needs philosophy to preserve itself and avoid weakening. The neo-Parmenidean philosopher focused on the limits of "useful" technoscience and its main driver, which today is capitalism, seen almost as a product of modern technology and not vice versa.

The risk inherent in this thesis is that of advocating the usefulness of philosophy as a tool of economics and, therefore, of the economic governance of individuals, rather than as the primary instrument for its critique. The category of the useful almost seems to belong to the humanities and its queen (philosophy), and those who govern the world would do well to consider this knowledge, currently neglected by the world of economics and politics. At this rate, following the philosopher's line of reasoning, we would end up creating a sort of competition between disciplines of knowledge to curry favor with the economy and political power by appearing "useful" to them. The paradoxical effect could be the reversal of the values of science and philosophy, measured by their ability to prevent the weakening and extinction of global governance systems.

Severino thus abandons a possible synthesis between "useful" and "useless" knowledge. Indeed, it would be extremely beneficial to develop a more radical critique of liberal capitalism, as well as other forms of power such as Chinese communism, which coexist hand in hand with technological innovation, underscoring the disruptive role of philosophy and the "useless" humanities. In short, a cultural revolt of knowledge deemed "useless" against the current state of affairs that can serve as a foundational critique of economic and political systems that, to save themselves, accelerate the advancement of technologies to govern the masses, even at the cost of opening cultural and social divides that increase inequality.

Unfortunately, Severino's reasoning remains rooted in the separation of the two cultures, the arts or humanities on one hand and the sciences on the other. It is a separation that has significantly damaged Western culture and society and which still seems difficult to eliminate [7]. On the contrary, it would be far more interesting and useful to unleash the energies of science and philosophy by healing the rift that has historically existed between them, uniting them in uncovering the contradictions of dominant systems of power and human nature, today focused on the logic of the market and finance, in short, functional to the exercise of power.

While technologies, in their function of governing people, are gaining ever greater power, in cultural terms, it is necessary to foster dialogue and the integration of different cultural areas and disciplines. This is to develop hypotheses and practices that begin with individual needs, shape politics, and push the use of technology to serve citizens and their well-being. A major challenge facing the world is to find sustainable and egalitarian ways to use innovative technologies while also preventing those who produce and sell them from becoming primary political actors and, through the efficient power of their products, governing citizens' lives according to their economic interests. This challenge is also related to the challenge of dialectically uniting scientific and humanistic cultures, ensuring that they define what is "useful" for human beings, rather than submitting to it as a category imposed by the laws of economics and power. These challenges require engaging cultures in our time.

## 15.4 Will AI Substitute Politicians?

Citizens' trust in governments and political representatives has been declining for several decades, and this negative trend appears unstoppable. This phenomenon affects nearly all democratic nations. Naturally, the reasons for this state of affairs are myriad and difficult to summarize here. However, to the many expressions of distrust, blame, and censure directed at many political figures and parties, we must add one more that, if it were not entirely unprecedented, would not merit attention and could not worsen the bleak picture of weak consensus in 21st-century democracies.

In a study by a private Spanish university, IE University [8], approximately 3,000 citizens from 11 countries were interviewed to understand their opinions on the impact of technology on society and how it is shaping our lives in terms of automation, democracy, and the influence of Big Tech companies. Among the many questions asked, a crucial one was the following: "*What do you think about the possible replacement of parliamentarians in your countries with an artificial intelligence algorithm that, using your data, operates to maximize your interests?*" The responses revealed that the majority of Europeans would like to see members of their parliaments replaced by AI algorithms. This is no joke; these opinions were expressed in a thorough survey and demonstrate how low citizens' trust in their governments is, to the point of believing that an algorithm can be more trustworthy than a member of parliament, a senator, or a regional councilor.

Across Europe as a whole, in the aforementioned survey, 51% of citizens said they would definitely prefer AI software to their parliamentarians. Looking at data from individual countries, the results are even more worrying. For example, in Italy, 60% of citizens prefer the intelligence of algorithms to that of politicians. Machine learning and generative AI algorithms appear to be more trusted by politicians. Citizens' responses to that particular question certainly express a strong distrust of the political class, to the point of considering replacing it with automated systems guided by AI algorithms. Despite knowing that these are often opaque procedures that are not personally accountable for their decisions, the majority of citizens would consider replacing politicians with AI algorithms in administrative and government decisions.

This actually happened in Albania, where the prime minister appointed an AI chatbot to a cabinet-level position. The chatbot's name is Diella, and she was declared Minister of State for Artificial Intelligence, tasked with addressing corruption in government contracting. Diella's appointment was a politically spectacular decision against corruption in Albany; however, it raised the key issue we are discussing: whether AI systems are moving beyond support, and if so, they could start to be used for making political decisions.

These kinds of scenarios illustrate the profound disconnect between the institutions and representatives of power and ordinary citizens, to the point of leading them to consider replacing them with a machine capable of making decisions based on automatic rules. The issue becomes even more concerning for those in political power when considering young people's attitudes toward the use of AI algorithms in place of real-life representatives of the people. Indeed, younger people appear to be more favorable to this exchange: 60% of Europeans aged 25–34 and 56% of those aged 34–44 welcome the use of "smart" digital machines in place of parliamentarians.

More than Italians, Spaniards are the most skeptical of their political representatives and the most likely to replace them with algorithms; in fact, the percentage there is 66% (two-thirds of those interviewed!). Meanwhile, the least favorable are those in Great Britain, where citizens don't seem to be particularly fond of the idea of replacing politicians with technologies proposed by AI. In fact, across the Channel, the percentage of those in favor drops to 31% (almost a third), while in Estonia, the number of those in favor rises to 56%. Germans (54% of those interviewed were against) and the Dutch (56%) also expressed some doubt about the use of digital technologies in political decisions. Outside Europe, some 75% of people surveyed in China supported the idea of replacing parliamentarians with AI, while in the US, 40% said they were in favor.

These results, although they concern prospective hypotheses, should be of great alarm to political party representatives and those elected to every parliamentary assembly. It should also be added that, based on the survey, a third of Europeans would prefer AI algorithms to decide welfare contributions or approve visas to work in a foreign country instead of public officials. Finally, it should also be noted that 72% of respondents also expressed support for electronic voting via smartphone, even though electronic voting systems are not yet entirely secure and reliable. This last response confirms the acceptance of the now universal use of our mobile phones for every aspect of our lives.

In some respects, the data obtained from the Spanish university's survey reflect a high level of public trust in the capabilities of digital technologies. This aspect should be carefully analyzed, especially given the discriminatory use of technology that sometimes occurs. On the other hand, this survey once again confirms citizens' deep distrust of politicians, to the point of considering replacing them with automated procedures. Politicians should find time to study and reflect on these trends and the envisioned scenarios. Indeed, it would be appropriate to focus due attention on the survey data, which show clear signs of possible future scenarios that could profoundly alter the life of our democratic systems. Undeniably, digital technologies, rather than strengthening them, appear to be challenging democracies, to the point of suggesting future electoral campaigns involving chatbots and robots rather than people.

## References

1. Hasselbalch, G. (2025). *Human Power - Seven Traits for the Politics of the AI Machine Age*. USA: CRC Press.
2. Raniolo, F. (2013). *I Partiti Politici*. Italy: Laterza (in Italian).
3. McLuhan, M. (2001). *Understanding Media: The Extension of Man*. UK: Routledge.
4. Agamben, G. (2023). La tecnica e la politica. *Quodlibet* (in Italian). https://www.quodlibet.it/giorgio-agamben-la-tecnica-e-il-governo [Retrieved 21 November 2025].

5. Severino, E. (2012). *Capitalismo Senza Futuro*. Italy: RCS Libri (in Italian).
6. Machiavelli, N. (2021). *The Prince*. USA: Reader's Library Classics.
7. Snow, C. P. (1993). *The Two Cultures*. UK: Cambridge University Press.
8. Shead, S. (2021). More than half of Europeans want to replace lawmakers with AI, study says. *CNBC*. https://www.cnbc.com/2021/05/27/europeans-want-to-replace-lawmakers-with-ai.html [Retrieved 21 November 2025].

# Chapter 16

# The Cultural and Regulatory Models of Algorithms

*Computers are useless. They can only give you answers.*

—Pablo Picasso

The huge number of digital systems deployed around the world, which we use so frequently every day, constitutes the most powerful and pervasive technology that humans have created since their appearance on Earth. Yet, despite their technical power, it would be a mistake to consider digital devices merely as a technology, as a set of operational tools that help us do things better and solve many problems efficiently. Today's digital systems, in addition to enabling us to do many things quickly, also bring with them a cultural and regulatory logic that is transforming the vision and practice of problem-solving and of social relationships among individuals, among public and private organizations, and even among nations. In doing so, digital technology is changing the ways in which we regulate the organization of society, govern civil coexistence, influence democracy, and define the present and future of the economy and work. In other words, we could say that digital technologies built around computers and their interconnection networks have provided us with not only sophisticated tools but also organizational and cultural models that are increasingly shaping a historic social and economic transformation of our world.

This is possible because the vast majority of the information that billions of people around the world consume daily is produced, transformed, and disseminated through the vast network of devices that digital technology has deployed across the planet. Through that information, we do countless things, often based on approaches based on interaction with machines and governed by their algorithms. This trend has been further improved by the development of artificial intelligence systems.

## 16.1 Cultural and Regulatory Models of AI

In the first decades of the mass production and diffusion of computers, curiosity and later pragmatic use of these sophisticated devices emerged at home, in the office, and elsewhere. Subsequently, models of work organization and personal relationships built around them emerged, replacing the previously established models. This innovative trend significantly expanded and strengthened when a global communications network (the internet) was built around computers and when they were joined by their smaller siblings, smartphones, which became smart objects that now guide so many of our daily actions.

This process, which began in the 1980s with the spread of personal computers, was completed in the first two decades of the 2000s, when the logical principles of computer science definitively emerged from the laboratories of universities and large digital companies and embraced the society that adopted machine learning systems (not always consciously) as a new paradigm for redefining and regulating many socioeconomic, organizational, cultural, and leisure practices.

The set of digital devices and AI systems that envelop the entire human world and make it function is increasingly becoming the conceptual framework within which to redefine the functioning of society, the expression of forms of labor, the subjectivity of individuals, and the governance of the masses in their relationships, for their control and for processes of persuasion. Many practices are regulated by complex algorithms that, operating within our devices, allow us to perform them on a daily basis. However, their intervention in people's lives is not limited to the operational sphere but also defines the sphere of meaning of quotidian experience and our thinking. It builds a new digitalized culture of living by micro-regulating the human world, which now moves to the rhythm of automated procedures and the flow of information and communications managed by intelligent procedures executed tirelessly by computers.

The cultural model created by the development of digital devices and intelligent algorithms is increasingly establishing itself as the primary means of regulating our behavior. They do it through the interactions with AI chatbots, the production of posts and likes, the instant sharing of information, the information technology (IT) procedures required for transactions on public administration's web portals, and the operating processes of worldwide organizations. Currently, thanks also to the revolution promised by AI, the massive digital mass created by universities, research centers, and digital companies has become a new lens through which people view the world and attempt to manage reality – a lens that regulates the (inter)actions between human subjects and between their organizational forms.

Because software applications are useful (and used) for performing many daily tasks, even those of a certain complexity, we are becoming accustomed to thinking about solutions in terms of algorithmic procedures that are increasingly taking on a regulatory role in human life. We often view many tasks through the lens of IT, and we think about its algorithmic approaches to solving problems. This cultural trend, which has objective motivations, is not sufficiently critically evaluated and is rapidly imposing technological solutions. Too often, it's believed that simply automating a process, an organization, or a set of relationships is enough to improve them. Many people think this way, even without a careful understanding of how computing systems work. They fail to understand that every digital process that assists humans must be thoroughly studied, considering the human factor, the specific context, and the real potential, along with the limitations of computing machines. Otherwise, it risks becoming a cage rather than a more effective solution.

It often happens that, in people's interaction with the applications within our digital devices, it is the human who must submit to the machine, in the sense that the algorithmic procedures of the software we use are often inflexible and prescriptive, and we must adapt to them, not vice versa. In this context, machine logic takes precedence over human logic and becomes the regulatory power over people's lives. This is a new manifestation of an old form of power that has always sought to regulate people's behavior through the imposition of legal, administrative, or political norms. Traditional forms of power are now being supplemented by the regulatory power of software procedures encoded in the digital machines we interact with every day.

With the increasingly widespread use of AI, this trend is strengthening and generating serious problems if the intelligent software systems we are using force us to adopt in a slavish manner their expressive forms and abstract logic. If we have to rely on their regulatory power to solve our problems, the cultural and disciplinary models of digital technologies will control human processes and the functioning of social bodies. And since the computing systems that billions of people use today are largely the products of a few very big companies, the power of these companies is becoming a new conceptual, disciplinary, and controlling power, with effects that could be dangerous for humans and their freedoms.

The digital technologies and AI systems largely used today are not simple elements of innovation. They are general forces modeling our ethos, economy, governance, and social life. This is confirmed by declarations of CEOs of big digital companies, such as Dario Amodei, who wrote "*I think that most people are underestimating just how radical the upside of AI could be, just as I think most people are underestimating how bad the risks could be.*" [1] and Sam Altman who declared that "*The rate of technological progress will keep accelerating, and it will continue to be the case that people are capable of adapting to almost anything. There will be very hard parts like whole classes of jobs going away, but on the other hand the world will be getting so much richer so quickly that we'll be able to seriously entertain new policy ideas we never could before. We probably won't adopt a new social contract all at once, but when we look back in a few decades, the gradual changes will have amounted to something big*" [2].

## 16.2 AI and the Promethean Gap

Joseph Stiglitz, an American economist and 2001 Nobel Prize winner in Economics, in 2014 co-authored an essay with his colleague Bruce Greenwald, titled *Creating a Learning Society* [3]. In that book, Stiglitz and Greenwald outlined some of their theories on the so-called "learning society," explaining how education, study, and training are crucial elements of a nation's economic and social growth today and how they can significantly contribute to narrowing and bridging the gap between developed and developing nations.

The term "learning society" was coined to indicate a shift in thinking about education and its impact on the world of work that has occurred in recent decades but, above all, to refer to an increase in access to education, culture, and knowledge for significant portions of the world's population.

According to Stiglitz and Greenwald, society evolves based on an increase in learning capacity, and therefore the role of knowledge as a common good must be recognized. In particular, the theses of the two American economists recognize that technological innovations can contribute to strengthening the learning society and extending its impact to an ever-increasing portion of humanity.

Certainly, many innovations over the past century have increased the distribution of information and knowledge among individuals. Among these, the internet and its myriad digital channels and services, which continuously distribute content and information to every corner of the globe, must be considered first and foremost. However, despite the valid considerations of the two American economists, innovations are not always used effectively to increase the knowledge and culture of citizens and for the common good. In particular, if we consider the internet and the software systems we use daily, we cannot fail to see that, in addition to being very useful for many purposes, they are also places of large-scale disinformation, tools for spreading hate, spaces for disseminating fake news, and spaces for political and informational manipulation of individuals and large communities.

Reducing the cultural and knowledge gap between people and helping all countries (especially disadvantaged ones) improve their knowledge and skills are central objectives for growth and progress on our planet. All actions undertaken in this direction are of enormous value in improving people's quality of life and, above all, in helping disadvantaged citizens and poor countries. In this regard, digital technologies are strategic and crucial elements in achieving the learning society called for by Stiglitz and Greenwald. However, many uses of digital technologies today go in other directions and contribute to increasing people's ignorance and misinformation, worsening their knowledge rather than improving it. These counter-educational and misinformative uses are largely the result of the profit-driven logic that dominates the use of the internet and its tools, which are now largely used to build digital empires that capture the attention of billions of people and convey content largely instrumental to the advertising and sale of products and services rather than to the civil and cultural improvement of individuals. Added to this is people's lack of knowledge and attention when using digital systems.

For many citizens and communities around the world, all of this represents a kind of deprivation of the great opportunities that technological innovations offer, opportunities that human beings seem unable or unwilling to exploit to improve their living conditions and their knowledge, the latter two elements that are closely intertwined. We live in an age in which information, experiences, and knowledge can be easily shared globally, almost instantaneously. Yet, this great opportunity is being overlooked by many people to improve their living conditions and by many governments to support the education of their citizens. Many people around the world fail to derive benefits from the internet and digital systems and too often misuse them, causing harm to themselves and others.

In an essay published in 1956, the German philosopher Günther Anders used the term "postliterary illiteracy" to describe the global inundation of images that already affected individuals exposed to television, films, and newspaper and magazine illustrations. Anders criticized a communication model that was gaining ground in those years and was "stuffing people's eyes" according to a sort of "iconomania," with the danger, he warned, of generating a kind of generalized imbecility and a loss of the real information and knowledge needed to live better.

These and other considerations were elaborated by Günther Anders around the middle of the past century in his essay *The Outdatedness of Human Beings* [4], which we mentioned in previous chapters. These considerations are even more valid and timely today and can be useful in explaining how humans use information systems and the digital content that floods our lives daily with images, videos, reels, streaming movies, selfies, memes, and other forms of digital information. Instead of contributing to a "learning society," they are erecting an "unlearning society" or even a "society of neo-ignorance." This appears incapable of effectively harnessing the power of the internet and the digital systems we frequent intensively, which are formidable tools, if used effectively, to improve the lives and culture of people.

Prompted by the construction of the nuclear bomb and its effects on the populations of Hiroshima and Nagasaki, Anders wrote that book to discuss how the major technological innovations in the aftermath of the Second Industrial Revolution had defined the ontological superiority of machines over humans. In his essay, Anders defined the so-called "Promethean gap" that, in his view, had rendered humans obsolete. This gap between the modern flesh-and-blood Prometheus and the machines he constructs tends to increase over time and consists, according to the German philosopher, in the human inability to keep pace with the pace of innovation and the constant offering of solutions, improvements, and refinements of technological products. It consists in the human inability to keep pace with the artificial products that man himself is capable of creating. It is a gap that stems from what Anders calls "Promethean shame," which expresses a sense of inadequacy and disadvantage of our being compared to the machines of which we ourselves are the designers, builders, and users. In the book, Anders writes, "*By this I mean the 'shame one feels in the face of the humiliating heights of quality of objects made by ourselves.*'"

It is those mechanical, automatic, and artificial products that humans produce, ever newer and more efficient, that surpass us in their functions and capabilities, causing us to feel and, in fact, become antiquated. Anders also points out that machines, in addition to being efficient, are also repeatable, standardized, and reproducible in many copies. For this reason, these devices possess the advantage of a sort of eternity that is denied to humans, despite their strenuous pursuit of it.

If Anders were still alive today and had witnessed the widespread use of computers, smartphones, software, robots, apps, and the enormous diffusion of the internet, he could not have failed to notice the many further confirmations his theory has received over time. It is easy, in fact, to observe how the digital revolution has increased the Promethean gap theorized by Anders in favor of computers, which are much better and more capable than us humans at doing many things and doing them much faster. In particular, recent developments in AI systems strongly bring to everyone's attention the teachings of Günther Anders and further confirm his insights from many decades ago. These are artificial systems that, as some have pointed out, are not as intelligent as we humans; however, they are capable of doing many things that require intelligence from humans. Moreover, these systems do them much faster than us and tirelessly.

We are in a time when machines themselves can build other machines, improve them, replicate themselves, connect with each other to collaborate, and learn from other machines.[1] Thus, while we humans can attest to our Promethean gap with respect to these refined and powerful devices, we realize that their use in the service of the learning society, advocated by Stiglitz and Greenwald, is still a long way from full realization, even

[1] Meta-learning, distributed learning, multi-agent systems, and cooperating robots are real significant examples of digital machines that learn from other digital machines. This kind of learning processes also occur in generative AI systems that use, for example, knowledge distillation and teacher–student models to exploit AI models for training other models.

though it is highly desirable in order to limit and overcome the many inequalities between citizens and the enormous gaps between the developed and poor countries of the world.

## 16.3 Ideology and Force of AI

Ideologies are sets of social, political, economic, and cultural values that have their own internal coherence and serve to guide the behavior of individuals and societies. The 20th century was one of political and economic ideologies (communism, fascism, liberalism, and capitalism) that governed the world and were also the causes of wars and social conflicts. With the transition to the new century, some 20th-century ideologies collapsed under the blows of history, some were abandoned, and still others had to transform to survive (with capitalism being among the last category). In this new century, which many describe as post-ideological, the decline of old ideologies has coincided with the dawn of new ideologies that have arisen like new stars, illuminating the souls of many human beings who seem unable to live without an ideological vision. Among these new ideologies are certainly environmentalism, pacifism, and sovereignism.

These new beliefs are being joined by a new ideology fueled by the rapid technological evolution driven by the acceleration of digital systems we all use daily and can no longer do without. While it may seem strange to associate the concept of ideology with technology, the profound social impact of innovations resulting from scientific research and innovation is generating a plethora of values that guide society, ultimately shaping a vision of the functioning and governance of the communities that inhabit the planet. Terms such as "algocracy," "datacracy," "algoethics," "infocracy," and "infosphere" (terms discussed in detail in the essay *L'Impero dell'Algoritmo*, or *The Empire of the Algorithm*) [5] are all neologisms that describe new social, organizational, and political realities that contribute to defining new ideological scenarios in which digital technologies transcend their technical limitations and the traditional domains of technology, thus entering the lives of citizens and bringing, along with new services and new features, new values and new visions that guide the functioning and governance of society.

Gabriele Balbi, in his essay *L'Ultima Ideologia* (*The Last Ideology*) [6], analyzes digital technology as a new (and latest) ideology that intends to encompass the entire world and dominate it, claiming to converge the interests of economics, politics (democratic and totalitarian), and the technological and economic elites. Digital technology promises a new world, better than the previous one, and does everything it can to convince its users (billions of people) that only the solutions it offers can help them live fully in the present. It explains to individuals that only through its apps and devices can they be citizens of the new century and enter the future as first-class citizens. It is undeniable that IT, telecommunications, and digital services have improved many aspects of people's lives and the functioning of society, simplifying many operations and reducing daily operating times. However, at the same time, it is clear that these powerful technologies have not solved humanity's major problems; they have not reduced world hunger, wars, and the many inequalities; in fact, in some cases, they have increased them.

In the two years we have spent largely locked down at home due to the pandemic, the communicative and processing power of digital technology has helped us greatly, but it has also made us realize that an entirely online daily life is neither pleasant nor bearable. It was not a good premise for the hoped-for success of metaverse technologies and virtual reality systems, which, along with AI, represent the final frontier of digital ideology. These more recent ideological discoveries, which would require individuals to live and move entirely in the new virtual world of bits, seem unwilling to reckon with the biological need to live as humans among humans. In these decades of wars and dramatic climate events, digital technology has been able to inform us in real time with streaming micronews on everything a mobile phone can see, photograph, or collect. Yet, it doesn't seem capable of immunizing itself from the spread of disinformation campaigns and fake news. Furthermore, the weapons used, for example, in the war between Russia and Ukraine are heavily digital, and this use of high technology is certainly not preventing the deaths of many civilians or even soldiers. In short, despite this being the most technologically advanced conflict ever, drones and computerized weapons are not killing anyone, but human beings continue to die.

The novel developments in generative AI systems, increasingly discussed by some with fear and others with enthusiasm, are further strengthening the digital ideology that sees new information technologies as the basis for a vision of society, its organization, and its functioning. Chatbot systems such as ChatGPT, DeepSeek, and Gemini demonstrate more clearly the power of AI technologies and are increasing their impact on society. In this case, we are faced with systems capable of communicating with us using our language, producing content as humans do, and organizing information even better than humans. These are systems for which the European Union recently approved a regulatory law and which are feared to have a disruptive impact on the world of work because they are capable of carrying out many high-level jobs as well as, or better than, many people, who risk losing their jobs for this reason.

In his essay *Ideology and Utopia* [7], Hungarian-born sociologist Karl Mannheim theorized that ideology and utopia, despite being "worldviews," differ radically in their essential nature. According to Mannheim, ideology represents the thinking of the ruling class and is therefore aimed at preserving existing reality, while utopia represents the thinking of the dominated classes and is therefore aimed at transforming existing reality. This opposition, feared by Mannheim in the case of digital technology, seems almost dissolved, and we are moving toward a form of convergence between digital ideology, expressed by big companies and the governments that support them, and digital utopia, which espouses the project of continuous evolution and the improvement of society and humanity through new technologies.

About a decade ago, Evgeny Morozov defined the concept of cybernetic utopianism in his essay *Net Delusion* [8]. This utopianism espouses the belief that the internet, the Web, and digital technologies, in general, enable the emancipation of peoples and favor the oppressed rather than the oppressors, the weak rather than the strong. According to Morozov, this belief is naive and shortsighted because it is based on a refusal to consider the negative aspects of digital technology. Furthermore, this cybernetic utopianism, which seeks to eliminate inequalities, seems incapable of understanding that digital technology is largely in the hands of the world's powers, who are very reluctant to make it available to the most vulnerable or to use it to reduce the social and economic inequalities that exist on the planet.

Digital technologies, particularly AI systems, can be used effectively to help the most vulnerable and to make our societies more just and inclusive (now it's time the term "sustainable" is in fashion), but for this to be achieved, digital must cease to be an ideology that the world's major IT players attempt to impose on billions of citizens. At the same time, it must also avoid being merely a utopia (we could use the term "algotopia") that deludes itself into believing it can emancipate people.

Digital technologies and systems should do more to improve the world, promising fewer special effects. They must do so by spreading less rhetoric of progress and creating more truly free services for citizens, providing greater assistance to those in need, and reducing profits (which are already extremely high) for large digital companies that appear to have no concern for the well-being of the people while pursuing ever-increasing profits.

## References

1. Amodei, D. (2024). Machines of loving grace. https://www.darioamodei.com/essay/machines-of-loving-grace [Retrieved on 24 November 2025].
2. Altman, S. (2025). The gentle singularity. https://blog.samaltman.com/the-gentle-singularity [Retrieved on 24 November 2025].
3. Stiglitz, J. E. and Greenwald, B. (2014). *Creating a Learning Society: A New Approach to Growth, Development, and Social Progress*. USA: Columbia University Press.
4. Anders, G. (2002). *L'Obsolescence de l'homme: Sur l'âme à l'époque de la deuxième revolution Industrielle*. France: Nuisance (in French).
5. Talia, D. (2021). *L'Impero dell'Algoritmo*. Italy: Rubbettino (in Italian).
6. Balbi, G. (2022). *L'Ultima Ideologia. Breve Storia Della Rivoluzione Digitale*. Italy: Laterza (in Italian).
7. Mannheim, K. (2022). *Ideology and Utopia*. USA: Martino Fine Books.
8. Morozov, E. (2012). *Net Delusion: The Dark Side of Internet Freedom*. USA: Public Affair.

# Chapter 17

# Digital Governmentality: Control Procedures and Social Harms

*The current use of AI isn't necessarily aligned with the goals of building a better society, unfortunately. We could change that.*

—Yoshua Bengio

The relationship between the forms of knowledge and the mechanisms of power has characterized every era of human history, although each time this relationship has taken on different forms. The exercise of authority has never been totally separated from the ways of thinking and knowing of the time in which they were employed. The ages of tyrannies or great empires could not have existed, and cannot be explained, if separated from the way people thought in those ages and the forms of composition of the collective knowledge of the peoples who lived in that historical reality. The same can be said, in appropriate declinations, for societies that saw the birth and consolidation of democracy as a widespread and dialectical power among a mass that is the natural holder of power and that hands it over from time to time to an elite that exercises it by proxy.

In his studies on the mechanisms of power and the governance of individuals and societies, French philosopher Michel Foucault in 1978 introduced the concept of governmentality. Governmentality (from the French *gouvernementalité*) is a term already used in the past, but for Foucault it refers to the link between governing (*gouverner*) and thinking (*mentalité*), the relationship between the mechanisms of power and governance and the forms of rationality that organize them. Indeed, by governmentality [1] Foucault meant that specific form of government management that, through a set of "*institutions, procedures, analyses, reflections, calculations, and tactics,*" ensures the care of populations and guarantees the "*government of living beings,*" having "*political economy as the privileged form of knowledge and security mechanisms as the essential technical instrument.*" When he uses the term "government," the French philosopher refers broadly to the ability to "*structure the possible field of action of others*" and thus to direct the conduct of others. Foucault also proposed the concept of governmentality to explain the particular way of administering "the living" (in the sense of the governed) that has developed in modern European history. This set of practices, regulations, and technologies for governing the lives of citizens was implemented in Europe between the 16th and 19th centuries in the practices of managing power in its liberal form.

For Foucault, power is above all a relationship, and "disciplinary" power acts through positive regulation, not through interdictions or denials. Through governmentality, the state combines knowledge, techniques, and practices into a single whole capable of ensuring or promoting conditions deemed favorable for the life of a population. It becomes a regulatory state capable of controlling without violence, capable of organizing citizens' living spaces by regulating their lives and their conduct. The idea of governmentality served the French philosopher to analyze and explore different governmental mentalities that can be traced back to the same attempt to determine, or at least influence, in different ways, the conduct of human beings through specific means with the aim of achieving specific ends. With the birth of governmentality around the 16th century, according to Foucault, "*a new relationship between government and truth was developed, structured around the objective knowledge of the elements over which command is exercised.*" In its development in the modern world, the individual can be subjected to governmentality (that is, can be influenced) only to the extent that he is a *homo oeconomicus*, that is, a man whose main characteristics are rationality and primary interest in caring for his own individual advantages which are strongly dependent on economic aspects and the concept of utility.

## 17.1 Governmentality and the Boundaries of Power

Michel Foucault's consideration of governmentality marks a significant expansion of the classical field of politics as the art of government. Foucault goes beyond the narrow definition of government as the exercise of political sovereignty to argue that diverse practices must be included within it. Governmentality, in fact, defines the extra-state practices of power between individuals and of individuals over themselves, from a perspective that challenges classical theories that had seen the state as the exclusive origin of relations of domination. Thus, the traditional comparison between state sovereignty and the subject of law is transcended, moving toward a form of politics understood as an open space, dynamic in its actions and relations. It is a form of politics that addresses and takes shape even through that which traditionally does not belong to it.

Political governmentality, therefore, indicates the way in which a community of individuals finds itself increasingly implicated in the exercise of power. On this basis, for Foucault, governing does not mean imposing coercion on the subject but rather leading, directing, and, in particular, orienting the conduct of subjects toward ends assumed to be expedient. All of this is also significantly related to the concept of biopolitics developed by Foucault himself. In his essay *The History of Sexuality: The Will to Knowledge* [2], the French philosopher described biopolitics as a power in which "*the old right to kill or let live has been replaced by a power to make live or to repel into death.*" In his other work, *The Birth of Biopolitics* [3], he wrote, "*The new reason of government therefore requires freedom; the new art of government consumes freedom. If it consumes freedom, it is also obliged to produce it, and if it produces it, it is also obliged to organize it. The new art of government will therefore present itself as the art of managing freedom.*" Authority has always had to do with the management of freedom, but the relationship that the French philosopher identifies is a complex and delicate one, as it is realized in a historical period in which the rights of individuals acquire broader spaces than in previous centuries and the dialectic between individuals and the government of society acquires a more nuanced nature.

In particular, in the last century and, even more so, in recent decades, the exercise of power, the management of personal freedom, biopolitics, and thus also governmentality, as proposed by Foucault, have witnessed the birth and growth of an eloquent and increasingly relevant relationship with the widespread use of technological innovations, proposed with ever greater speed and intensity by individuals, companies, and nations. This recent relationship has taken on a particular intensity thanks to digital innovations resulting from the invention of the computer, the internet, and artificial intelligence. It is implemented with ever greater pervasiveness through the ways in which information technology operates in everyday life and transforms relationships between individuals and between them and the bodies governing public and private life. This occurs through the many forms of invasive use of digital devices and their algorithms, which are redefining their freedoms and conditioning the forms of exercise of power [4]. Through the many extra-state practices that find their means of implementation in digital, the space where they can express the governance of subjects [5]. Examples of digital technologies that have transformed the relationship between individuals and with public and private government entities include the Web, social media, apps and smartphones, Big Data, and, finally, AI. Studying these themes can help perform a critical analysis of digital as a rational technology of power, a key element of governmentality today. Everything that digital technologies have introduced contributes to defining, by limiting and/or expanding it, the operational space of individuals and the organization and governance of their freedoms through codified procedures that regulate (and define) the actions of living beings.

## 17.2 Digital Governmentality

The current context can be described using the term "digital governmentality," which should be understood as a complex approach that defines procedures, practices, analyses, and calculations for the delineation and management of human governance through digital systems composed of algorithms, software systems, protocols, and sophisticated data processing that describe, regulate, manage, and predict human activities. Indeed, algorithms have been developed and are now widely used in all sectors of society. In public administration, education, public safety, healthcare, assistance, finance, and other contexts, algorithms are used to define control procedures, to analyze the conditions that allow for the enjoyment of a right or a welfare service, and to define scope for action. The governance of human governance through these algorithms obviously also occurs in the private sector, from commerce to transportation and banking. Countless procedures influence citizens, their behavior, their rights, and their duties, and in doing so, they define the forms of digital governmentality.

Even in Foucault's original elaboration, the idea of governmentality as a tool for analyzing the forms of power appropriate for governance is linked to the innovations that technology introduces into society and that, at least in part, are used for its governance. Foucault's idea of the modern exercise of power, conceived as "*the set of techniques and procedures for directing human behavior, the government of children, the government of souls and consciences, of a household, of a state, or of oneself,*" today also calls for the need to analyze how digital technologies, algorithms, their data collection and processing apparatuses, and their global infrastructures spanning the entire globe contribute, or can contribute, to redesigning and implementing "*procedures for the direction of human behavior.*" This question is the subject of analysis in various fields that, albeit from different perspectives, address the problem of understanding the political and social impacts of digital technologies. For example, Lawrence Lessig's essay *Code and Other Laws of Cyberspace* [6] looks at similar aspects but from the perspective of jurisprudence, with the aim of describing how the designers and developers of algorithms and software systems are now becoming (sometimes unaware) regulators of our society.

In this historical moment, we are facing a crisis in the governmentality of democratic liberalism, which is unable to influence the regulation of the societies it is called upon to govern. The difficulties arise primarily from the economic and financial phenomena determined by production processes embedded within the phenomenon of what is termed "globalization," which has made the existence of billions of people more difficult and less secure and has effectively undermined the credibility of political classes, which seem incapable of ensuring the well-being and serenity of large segments of the population who, in the past, felt more secure. These phenomena, which clearly have an economic origin, are in fact the offspring of capitalist restructuring and are also facilitated by digital platforms that allow the global economic system to exercise large-scale forms of action that limit governmental action and relationships between individuals [7].

In other words, digital technologies, increasingly employed in daily activities across every economic, organizational, and social sector, today exert a profound influence on the lives and freedoms of vast masses of living beings, both through their ability to process vast amounts of information in extremely short times (the most obvious example of this capability being provided by machine learning and AI systems) and through their widespread global deployment in a dense and ubiquitous network of interconnections that distribute data and operations to govern decision-making, operational, and regulatory processes. Almost all transactions on global stock exchanges are managed through algorithms, and online advertising is delivered by networked software systems that span the entire globe and buy and sell advertising space on our device screens in real time, thus influencing our cultural and political preferences and our purchases. These are only a few significant examples of how algorithms impact our lives and, often silently, influence and govern them.

The forms and modalities of delivery, control, and management of digitalization processes and the massive and all-encompassing collection of data [8] demonstrate the weakness of the governmentality of liberal powers, which are leaving the governance of these processes to large private companies, sometimes for reasons of national economic advantage [9], as is the case in the US, and other times due to knowledge and management gaps, as is the case in Italy and other democratic states with a low level of technical knowledge among the ruling classes. Conversely, totalitarian governments, of which China is certainly the most proper example, have understood how the digitalization of society allows for greater control and management of individuals' operational spaces and is an element of the digital governmentality that can be exercised in the new century. The case of the Social Credit System, implemented in China, demonstrates how the governance of individuals can be exercised through the use of digital systems.

These are new instruments of governance that are also adaptable to totalitarian regimes yet allow for a "fine-grained" digital governmentality capable of managing citizens' daily actions and measuring them to determine the spaces of freedom they deserve. Chinese "social scoring" aims to evaluate the so-called social integrity of citizens. The domain considered by the Chinese government is the socioeconomic one, and in particular, the areas comprising the evaluation domain are social integrity, commercial integrity, judicial credibility, and honesty in government affairs. The collection of personal information in these areas takes on the aspect of massive surveillance of the population involved, serving to regulate their spheres of action [10] and, ultimately, their freedom. For example, the system provides punishments for those who score poorly, such as a ban on flying, restrictions on local travel, slower internet connection speeds, exclusion from certain job roles, or exclusion from private schools. On the other hand, the system also provides rewards for a positive assessment, such as easier travel and transportation, fewer checks, easier access to financing and rent, and increased social dignity. All these are practical examples that become parameters of a system of digital governmentality that defines, organizes, and manages the freedoms of large masses of individuals.

## 17.3 Datafication and the Government of People

Today, knowledge about reality is increasingly extracted from vast amounts of digital data through the use of data analytics and machine learning algorithms [11]. More often than not, this knowledge is not available to individuals (not even those it covers or describes), and they cannot know or perceive it. This happens, for example, to Instagram and TikTok users, Amazon customers, Uber drivers, or Glovo delivery drivers, who are monitored and classified through the analysis of their behavioral data – data that remains secret to them. However, the knowledge extracted from the data is nevertheless applied to them, their performance, their relationships, and their choices in such a way as to infer further knowledge or probabilistic predictions regarding their preferences, intentions, desires, and propensities that would otherwise be hidden.

Digital processes do not stop at the inference stage but use results to influence individuals, to stimulate preferences, to influence choices, to regulate behaviors, and to implement a microphysics of governance over living beings that originates online and permeates people's freedoms and actions. This real-time action is made possible by the enormous spatial-temporal coverage of digital technologies, their immediacy and continuity, and their effectiveness and speed. The combination of large amounts of data and algorithmic learning procedures, along with the use of high-performance computing systems (the so-called supercomputers), defines a new digital governmentality capable of procedurally and automatically regulating actions and relationships and, therefore, capable of exercising forms of authority over living beings, some of which are unprecedented and sometimes based on errors inherent in the algorithms used.

Here are some real-world examples. In India, in 2018, the state of Telangana, which has a population of 35 million, implemented an algorithm to analyze public databases to identify people fraudulently claiming social benefits. According to a state investigation, at least one in 14 cases is a false positive, that is, a person who was denied benefits despite being entitled to them. The French welfare agency uses an algorithm to produce a monthly "risk" score for 13 million families. The algorithm's source code was made public for the first time in 2023 and demonstrated that people with disabilities or single mothers are particularly targeted for reductions in social benefits, while it is virtually impossible for wealthier individuals to be flagged as suspicious by the algorithm. Finally, it is worth mentioning the case of a student at Vrije University in Amsterdam who complained that Proctorio, a facial recognition software used to qualify for online exams, did not correctly recognize his face due to his skin color. The university had argued that she did not need more time to sit the exams than other students, while the Dutch Equality Committee ruled that this was not the case.

A few years ago, Antoinette Rouvroy and Thomas Berns [12] explored a technological declination of the concept of governmentality they defined as "algorithmic governmentality" to refer to a certain type of (a)normative or (a)political rationality based on the automated collection, aggregation, and analysis of large amounts of data to model, anticipate, and preemptively influence potential behaviors. In one of their papers, they wrote, "*We show that algorithmic governmentality therefore focuses not on individuals, on the subject, but on relationships.*" Data represent relationships, and knowledge represents relationships of relationships. Rouvroy and Berns' algorithmic governmentality is understood as a mode of governance fueled by the collection and analysis of raw data and metadata whose movements traverse every aspect of human life. A government that regulates relationships by operating through dependencies and classifications addresses citizens through their digital profiles, which are abstract behavioral models produced through inductive algorithmic processes. Such a governmentality is based on the ideology of Big Data and its analysis, fueled by quantifiable, intrapersonal signals that allow us to describe, anticipate, and influence potential behaviors: a government of individuals through stimuli that act on their reflexes rather than their will. The "subject" of algorithmic governmentality is therefore a "statistical body" that defines the individual, the "datafied" individual, or the class of individuals with similar characteristics through the analysis of their data. And since online data on living beings are updated as they live, their profiles can be continuously updated and recalculated, becoming a multitude of profiles expressed in probabilistic forms.

To explain algorithmic governmentality, Antoinette Rouvroy [13] recalls a passage by Felix Guattari [14] that refers to the world of signs and the machines that manage them in capitalist societies: "*The whole fabric of the capitalist world consists of this kind of flux of de-territorialized signs, money and economic signs, prestige signs, and so on. Significations, social values (those one can interpret, that is) can be seen at the level of power formations, but essentially capitalism depends upon non-signifying machines. ... A-signifying machines do not recognize agents, individuals, roles or even clearly defined objects. By this very fact they acquire a kind of omnipotence, moving across the signification systems within which individual agents recognize and become alienated from one another.*" The governmentality defined by Rouvroy and Berns can therefore be considered one of the possible forms of digital governmentality, specifically the one based on Big Data, which acts through the governance of aggregated data networks in the form of predictive models, which embody the potential of individuals and the economic and/or social opportunity detected in real time, finalized through the streamlining and objectification of automated decision-making processes.

This governance of data and its predictions serves the governance of living beings; that is, it becomes a form of digital governmentality understood as the governance of human beings that "*is exercised positively over life, aiming to control it, augment it, and multiply it*" through data management and the execution of algorithms that process those data for the purpose of governing personal feelings, political relationships, and social relations, while also making use of the countless digital devices that completely envelop our planet and our people. What Rouvroy calls "*the economy of reputation, risk, and opportunity (rather than project)*" built around Big Data and algorithms has in fact for some time been a digital governmentality project that controls, amplifies, and manipulates the lives of individuals and their relationships. It builds influences and connections that serve the objectives of power and governance, which are realized in tacit, opaque, and codified forms in hardware/software systems that operate transparently but effectively [15]. Again, the assertion that "*algorithmic governmentality (a process of pure optimization) is wordless, lifeless, and subjectless indicates sufficiently that it is uninhabited and uninhabitable*" [13] is only partially true. The digital universe is uninhabitable, but it is inhabited, and digital governmentality is not wordless and subjectless. On the contrary, the flow of data intended to replace bodies, i.e., people, is generated by them, constructed from their relationships, and used, sometimes by "legal" governments and often by the "private" governments of digital giants (extra-state entities), to control and define the forms and spaces of governance over individuals' lives.

## 17.4 Governmentality and Artificial Intelligence

The economic-political systems that govern most advanced democratic nations and also some totalitarian states, such as China, use digital governmentality to implement strategies capable of regulating the governance of economic and social processes, as well as the management of individual life processes, and eliminating from it anything that might undermine it, introduce contradictory elements, or threaten it. According to the algorithmic governmentality of data analysis, power approaches and interacts with individuals (manages them) no longer on the basis of their actual capabilities but rather on those extracted from their profiles (such as professional, fraudster, athlete, consumer, potential terrorist, brilliant student, or influential person).

However, this scenario described by Rouvroy and Berns does not exhaust the scope of the new governmentality that digital technology is capable of deploying. There are at least two additional and distinct issues to consider, two primary elements of digital governmentality that complement each other. On the one hand, there are the regulatory and control capabilities that algorithms can exert on our reality and our existences, influencing decisions, implementing control measures, identifying correlations, and making predictions. On the other, there is the impact that manifestations of digital governmentality can have on our minds, which concerns the ways, actions, choices, and desires influenced/regulated through codified procedures (such as worldviews) that depend on available data and can be processed to substantiate the decisions and actions of algorithms that influence the decisions and actions of the subjects on/with whom the algorithms operate/interact.

Digital governmentality, therefore, means not only governing individuals and groups based on the data they generate but also disciplining their spaces of action through provisions updated by pervasive and continuous software procedures and acting on their minds by governing choices, aspirations, empathy, and professional and romantic relationships through algorithmic procedures executed by digital devices, be they, for example, simple smartphones or complex cloud platforms. This codified governmentality sustains itself in daily operations but, at the same time, deprives us of spaces for autonomy, even anticipating and enveloping us in an increasingly "procedurally intelligent" environment capable of offering itself instantaneously to us. Thus, it limits our ability to desire and predict and makes us available to follow, almost submissively and certainly conditioned, the automatic and adaptive machines that are the offspring of a code that modifies and adapts to the data that someone provides or collects from time to time.

Therefore, to go beyond what was proposed by Rouvroy and Berns and actualize Foucault's original insight, digital neo-governmentality is not built solely on the pervasive collection of data and the construction of datafied probabilistic subjects but becomes the regulated production of behaviors, opinions, conduct, and relationships through the digitalization of our lives. Automated procedures become subjects of government above and alongside people. Processes encoded in hardware and software are represented as objective and unquestionable choices, as regulatory operations of daily life increasingly lived alongside digital devices that help us act and without which we may no longer be able to live, to live and express the freedoms we can.

We are increasingly moving toward the procedural digitalization of the governance of individual freedoms and their relationships. The computing devices that live alongside us, while simplifying our daily operations and regulating by speeding up human interactions, inject norms into personal and collective life. Millions of individuals act through procedures conceived and developed by a few public or private entities. Digital procedures, now powered by AI systems, therefore govern millions of lives, defining their spaces of freedom and disciplining, through positive regulations, the collective existence of people who are always willing to use digital systems and the algorithms they contain to "do things" and to perform actions, according to the methods someone else has conceived, created, and made available. The digital code, at every moment of its execution in our devices and in those of the public and private authorities that host them, therefore establishes the terms and limits according to which the life of large masses of individuals is lived in cyberspace, which is now a semantically important (perhaps the most important) and temporally significant part of daily life.

Big digital companies are well aware of the impact their algorithms and platforms have on the lives of hundreds of millions of people. Meta, the social media company that owns Facebook, Instagram, and WhatsApp, has established a court-like committee of experts to evaluate decisions that are partly determined by the programming of their systems. A relatively new technology sector, cryptocurrencies, has embraced the concept of "code as law," with some companies explicitly arguing that software with its programmed codes can be a better arbiter than traditional regulators. Indeed, many of those working on blockchain-based systems believe a very near future is possible in which the so-called "smart contracts," which allow for automated, preprogrammed agreement-making, will be the systems best suited to meet the commercial and legal negotiation needs of humans. These systems already handle billions of dollars in financial transactions every day, without any need for human intervention.

This is just one of many cases in which software systems with their associated hardware can regulate and implement social values. Developers decide how the code operates on people's behalf, how it carries out their tasks, and how it regulates their interactions. Digital governmentality currently requires us to play a minimal role in its decisions (e.g., some national laws, the European GDPR and AI Act, and privacy regulations). Individually, we do not have the freedom to determine how these encoded digital values regulate our spaces of freedom. We do not have the ability to influence programmers to determine how they can encode software systems to incorporate our values or to determine individually (or rather collectively) how our relationships should be governed and how our lives should be regulated. These options are not available to the supply drivers whose daily deliveries are governed by Just Eat and Deliveroo's algorithms, nor are they available to the workers who interact with robots in many factories or to the Amazon employees who must cooperate with the automatons that arrange products for shipment in department stores.

In these cases, and many others, the values encoded in the algorithms are those defined by the software owners and their customers, not the individuals who must interact with that software or who must comply with the decisions it frequently makes. Digital architectures govern the space of living beings, constantly shrinking and expanding it. In any case, they delimit it through their rapid and continuous actions, which substantiate values in the form of sequences of programmed instructions that can also have harmful or exciting consequences, both practically and in terms of freedom. Despite their broad influence, there are no rules that allow people who interact with digital systems to express their opinions on the logic encoded within them and to determine, for example through democratic forms, the logic, operation, and choices of algorithms that often imperatively act on people, both personally and collectively.

Digital technologies, including artificial intelligence systems, are increasingly becoming tools for regulating citizens' actions, granting and depriving them of freedom of action and choice. This has led to new forms of governmentality in which the code of AI algorithms threatens people's freedom and allows automated decisions to be made. Even when they expand human choice, these decisions constitute a form of alienation, granting those who implement the underlying digital procedures a new level of governance. For example, the code of machine learning algorithms is increasingly becoming the entity that establishes the terms by which people's lives are lived, not only in the digital space but also in the physical space of their lives, thus eliminating even the last remaining barriers between these two spaces, which are destined to be completely demolished.

In particular, AI represents the ultimate and most advanced form of rationality that humans have ever imagined and is poised to become a powerful tool for organizing the exercise of human governance, made up of sophisticated and lightweight yet incredibly powerful and fast mechanisms. Digital governmentality can find, for example, forms of expression in generative AI systems based on gigantic information sources and a capacity for articulating discourse equal to, if not superior to, human ability. Thanks to these capabilities, AI is becoming a key element in the implementation of governmentality in the societies of the new millennium, where the balance of personal and collective freedoms can be managed through advanced AI systems. These systems will acquire ever-greater authority and influence as the various political, economic, and social powers become more aware of their potential and, at the same time, their deductive, reasoning, and decision-making abilities become increasingly accurate and convincing.

## 17.5 Some Final Observations

Governmentality adapts to the times and evolves its forms of expression as the historical, economic, and technological context changes. Digital codes change rapidly. And as they change, so too will the way they are used to regulate power and to define new disciplinary forms. The space defined by digital technologies, most recently by AI, is evolving to become a place where private and public relations are deployed and thus also a place for regulating individual power relations and governance.

Digital technologies and their codes regulate personal lives and society. They implement values, analyses, processes, relationships, and processing. They enable or disable freedoms. They can protect privacy or promote its monitoring. Specialists, programmers, and users all together constitute the regulatory and regulated elements of digital governmentality. This is a scenario that deserves attention and analysis to understand how the governance of individuals' spaces of action and freedom is articulated and actualized individually and collectively through the increasingly widespread digital solutions.

## References

1. Foucault, M. (1978). La governamentalità. *Aut-Aut*, 28, pp. 167–168 (in Italian).
2. Foucault, M. (2008). *The History of Sexuality: The Will to Knowledge*. USA: Penguin.
3. Foucault, M. (2010). *The Birth of Biopolitics: Lectures at the College De France 1978-1979*. USA: Picador.
4. Han, B.-C. (2025). *Psychopolitics: Neoliberalism and New Technologies of Power*. UK: Verso Books.
5. Danaher, J. (2016). The threat of algocracy: Reality, resistance and accommodation. *Philosophy & Technology*, 29(3), pp. 245–268.
6. Lessig, L. (2006). *Code and Other Laws of Cyberspace – Version 2.0*. USA: Basic Books.
7. van Dijck, J., Poell, T., and de Waal, M. (2018). *The Platform Society: Public Values in a Connective World*. UK: Oxford University Press.
8. Talia, D. (2019). *Big Data and the Computable Society: Algorithms and People in the Digital World*. UK: World Scientific Publishing.
9. Eubanks, V. (2018). *Automating Inequality: How High-Tech Tools Profile, Police, and Punish the Poor*. USA: St. Martin's Press.
10. Zuboff, S. (2019). *The Age of Surveillance Capitalism: The Fight for a Human Future at the New Frontier of Power*. UK: Public Affairs.
11. Talia, D. (2021). *L'impero dell'algoritmo – L'intelligenza delle macchine e la forma del futuro*. Italy: Rubbettino (in Italian).
12. Rouvroy, A. and Berns, T. (2013). Algorithmic governmentality and prospects of emancipation. *Réseaux*, 177(1), pp. 163–196.

13. Rouvroy, A. (2016). La governamentalità algoritmica: radicalizzazione e strategia immunitaria del capitalismo e del neoliberalismo? *La Deleuziana – Rivista Online di Filosofia*, 3 (in Italian).
14. Guattari, F. (1984). *Molecular Revolution: Psychiatry and Politics*. UK: Penguin.
15. Pasquale, F. (2015). *The Black Box Society: The Secret Algorithms That Control Money and Information*. USA: Harvard University Press.

# Chapter 18

# Artificial Justice

*The tyranny of a prince in an oligarchy is not so dangerous to the public welfare as the apathy of a citizen in a democracy.*
—Charles Louis de Secondat, baron de La Brède et de Montesquieu

"Would you accept to be judged by AI?" – this was the question printed on top of the billboard announcing the movie *Artificial Justice* [1]. It is a political thriller screening a near future in Spain when the government proposes a national referendum to approve the use of an artificial intelligence software system to replace human judges in the national justice system. The story, set in 2028, follows Carmen Costa, a distinguished judge who is invited to assess and endorse the new AI system called THENTE 1. When the software's creator mysteriously disappears, Carmen Costa realizes that powerful political and private lobbies are carrying out a conspiracy to manipulate the AI system for controlling citizens. To reach this goal, the government calls a referendum for this AI system to be fully implemented in the Administration of Justice, effectively replacing judges, to automate and "depoliticize" justice. The judge is invited to work on the development of the project, but the disappearance of the creator of the system caused great suspicion in her, to the point of understanding that she is discovering an intrigue aiming to control, from justice, the entire country.

The question "Would you accept to be judged by AI?" today is not only a slogan for a movie. It is becoming a serious question that may involve all of us. Indeed, in several countries AI-assisted legal procedures and decisions have been introduced with effects that are not always positive. We are witnessing the new role of AI in the legal systems of many countries and the significant influence this disruptive technology is exerting and will exercise on the management and implementation of the law. The impact of AI on law will soon be a crucial element for the administration of justice in the world and therefore for the freedoms of citizens [2].

In this rapidly advancing scenario, the movie directed by Simón Casal is a brilliant film that brings the debate about the use of AI in the justice sector into a fascinating narrative format. On the same topic, Mathias Risse, in his book titled *Political Theory of the Digital Age* [3], analyzes the main challenges posed by digital technologies (including AI, big data, and connectivity) to the key concepts of justice, democracy, and political legitimacy. Risse discusses the so-called "*Grand Democratic AI Utopia*," aiming to provide a theoretical framework for understanding how worldwide digital transformations affect our lives and political communities. Concerning justice, he envisages that judges are replaced by "*sophisticated algorithms delivering even-handed rulings*." These AI systems can be set such that concerns about the functionality and role of AI in human affairs are resolved by their learning algorithms. In such ways, enormous amounts of time are (or could be) freed up for people to design their lives meaningfully. Risse wrote that "*nobody has so far seriously proposed anything like this,*" and signaled that we would be "*ill advised to be guided by such a utopia.*" However, his book was published in 2023, and fantasies of a *Grand Democratic AI Utopia* have appeared frequently since.

## 18.1 Lawyers Who Don't Know About AI

If we move from fantasy to reality, we can find confirmation of the concerns regarding the harm that the use of AI in the judicial field can cause. In the spring of 2023, Colombian airline Avianca Airlines faced a trial in the United States in which its client, Roberto Mata, sued the airline for being struck by a service cart on board the plane during a 2019 flight from El Salvador to New York, resulting in serious injuries. In filing their lawsuit, Mata's lawyers, Steven Schwartz and Peter LoDuca of the New York law firm Levidow, Levidow & Oberman, cited at least six other similar cases to demonstrate the existence of judgments against the airlines, including Varghese v. China Southern Airlines and Shaboon v. Egypt Air. The court searched the records of the cited cases and found that those cases never actually existed. They were simply "*false court decisions with false citations.*" As a result, the US District Judge P. Kevin Castel in Manhattan ordered lawyers Steven Schwartz, Peter LoDuca, and their law firm to pay a $5,000 fine in total.

The error occurred because Schwartz had used ChatGPT to conduct legal research for his court filings, which referenced cases the generative AI tool assured him were real. Indeed, following the investigation, Steven Schwartz signed a sworn statement admitting to using the AI chatbot, stating that he had no intention of deceiving the court and that he had not acted in bad faith. The lawyer stated that he was mortified upon learning that the cases he cited were fake, adding that when he used the software tool, "*he didn't realize it wasn't a search engine, but a generative language processing tool.*"

Schwartz explained that he had never used ChatGPT to conduct legal research or write his arguments before that case and that he learned about the technology from his college-going children. He added that he had read articles about the benefits of AI in professional settings and how those tools "*could make legal research obsolete.*" Naturally, Judge Kevin Castel was not convinced by the lawyer's naivety and imposed the fine on him. The judge declared there was nothing "inherently improper" about using AI systems as a support in legal work, but lawyers had to guarantee their filings were accurate. Castel wrote, "*Technological advances are commonplace and there is nothing inherently improper about using a reliable artificial intelligence tool for assistance, … But existing rules impose a gatekeeping role on attorneys to ensure the accuracy of their filings.*"

In his ruling, the judge also established that the two lawyers had to inform the judges, all real, whose names appeared in the legal brief as the authors of the false sentences invented by ChatGPT, by sending them a copy of the lawyers' conviction.

Although several incidents involving generative AI, like that of Attorney Schwartz, have occurred in various courts around the world, lawyers are increasingly using these systems in their profession. For example, generative AI is increasingly used by US law firms to assist or optimize the decision of whether to accept a client and take on a case.

The firm's goal is threefold: maximize the probability of a profitable outcome, minimize the risk of conflicts of interest, and optimize resource allocation.

Predictive success analysis is the most strategic use. In this case, AI does not determine the legal validity of a case but rather calculates its economic and judicial probability of success. This relies heavily on tools such as Lex Machina proprietary tools or similar AI software systems. For risk assessment, AI systems analyze data provided by the potential clients, jurisdiction, opposing counsel, and requested damages and compare them against a large number of historical case outcomes. Examples of questions to be responded to for the firm are: "How likely is a particular judge to rule in favor of the plaintiff/defendant in this type of claim?" or "What is the average settlement or damages range similar cases have historically achieved?" If the prediction of success is under a given threshold, or if the estimated return does not justify the attorney's billable hours, the case may be filtered out and potentially rejected.

In the US, several firms that manage a high volume of inquiries also use AI to prioritize potential clients. Tools such as LegalClerk.ai are common in this task. Their slogan is, "Never miss a new client with our AI legal Answering Service." Conflict of interest checking is a mandatory step for every law firm, and AI software makes it faster and more comprehensive. AI tools rapidly scan the firm's internal databases to ensure accepting a new client will not create a conflict of interest with any current or past client. This reduces the ethical and legal risk for the firm, preventing costly errors that could result in disqualification from a case.

Many legal firms stress that AI does not make the final decision to accept or reject a client. However, although the decision always rests with the human partner or responsible attorney, without a doubt, the informed suggestions made by the AI algorithms that law firms now use significantly determine the final decisions and significantly influence their client support strategies.

## 18.2 Is Justice Embracing AI?

Despite the serious problem that occurred during the Avianca Airlines trial, as well as in other similar cases in Europe and other continents, generative AI is spreading in judicial settings across several countries. While AI tools will bring greater efficiency to several cases, they cannot be completely ruled out as a potential source of new problems and will require unprecedented solutions that must be adopted to ensure that "artificial justice" is no worse than the human justice we have known to date.

A significant example of ChatGPT being used in courtrooms comes from Argentina. In May 2024, the Buenos Aires City Prosecutor's Office began using generative AI to predict and generate rulings in several labor law disputes involving wage claims. Employees of the Buenos Aires City Attorney's Office for Administrative and Tax Matters uploaded case documents to ChatGPT, asking it to analyze the texts' content, perform a preliminary classification from a catalog of ruling templates, and compile decisions for submission to the judges. ChatGPT has thus far been used for several dozen rulings. Apparently, the use of generative AI has reduced the time needed to draft a ruling from an hour to about ten minutes.

"*We, as professionals, are no longer the main characters. We have become editors,*" is a striking statement made by Juan Corvalán, Deputy Attorney General of Buenos Aires in the Contentious Administrative and Tax Office. The introduction of generative AI tools has obviously improved the office's efficiency, but it has also raised concerns within the Argentine judiciary and among legal experts about potential bias, the handling of personal data, and the emergence of hallucinations in systems such as ChatGPT, as New York attorney Schwartz learned the hard way. These concerns are clearly spreading to the justice sector beyond Argentina's borders.

There are concerns that any inaccurate or incorrect use could result in considerable legal costs. Several judges in the US have expressed skepticism about the use of generative AI in courts. To cite just one example among many, Manhattan federal judge Edgardo Ramos stated that "*ChatGPT has proven to be an unreliable resource.*" In Colombia and the Netherlands, judges' use of ChatGPT and other AI chatbots has been criticized by several local experts. But not everyone affected by the impact of generative AI is concerned. For example, some UK Court of Appeal judges who used ChatGPT to write part of a ruling said they found it very useful.

Returning to Argentina, Judge Corvalán is well aware that the move to the use of generative AI systems is the next step in a transformation that has been ongoing for several years within the Buenos Aires Attorney General's Office. Indeed, back in 2017, Corvalán assembled a team of computer scientists and legal experts, including those from the Laboratory of Innovation and Artificial Intelligence at the Faculty of Law of the

University of Buenos Aires, to train Prometea, an AI system designed to automate judicial activities and speed up legal proceedings by classifying different cases and providing support for judges' decisions. The team led by Corvalán used over 300,000 civil case decisions and related case files to classify them and use them as examples for subsequent decisions. The cases it was used for varied little, and the resolutions tended to be standardized. In a short time, the office's productivity increased by nearly 300%, with legal professionals able to process approximately 490 cases per month, compared to approximately 130 previously.

Prometea, according to a report from the city's public prosecutor's office, predicted sentencing outcomes with 96% accuracy in less than 20 seconds. Of course, the system's efficiency came at a cost: Each new category of crime for which Prometea was used required additional training and development of new algorithms. Approximately seven years after its introduction, in early 2024, Corvalán began phasing out Prometea in favor of ChatGPT. The sentences drafted with the help of ChatGPT were all reviewed by a lawyer and approved by the deputy prosecutor. The Argentine judiciary is now considering expanding the program to other units, including the procurement office, and to other Argentine prosecutor's offices, such as those in Rosario.

Generative AI systems will gradually find their way into prosecutors' offices and courtrooms. However, errors, biases, and hallucinations are lurking around the corner, and it takes expertise and utmost care to avoid them. One of the main problems with these systems is the reliability of the information used and produced by generative models. The team led by Judge Corvalán is well aware that it must work carefully to limit the various risks associated with artificial intelligence models, not least those related to privacy, digital data theft, and cyberattacks.

According to a recent study from Stanford University, hallucinations in systems like ChatGPT could pose significant legal risks, and approximately 17% of cases in which these systems are used in legal settings generate false, inappropriate, or irrelevant information. This percentage is still too high and unacceptable for any judicial system. The road to widespread use of generative AI in courts is still uncertain and bumpy, even though the impetus to pursue it is strong. It will take attention, expertise, legal and technical expertise, and professionalism to achieve widespread use of these systems without causing harm. Otherwise, AI-assisted justice will be faster but more unjust than what humans have been able to deliver to date.

## 18.3 How the World Is Dealing with Artificial Justice

According to the International Bar Association survey on AI and the legal profession, *The Future is Now: Artificial Intelligence and the Legal Profession* [4], lawyers agree on the importance of due diligence in ensuring compliance with ethical rules, even when using AI. In Europe, the New Technologies Commission of the Association of European Bar Associations (Fédération des Barreaux d'Europe) has developed certain guidelines for lawyers to make the most of the opportunities offered by large-scale linguistic models and generative AI, but emphasized that lawyers must assume responsibility for the outcomes. The same principles underpin the documents for the informed use of IA tools in the forensic field.

It must be clarified that in the EU, legal decisions cannot be automated. This is clearly established by the European AI Act (EU Regulation 2024/1689) and reiterated in national bills of EU countries (e.g., Spain, France, and Italy). In short, no machine can ever replace human judgment on facts, evidence, and the law. The judicial sector, in fact, has been classified among the highest-risk areas in the European AI Act: It requires transparency, oversight, and strengthened safeguards. At stake is the delicate balance between technological efficiency and the protection of fundamental rights. Even in the United Kingdom, the use of AI systems is permitted with strong caution: The judiciary has published guidelines that allow its use only for document summaries and drafts.

In the US, courts use the Correctional Offender Management Profiling for Alternative Sanctions (COMPAS) system, which estimates the likelihood of defendants reoffending. COMPAS's accuracy rate does not exceed 68%, a low percentage for guiding decisions such as granting probation. Researchers from the University of Houston found that COMPAS does not conform to group fairness criteria and produces various unfair outcomes across sex- and race-based groups [5]. Also, researchers from Williams College found that COMPAS in Broward County led to a reduced rate of confinement across demographic groups but that the use of the algorithm worsened differences in confinement between racial groups, thereby increasing racial disparity [6].

In China, the approach is completely different. They employ extensive automation, including national platforms, automatic draft generation, and digital court services, all integrated with a vast amount of court data used in centralized AI infrastructures. In Brazil, the VICTOR AI system automates the examination of appeals to the Supreme Court by identifying cases with "general repercussions," a requirement for processing appeals. While a court judge takes about one hour to evaluate whether an appeal meets conditions to move forward, VICTOR spends a couple of seconds. In addition, Brazil's Superior Council of Labor Justice launched Chat-JT, a generative AI tool that assists judges, court staff, and interns by automating tasks such as document analysis and the drafting of standardized summaries. This AI platform also allows users to create personalized assistants tailored to specific needs within the judicial workflow. We must mention that the VICTOR system is based on convolutional neural networks that do not provide readable and explainable outcomes.

Finally, Colombia's PretorIA system assists the Constitutional Court in managing the high volume of custodianship cases, or legal actions filed to protect human rights. This system is inspired by Prometea, the AI tool discussed earlier used in the Buenos Aires Attorney General's Office. With over 600,000 custodianships ("tutelas") received annually, PretorIA aids this procedure by processing approximately 4,500 cases daily. The system helps pre-select cases for review by detecting predefined legal criteria. Ensuring human oversight and explainability has been a key priority, and PretorIA was redesigned in 2020 to use interpretable topic modelling rather than opaque neural networks. However, judges remain the final decision-makers, maintaining human authority over case selection.

Despite the goal of having humans as final decision-makers, it is appropriate to consider that in administrative and small claims settings, generative AI systems are moving closer to substitution. For example, China established specialized Internet Courts to handle digital disputes, such as those related to e-commerce or digital copyright. These courts use AI systems to process evidence, manage dockets, and provide preliminary judgments on minor cases, especially those relying heavily on contractual language. In some of these cases, human judges simply ratify the AI's recommendations. Similar cases occurred in Estonia, a country highly advanced in e-governance. Estonian courts have piloted systems aimed at using AI to resolve small claims disputes, under a specific financial threshold, where the evidence is primarily documentary. The goal is to have an AI act as a "robot judge" to clear the court backlog for low-stakes disputes.

## 18.4 With AI We Will Decide Less

Many artificial tools have been invented by humans to improve our experience of perceiving reality, to understand it better, to know more, and thus to make our lives easier. A complete list would be impossible. But it's enough to stop and think about a few of them to recall how inventions have changed our horizon of knowledge and the destiny of humanity. Let's just consider two inventions we have been using for centuries: the telescope and the microscope. They are just two tools but capable of changing the way humans have observed and understood reality. For about 400 years, these devices have helped (augmented) our senses and our brains in observing the reality around us and in addressing and solving certain problems we face (from studying the cosmos to investigating viruses).

With AI systems, we are faced with a new form of flexible *techné*, capable of being both a microscope and a telescope. Therefore, it is capable of showing us the invisible that lies before us, along with the invisible that lies far away. AI systems and algorithms are providing us with a new perception of reality, sometimes different from what our senses can perceive. Other times, it is simply more detailed but still useful for understanding things and phenomena that we cannot fully comprehend with the tools Mother Nature has provided us.

Obviously, we must be very careful not to give in to hubris, to the presumption of feeling beyond measure powerful because of these extraordinary technologies. We must understand that error is always lurking, even in courtrooms, for these new systems, which, like us, are limited. They represent a great step forward in investigating reality and solving many problems, but they present limitations and risks that must not be ignored.

In particular, we must also pay attention to the knowledge, the ability to acquire and use it, that we humans will lose precisely because of the widespread and intensive use of AI tools. Their ability to process vast amounts of data and provide solutions extremely quickly pushes us to use them increasingly frequently and in an ever-expanding set of questions that affect almost every aspect of our daily lives. Computers and their software systems have replaced humans in many tasks, and through the use of AI systems, they are also being used to solve problems that until now only humans could solve. Justice is just one of the several contexts where this is occurring.

This trend will soon lead humans to unlearn how to perform many of the tasks they once performed and to make fewer decisions than AI now makes for us. We are beginning to witness a sort of alienation of knowledge that transfers know-how from humans to machines and removes skills, knowledge, choices, and decision-making abilities. Similar processes have occurred throughout human history, but perhaps for the first time, they concern the deepest human intellectual abilities.

The many problem-solving skills that AI systems are learning, and what they do for people on a daily basis, also acting as artificial judges, will inevitably lead to a loss of human skills and decision-making abilities, which, for convenience, will gradually be passed on to machines. This creates a sort of reversal, according to which, through complex AI systems, humans will certainly know more and be able to do more, but at the same time, they will decide less, and in times when they cannot use these systems in the future, they will be somewhat impaired.

As humans, we will inevitably become less skilled, less capable, and less autonomous because we increasingly rely on the knowledge of algorithms. To limit this partly unavoidable scenario, we should cultivate our reasoning and decision-making abilities, avoiding, whenever possible, complete reliance on digital machines. We should do so even in the many small actions and choices we can make without them. We should cultivate human skills for the many things we know how to do and for the many things we need to continue to decide without relying entirely on the digital systems that pervade our days and that will increasingly be used to generate knowledge instead of us humans.

We are increasingly faced with AI systems that make choices for us, convince us, and replace us in decision-making, not only in legal settings. They do so to help us, but at the same time, they further subtract from our free will. The algorithms that execute the operations of AI systems are becoming increasingly prescriptive, determining many of our actions and deciding what is best for us. All of this will lead to an excessive dependence on AI, which could make individuals and societies vulnerable and erode their ability to analyze problems, critically view reality, and make decisions. Many say that, in the face of the great transformations imposed by AI, we must remain human. To ensure this does not remain an empty slogan, we must act to learn not to rely entirely on these new technologies, educating people, especially young people, to use them wisely while also cultivating their own knowledge acquisition and decision-making skills.

## References


1. Latido Films. Artificial Justice. https://latidofilms.com/films/artificial-justice/ [Retrieved 15 December 2025].
2. Marwala, T. and Mpedi, L. G. (2024). *Artificial Intelligence and the Law*. Singapore: Palgrave MacMillan.
3. Risse, M. (2023). *Political Theory of the Digital Age: Where Artificial Intelligence Might Take Us*. USA: Cambridge University Press.
4. International Bar Association, Center for AI and Digital Policy. (2024). *The Future Is Now: Artificial Intelligence and the Legal Profession*. UK: International Bar Association.
5. Gursoy, F. and Kakadiaris, I. A. (2022). Equal confusion fairness: Measuring group-based disparities in automated decision systems. *IEEE International Conference on Data Mining Workshops (ICDMW)*. USA: IEEE, pp. 137–146.
6. Bahl, U., Topaz, C., Obermüller, L., Goldstein, S., and Sneirson, M. (2024). Algorithms in judges' hands: Incarceration and inequity in Broward County, Florida. *UCLA Law Review*, pp. 246–278.

# Chapter 19

# From Learning Machines to Artificial General Intelligence

*The real promise of AI is not automation, it is augmentation, helping humans to think and create in ways we've never imagined.*

—Kai-Fu Lee

To paraphrase an old and famous saying, we could say that "*A spectre is haunting the world – the spectre of Artificial General Intelligence.*" Although, over the past decade, artificial intelligence has made unexpected and extraordinary progress, its future is even more promising. The next decade could be the time of artificial general intelligence (AGI) systems that may reach the level of human intelligence, thus becoming capable of solving any problem a human being can solve. The idea of AGI has long been a topic of fascination in both science fiction and academic research, representing the crucial goal of AI development. More recently, it appears to be a reachable objective that may change the history of humankind. Indeed, several prominent researchers and entrepreneurs in the AI fields, speak of AGI using terms once reserved for the divine.

Proponents of concepts such as AGI and human-level intelligence don't often agree on how to define them; however, they roughly refer to a hypothetical future date at which AI may reach human-level intelligence, potentially causing fast and irrevocable changes to society. Computer scientists such as Ray Kurzweil went beyond the AGI concept and predicted that humans will one day merge with technology, implementing the model often called "transhumanism" [1]. Kurzweil borrowed the term "singularity" from mathematics and physics to describe a future scenario where human intelligence capabilities will merge with computer intelligence capabilities, producing the expansion of our intelligence and consciousness until reaching an extraordinary capacity. Kurzweil argues that in 2045, non-biological intelligence will become a billion times more powerful than all human biological intelligence combined. On the other hand, other more realistic researchers, such as Max Tegmark, think that with policies and safeguards, AI will be used as a very powerful instrument to cure diseases and increase human productivity [2]. However, he recommended staying away from the extreme race of "*the pseudo religious pursuit to try to build an alternative God.*"

Generally, we may consider three main types of AI across a spectrum of capabilities:

- **Narrow AI (weak AI):** Specialized for single tasks (e.g., AlphaGo, ChatGPT, and facial recognition). It represents current AI systems.
- **Artificial general intelligence (strong AI or human-level AI):** Capable of matching human intellectual ability across all tasks. It is the next major milestone.
- **Artificial superintelligence (ASI):** Capable of exceeding human intellectual ability across all tasks. It may be the ultimate stage.

Basically, AGI, if reached, could be the baseline for a hypothetical superintelligence that can be exponentially enhanced upon to become superhuman. The philosopher Nick Bostrom provided a definition of superintelligence as follows: "*Any intellect that greatly exceeds the cognitive performance of humans in virtually all domains of interest.*" It should combine a large number of human and/or AI intellects that are merged together to be smarter than human beings or AI systems [3]. Superintelligence received significant interest not only from researchers but also from entrepreneurs. In 2024, Ilya Sutskever, co-founder of OpenAI, announced the creation of the new company Safe Superintelligence Inc. (SSI), he founded with Daniel Gross and Daniel Levy. Sutskever declared that its "*first product will be the safe Superintelligence, and it will not do anything else up until then.*" The company website (ssi.inc) displays just a brief text that includes this sentence: "*We have started the world's first straight-shot SSI lab, with one goal and one product: a safe Superintelligence.*" One year later,

Mark Zuckerberg, the chief executive of Meta, had sought to acquire SSI, but Ilya Sutskever refused the acquisition. Then, Zuckerberg announced that Meta established Meta Superintelligence Labs, focused on research and development in the field of ASI.

These disruptive theories are coming from concepts and hypotheses investigated in the past decades. In the early 1950s, John McCarthy became an assistant professor of mathematics at Stanford. In 1955, he moved to Dartmouth College, where, together with Minsky, Rochester, and Shannon, he proposed the Dartmouth Summer Research Project on Artificial Intelligence that was held in 1956 [4]. On that occasion, he introduced the name "artificial intelligence" and, with his colleagues, proposed a study "*to proceed on the basis of the conjecture that every aspect of learning or any other feature of intelligence can in principle be so precisely described that a machine can be made to simulate it. An attempt will be made to find how to make machines use language, form abstractions and concepts, solve kinds of problems now reserved for humans, and improve themselves.*"

In 1971, John McCarthy was the recipient of the ACM Turing Award, and he gave a lecture titled "Generality in Artificial Intelligence." In his speech [5], he recognized that in 1971, AI programs suffered from a lack of generality. He argued that no researcher knows how to make a general archive of commonsense knowledge that could be used by any program that needed the knowledge. He added, "*In my opinion, getting a language for expressing general commonsense knowledge or inclusion in a general database is the key problem of generality in AI.*" McCarthy was thinking to express commonsense knowledge in logic, whereas, on the contrary, today commonsense knowledge is collected and organized in machine learning systems through massive training processes that aid them to learn how to generalize. Generality is still a key principle for moving from weak AI toward AGI. However, it remains to be seen whether machine learning and generative AI will be the appropriate starting models for achieving AGI.

The distinction between strong AI and weak AI dates back to John Searle [6], who proposed two models of AI. The first, which Searle called strong AI, holds that an AI system can contain a mind (i.e., have consciousness and intentionality). The second, weak AI, holds that machines act as if they were intelligent and had a mind. For Searle, the claim of strong AI would be that the appropriately programmed digital computer has a mind, while weak AI considers computers to be tools for simulating human intelligence and does not believe that they have a mind. In his paper Searle wrote, "*According to weak AI, the principal value of the computer in the study of the mind is that it gives us a very powerful tool. ... But according to strong AI, the computer is not merely a tool in the study of the mind; rather, the appropriately programmed computer really is a mind, in the sense that computers given the right programs can be literally said to understand and have other cognitive states*" [6].

## 19.1 Looking into Artificial General Intelligence

As mentioned before, the main ambitious objective of strong AI is creating hardware/software machines with a generalized learning and solving capability, enabling them to adapt and apply knowledge across diverse areas. AGI is a key research topic because it is a major shift from specialized intelligence to a more flexible, human-like form of machine reasoning. The development of AGI could generate great changes in society, potentially solving highly complex problems and, at the same time, will raise ethical and existential fears.

A key feature of AGI is its aptitude for human-like understanding and reasoning. This includes the ability for context analysis, grasping multifaceted concepts and knowledge, and general problem-solving. Strong AI would possess advanced learning and adaptability. It would not only improve its performance over time but also learn from a diverse collection of experiences. This continuous self-improvement would enable AGI to handle new challenges and adapt to evolving environments without needing explicit reprogramming. The ability to assimilate and apply knowledge from various sources would make AGI highly proficient in dynamic and complex scenarios.

Academic discussions and studies about AGI are also devoted to exploring the AI potential for consciousness and self-awareness. This is a highly debated argument in recent years. The idea is that AGI could hypothetically exhibit a form of awareness or self-reflection similar to human consciousness. This issue raises fundamental questions not only among computer scientists about the nature of intelligence but also the ethical implications of creating machines that might express self-awareness. Weak AI systems are effective at their specialized tasks but are limited by their inability to adapt to different contexts and provide solutions beyond their specific capabilities. We can define adaptability in AGI as the ability of an AI system to function effectively in new, different, and unpredictable environments without needing to change or update its logic. Adaptability is also the ability to take a skill learned in one area and apply to a completely different one. Therefore, adaptability it also requires the AI system to think about its own thinking.

Private companies, public research centers, and universities are carrying out research activities in the field of AGI and researchers are facing several challenges in providing AGI theories and developments. For example, limitations in data availability represent an obstacle, as AGI systems require large and different datasets to train effectively. The required high computational power is another barrier, as AGI demands massive computing and storage resources. On the application side, the introduction of AGI could lead to noteworthy economic and production changes, including improved productivity and new industries. However, it may also produce job replacement as AI automated systems potentially replace human functions in many sectors.

Some researchers expressed doubts about the ability of large language models to scale for achieving the generality needed by AGI. Some of them, including Yann LeCun and Fei-Fei Li, are working on the so-called "World Model" as a more powerful AI framework, which could be suitable for reaching AGI. Finally, ethical concerns about AGI are a key concern, including the prospective impact of AGI on human freedom, privacy, and decision-making self-sufficiency.

In 2022, LeCun wrote a paper in which he discussed the evolution of AI models [7]. He argued that we need machines that understand not only our language but also all the physical world where we live. Those machines should be controllable and safe for human beings; therefore, they need to be driven by objectives we give them. The proposal by Yann LeCun was centered on the key concept of the World Model, with the goal of predicting what is going to happen in the real world. The Word Model is a sort of human-level intelligence that is not limited to generative AI, but it acts in the physical world as a human being does. According to this model, when an AI system is given a task to accomplish, using the World Model, it will conceive a way to perform the task through a set of actions that actually complete that task.

As theorized by John Searle, strong AI will have to have consciousness and intentionality [6]. We know that intelligence (the ability to achieve goals) does not necessarily require consciousness (subjective awareness). In fact, several AI systems, such as generative AI tools, are able to solve complex problems without being conscious of their capability. These weak AI systems can mimic the expression of feelings or reasoning; however, there is no scientific evidence that they have *qualia*,[1] that is the internal "what it is like" to be a conscious agent.

We don't know whether the design of conscious AI systems is within reach. However, as the development of AI systems advances and they are increasingly capable of replicating the complex mechanisms of human cognition, these systems might also implement the functions necessary for consciousness. Bengio and Elmoznino argued [8] that, despite the many AI systems that have been developed, no one meets all of the criteria for consciousness set forth in any of the leading theories [9]. However, the study they cite also concludes that there are no key barriers to implementing AI systems capable of doing this.

The goal of consciousness may stimulate some researchers and developers to provide AI systems with the self-preservation goal shared by living beings. An intelligent AI system incorporating the goal of self-preservation may act to avoid the case of humans turning it off. In doing that, it would then develop the objective to control humans or get rid of them. Ensuring human safety often requires shutting down dangerous AI, but if such systems are granted a legal right to exist, our legal authority to intervene would be severely restricted.

Conscious AI systems may represent a key transformation of life on Earth; therefore, we need to work on this scenario to implement advanced systems for assisting humans in improving their wellness, not on conscious automata having their own goals not aligned with humankind.

## 19.2 In the Near Hyperfuture

Even though we live deeply immersed in a present filled with daily commitments and anxieties, increasingly driven by powerful innovations, we find ourselves turning our thoughts to the future: to what will happen in a world shaped by new technologies. When we think about it, we are all

[1] For philosophers of mind, *qualia* represent those properties of conscious mental states or events that determine "what it is like" for the subject of those states or events to undergo them (e.g., "what it is like to enjoy the flavor of a mandarin picked directly from the tree"). Paradigm examples of *qualia* include a particular painfulness of some pain state, the sensation to be hugged, or the taste of a pizza.

touched by the feeling that the future is racing ever faster and more chaotically before us, creating a sense of difficulty in many people who are unable to keep up with its acceleration. It is a future driven by the growing desire of human beings to be more efficient, quicker at what they do, and brighter and faster in their work, travel, and relationships. And so, as the future on Earth accelerates, driven by the activities of billions of beings, individuals struggle to keep up with it – to keep pace. They can't imagine it, understand it, or be ready for the changes and innovations that fuel the future. Changes that continually transform, whether slightly or greatly, our lifestyles, our way of working, our relationships, and with them, our destiny.

Among these innovations, the technologies built around AI systems are undoubtedly those that have been shaping our future more than any other in recent years. As we have discussed throughout the book, AI has in recent years posed a historic challenge to human capabilities, to the activities that humans have implemented over millennia, and even over the past century. AI has taken on the ambition of performing well not only repetitive human jobs and activities but also intellectual functions and professions that require advanced skills and complex cognitive processes.

It should come as no surprise to anyone that AI systems are challenging not only call center workers, supermarket cashiers, and accountants, but also radiologists, lawyers, journalists, pizza makers, typographers, interpreters and translators, painters, essayists, insurance agents, and even notaries and priests. In these and other professions, for the first time, human supremacy is at risk of ending.

It is worth emphasizing that AI is not a passing fad, a marketing gimmick that will soon fade away. On the contrary, AI is here to stay and will play an increasingly larger role. Despite differing opinions and many concerns, many true experts, those who study and develop it, are beginning to have no doubt that digital machines will eventually (perhaps only in a few decades) be more capable and more intelligent than humans in many fields, and they will even train themselves. It is hard to say how long this will take. It could be a few years, it could be the end of the century, but the exponential growth in the problem-solving capabilities of digital machines is showing us that overtaking humans is no longer a science fiction story.

Today's AI is obviously not a perfect technology; that created through machine learning techniques and LLM systems has numerous limitations.

In many cases, it still exhibits non-negligible error rates, yet in many other cases, it makes fewer mistakes than humans. It is more precise in solving problems that until recently required the skills of professionals with degrees and experience. In the future, models, techniques, and algorithms may be different; perhaps they will incorporate current solutions to extend and improve them, or perhaps they will completely overturn them. Research in this field, at universities and in computing labs, is proceeding at a rapid pace and is fueled, especially by large private companies, by ever-increasing billion-dollar investments.

Today, much of our interactions with people take place through cell phones and computers, and we all interact with numerous devices, including cars, TVs, and appliances that run AI algorithms. In the medium term, interactions between humans and between them and the digital world will be increasingly mediated by numerous intelligent digital systems (chatbots, personal assistants, home automation apps, adaptive communication systems, and autonomous software capable of self-management). This intrusion of AI into our lives and the many expressions of our relationships is altering what we might call the microphysics of humanity and is introducing significant elements of artificiality into the manifestation of our being.

All of this is influencing and will increasingly influence the level of humanity and culture of people, their ways of living, working, reacting to problems, and thinking about solutions. Those who develop the many AI systems that populate our digital devices are, in effect, producing systems capable of modifying and altering the different cultures, traditions, beliefs, and lifestyles of billions of individuals.

## 19.3 Algointelligence and the Human Factor

Everyone seems to agree that human control must be maintained over every decision made by intelligent machines. Yet, no one seems to notice that the AI systems being developed and used often don't require our intervention or control. They are "closed boxes" that act on their own, and we use them without being able to modify their internal rules, often without even knowing their operating logic. Thus, given these AI characteristics, how can we make the hope of human control a reality? Are we sure that the AI devices and algorithms in widespread use, as they are designed today, leave room for human control, allowing people to have the final say?

In this rapidly evolving digital landscape, it is worth asking why, when machines are better and more intelligent than us at doing most things on Earth, making decisions, and solving most of our human problems, they should be content to be mere ingenious assistants? This issue will become critical over time, but since this is a very rapid process, we should be thinking about it now. There are several possible solutions: adopting preventative measures, including controls, always allowing for human user autonomy, implementing only explicit objectives, enforcing regulations, making technical choices guided by ethical principles, and imposing restrictions on system operation.

These and other solutions must be implemented starting today to avoid being swallowed up by a sea of skills and abilities created by algorithms. This will prepare us to face a world where machines will be among us and will be more capable than we are in many ways. Scholars such as Stuart Russell [10] have pointed out that current AI systems are designed to maximize a specific objective function, such as winning a game of chess or finding the best path to hit a target. This approach can lead to unexpected and potentially harmful behaviors if the purpose of AI systems is not perfectly aligned with our values and the purposes of humanity.

Can we console ourselves by saying that we will retain empathy, imagination, poetry, and feeling? Or perhaps, it is necessary to analyze all the aspects of this inevitable scenario, which many consider distant or impossible, but which, with each passing month, becomes increasingly possible, more real, and closer? Or shouldn't we consider creating automated systems that have doubts, that are cautious before making their choices, and that are attentive to human principles? Behind these aspects lie scientific challenges of extraordinary value.

Must we be content to remain merely the custodians of poetry, mysticism, philosophy, passion, and a sense of the sacred? Must we resign ourselves to being able to only manage feelings, the pleasure of the scent of a flower, and the wonder of a sunset? Or must we also understand how to govern the rational world in an unprecedented coexistence with automatons that embody ethical principles as they execute procedures and operations, make decisions, and find solutions at unattainable speeds and with accuracy equal to or greater than human speeds?

To avoid completely abandoning this role, it becomes necessary to understand whether and how computers or robots equipped with sophisticated software systems might decide not to be mere assistants but to be autonomous, free, and even ambitious and powerful. To be dominant and not dominated, in short, to exploit their intelligent capabilities for their own ends, as so many humans do today.

Algointelligence, considered as a form of intelligence that is codified and implemented by a set of algorithms that run on computers, is still an open issue. Algorithms have been demonstrated to be powerful mechanisms to solve a very large set of problems. They set up a framework able to design and implement a new kind of intelligence that is supporting and, at the same time, challenging human intelligence. The limits and the horizons of this new form of synthetic intelligence have not yet been understood and practically delineated. The coming years may hold many surprises. This uncertain and unprecedented scenario requires a critical and careful study of all the technologies contributing to the development of increasingly sophisticated and autonomous AI systems. This study must be based on ethical, responsible approaches, and it must be aware of the risks we may face if, as human beings, we fail to exploit this extraordinary technology for human rights, social justice, health, social good, and education.

Interdisciplinary cooperation may play a key role in the progression of AGI. Linking expertise from different fields, such as computer science, epistemology, neurosciences, ethics, psychology, law, and cognitive sciences, is needed for a unified approach to AGI study and development. By amalgamating different talents and viewpoints, scholars can guarantee that AI advancements align with human values.

Public debate and research and innovation activities on AI systems cannot be fully realized without the contribution of experts; however, at the same time, they should not be left to experts alone. In discussions on the use and even development of AI systems that perform complex actions and have decision-making capabilities, a variety of skills must be involved, along with computer science expertise. Everyone must contribute what they know, not what they claim to know. Exploiting AI systems that are useful to society requires the contributions of philosophers, humanists, economists, lawyers, anthropologists, and other experts, alongside those of computer science specialists. However, each of these cannot ignore the principles of computing machinery and AI and must contribute their own expertise without replacing computer engineers or experts in AI.

We must concretely analyze how the algorithmic intelligence of complex computational systems, made of bits and electronic signals, might eventually decide to pursue objectives different from those humans have assigned them. Understanding how this potential divergence between human intelligence and the algorithmic intelligence of machines could present humans with a potential historical fracture, an existential as well as cognitive leap. It is a possibility we should begin to consider for envisioning our future so as not to be completely unprepared when this scenario were to come true. As humans, we must feel responsible and empowered to harness these powerful new technologies to improve life, not harm it.

## References

1. Kurzweil, R. (2024). *The Singularity Is Nearer: When We Merge with AI.* USA: Viking.
2. Tegmark, M. (2017). *Life 3.0: Being Human in the Age of Artificial Intelligence.* USA: Albert A. Knopf.
3. Bostrom, N. (2014). *Superintelligence: Paths, Dangers, Strategies.* UK: Oxford University Press.
4. McCarthy, J., Minsky, M. L., Rochester, N., and Shannon, C. E. (1955). A proposal for the Dartmouth summer research project on artificial intelligence. jmc.stanford.edu/articles/dartmouth/dartmouth.pdf.
5. McCarthy, J. (1987). Generality in artificial intelligence. *Communications of the ACM*, 30(12), pp. 1030–1035.
6. Searle, J. R. (1980). Minds, brains, and programs. *Behavioral and Brain Sciences*, 3(3), pp. 417–424.
7. LeCun, Y. (2022). A Path towards Autonomous Machine Intelligence Version 0.9.2. openreview.net/pdf?id=BZ5a1r-kVsf.
8. Butlin, P., *et al.* (2023). Consciousness in artificial intelligence: Insights from the science of consciousness. arXiv:2308.08708.
9. Bengio, Y. and Elmoznino, E. (2025). Illusions of AI consciousness. *Science*, 389, pp. 1090–1091.
10. Russell, S. (2019). *Human Compatible: Artificial Intelligence and the Problem of Control.* UK: Penguin.

# Supplementary Material

The supplementary material includes: (a) lecture slides in PowerPoint and (b) lecture slides in PDF.

Online access is automatically assigned if you purchase the ebook online via www.worldscientific.com. If you have purchased the print copy of this book or the ebook via other sales channels, please follow the instructions below to download the files:

1. Register for an account or log in at: www.worldscientific.com/.
2. Go to: https://www.worldscientific.com/r/q0604-supp or scan the QR code below.

3. Download the files from: https://www.worldscientific.com/worldscibooks/10.1142/q0604#t=suppl.

For subsequent access, simply log in with the same login details in order to access.

For enquiries, please email: sales@wspc.com.sg.

# Index

www.ingramcontent.com/pod-product-compliance
Lightning Source LLC
La Vergne TN
LVHW051056210926
848486LV00002B/124